The Mass Media, Public Opinion, and Public Policy Analysis: Linkage Explorations

James C. Strouse

University of Maryland

CHARLES E. MERRILL PUBLISHING COMPANY
A Bell & Howell Company
Columbus, Ohio

To my beautiful wife, Darla,
who makes everything worthwhile

Published by
Charles E. Merrill Publishing Company
A Bell & Howell Company
Columbus, Ohio 43216

This book was set in Schoolbook.
The Production Editor was Linda Gambaiani.
The cover was designed by Will Chenoweth.

ISBN: 0-675-08701-5

Library of Congress Catalog Card Number: 74-31979

1 2 3 4 5 6 7 8 — 82 81 80 79 78 77 76 75

Printed in the United States of America

Preface

The purpose of this book is to explore the effects of public opinion on governmental policy making with a special focus on the role of the mass media in this process. The area is a fascinating one; however, the studies completed to date are inconclusive and suggestive. The areas I chose to focus upon were political campaigning, the president and the press, blacks and the media, and cable television. The speculation concerning media and the opinion-policy process and the relative dearth of good empirical studies must be remedied. Communications theory is extremely important and may offer the first testable paradigm for political science.

Chapter 1 deals with formal linkage models that reflect the public opinion-public policy analysis process with specific consideration of the effects of the mass media. How does public opinion generate, change, or force governmental policy making? Are certain types of policies easier to change than others? Are there identifiable limits to the effect of the media and public opinion? What are the different roles the media play in this process? Policy impact is explored since the media and public opinion play a significant role in this all-important area as well. While a definitive model is suggested, the model and its implications must be refined considerably through empirical studies before a satisfactory model can be developed.

How Americans nominate and elect their leaders are central concerns for all persons interested in policy making, since these leaders shape and determine governmental decisions. Chapter 3 deals directly with how and why Americans vote as they do. It explores the decline in influence of the party machine and the complex problems of changing and influencing voters' minds. Voting studies and experimental attitude-change research efforts are compared. Finally, the chapter examines the influence of party identification, issue orientation, and candidate orientation on the voter with special attention being paid to the independent voter.

Chapter 2, "Professional Public Relations and Political Power," deals specifically with the uses of the media in political campaigns. Among the topics explored are early professional public relations campaigns, the 1966 Agnew-Mahoney gubernatorial campaign, the behavioral independent and image voting, and how to wage a political campaign in the new media politics. The use of historical perspective and case studies enables us to focus on the definable influence of the mass media. While the orientation of chapters 2 and 3 is on how the media help determine the elections of policy decision makers, chapters 4 and 6 examine the influence of the mass media and public opinion on the generation and manipulation of public issues.

One of the most controversial areas of opinion-media influence on public issues centers around the relationship between presidential control and manipulation of opinion and information to the bias of the newspaper and television press. Innumerable stories are written about the influence of Walter Cronkite's raised eyebrows or the impact of the stories of Jack Anderson. Chapter 4 reviews the conflict between the president and the press and explores a case study: the Pentagon's attempted influencing of public opinion on Vietnam policy. Chapter 5 is a special chapter on the Watergate scandal especially as it relates to the public opinion-public policy process.

One of the most explosive policy issues in American history concerns the civil rights movement and the riots in the cities. To some, it seemed as though the very fabric of the nation would be torn apart. Chapter 6 examines the role of the media in the civil rights movement with some discussion of urban riots and protest politics in general. Student demonstrations, protests by Indians, Chicanos, and women's liberation groups signalled an emerging area of direct participation in policy making by those affected by the policy. The media played a central role in legitimatizing and publicizing the demands and actions of these groups.

Chapter 7 explores the various theories of media influence and attitude change. The "hot" and "cold" media ideas of McLuhan are examined as well as communication theory as it applies to studies of political systems.

An empirical examination of media effect is the focus of chapter 8 using the wealth of data collected by Donald R. Matthews and

James W. Prothro for their *Negroes and the New Southern Politics.* A statistical analysis attempts to show the independent effect of the mass media on political attitudes and race relations.

Chapter 9 explores the social and political implications of cable television. Besides the obvious advantages of CATV such as sending and receiving all mail and telephone conversations, shopping, or conversing with select groups interested in a particular issue such as pollution, CATV offers the possibility of massive political change. Voting by CATV, direct democracy with all receiver sets having the capacity to monitor all legislative debate on public issues, campaigning by cable television with the ability to address only those voters in a specific district — all are among the seemingly limitless possibilities of CATV. The dangers of CATV are also explored, especially the possibility of governmental surveillance. If the receiving sets are wired for it, a central control facility can turn on the sets at will and monitor conversations and actions of persons in each home.

The aim throughout the book will be to examine the impact of the media upon policy making in the United States. While much of the information available is indirect and superficial, a thorough examination should reveal some conclusions on a very vital part of the American political process.

I would like to thank a number of people who aided and encouraged my research. Professors Bob Alperin, Richard Claude, Don Devine, M. Margaret Conway, Clarence Stone, Mary Berry, and Mel Hollis read portions of the manuscript and made a number of useful suggestions. Professor James W. Prothro deserves special mention because of his encouragement of my work. Bill Setten also was very helpful in the initial planning stages of this book. A very special thanks goes to Dean Ray E. Hiebert who helped in many ways. My graduate assistant, Sewahn Kim, helped in much of the detail work that goes to complete a book. Also, thanks to Mary Keener, Susan Finn, and Molly Parker for their excellent typing. A special word for my editor, Fred Kinne — his efforts alone probably saved six months to a year in getting the book completed. He has been a terrific editor and deserves a great deal of praise. Finally, many thanks go to Ms. Linda Gambaiani, production editor in political science, for her invaluable help in getting the book to press.

Contents

Introduction

The mass media, defined as newspapers, radio, and television, have always played a central role in governmental policy making. From the "yellow-journalism" of the Hearst newspapers to the biased analyses of presidential speeches, the media have had a long history of central involvement in American governmental affairs. This book will explore the influence of the mass media on the public opinion-public policy process.

Marshall McLuhan tells us that the electronic media are changing the very nature of our lives.[1] Just as the printing press, the industrial age and its inventions, and the wheel changed the way people lived, the radio and especially the television are changing the very environment in which the citizens of the world live. Now instant communications are available to almost all; one can see the world's events recorded before his eyes. Our view of the world is vastly expanded; our view of our fellow human beings (both American and foreign) is significantly altered; our entire manner of doing things is seriously changed. Thus, McLuhan argues, the media themselves, not their contents, are the most significant factors in the world today.

Few would need convincing that the media are extremely important in governmental affairs. In Communist and other authoritarian countries, all media are subject to strict control and censorship. The citizenry will see, hear, and read only that which the government approves. Even in democracies, the media, especially television and radio, have been controlled to some degree. In France, there is only government television. Until a few years ago, even Great Britain had only government-controlled television available to its citizens. In the United States, television has been given con-

siderably more independence from control, although the Federal
Communications Commission can revoke licenses of television stations. In practice, the FCC has rarely asserted itself. Informal control does exist, however, with presidents of the various networks
placed on advisory commissions and subject to angry telephone
calls and meetings with high governmental officials on occasion.

During wartime, most news accounts are censored and the information channels are subject to careful review. Information is power
and the person who controls the channels of communication is, by
definition, powerful. *The Pentagon Propaganda Machine*,[2] *The Hidden Persuaders*,[3] the TV special "The Selling of the Pentagon" —
all suggest that people can be manipulated by propaganda and
advertisements on the mass media. The recent debates over the
policy implications of cable television (CATV) indicate that control can be much more widespread, raising the spector of "Big
Brother" even before 1984.

With all citizens wired for CATV, mail could be received and
sent via the TV; productions could be produced in millions of homes
throughout America; the government could watch all its citizens
through cable and a hundred other uses could be found for this
communication innovation. Because of adamant opposition to cable
by the three major networks, the development of it and its myriad
of possibilities will be slowed. Yet few would deny that society
itself will be changed, as McLuhan has argued, if cable television
approaches its potentialities.

The Media and
Public Policy Making

The central thrust of this book is to examine the specific impact
the mass media have on governmental policy making. Most are
aware that the government is extremely conscious of publicity.
Foreign policy experts in the State Department and the White
House carefully review the columns of nationally syndicated columnists. Bureaucrats at all levels have been "energized" by direct
actions such as sit-ins and protests by various interest groups.
The media can influence policy by simply exposing it to the public.
However, to point to the specific influence of the media in any one
event or one policy is quite difficult.

Policy making is defined as the purposeful actions of government to solve or settle some specific problem. Many scholars have
pointed out the difficulty in analyzing decisions or programs.
Various systems such as PPBS (planning, programming, budgeting

system) and rational decision-making models have been proposed to simplify the process. Some governmental advisors such as Daniel Moynihan have suggested that much of the policy making that goes on in government is accidental, simply the result of a strange conglomerate of events or the by-product of a planned policy that failed.[4] Others suggest that all policy making is strictly a "process of muddling through."[5] The slow, additive, uneventful nature of such policy making could be predicted simply by looking at what was done previously.

Some have suggested that the media's role in this process is to spotlight the program and place it on a priority list. Thus, the media helped make pollution a topic for national concern by showing what was happening to our natural resources and indicating that much of the damage could be corrected. The entire civil rights movement was enhanced and legitimized by the media showing the injustices being done to blacks in the South (and in the North also). The media, then, can be viewed as an important part of the action process that highlights and then stimulates government programs and decisions.

The media's role in different policy areas will be different. In some, they will play a role as a central, action catalyst, and in others, the media will be peripheral to policy determination. In this book we will investigate the media's roles in some crucial areas of American life and governmental policy making. Although the information presented sometimes will be limited because of a dearth of conclusive studies, when it is fairly complete, conclusions will be drawn.

While discovering the exact role of the media in making, changing, or defining a public policy is difficult, an even harder job will be examining the policy impact of the media. It has been observed that the impact of a policy is considerably more important than the policy itself, for the impact denotes just what changes the program makes upon the citizenry. The media play a role in the impact area. However, without good panel (before–after) surveys or intensive historical studies, impact analysis is difficult at best. Assessing the role of the media will be equally difficult.

NOTES

1. Marshall McLuhan, *Understanding Media: The Extensions of Man* (London: McGraw-Hill, 1965), *passim.* See especially part I, pp. 3-62.

2. J. William Fulbright, *The Pentagon Propaganda Machine* (New York: Vintage Books, 1971).

3. Vance Packard, *The Hidden Persuaders* (New York: McKay, 1957).

4. Daniel P. Moynihan, "The Presidency and the Press," *Commentary* (March 1971), pp. 41-52.

5. Charles E. Lindblom, "The Science of Muddling Through," *Public Administration Review* 19 (Spring 1959): 79-88.

1

Linkage Models, Public Opinion, and Media Effect

A democratic system, if it aspires to an open, accessible society, requires an informed, interested, rational, and participatory public.[1] This public should have the ability and willingness to express itself collectively and individually on specific issues at all levels of government. Most observers of the American polity — from Walter Lippmann[2] to V.O. Key[3] — have suggested a far different American public. Rather than being interested, informed, and participatory, the American electorate is uninterested and usually apathetic to most issues at the national, state, and local levels. Some have suggested that American democracy has profited from this dismal situation, claiming that elites govern better and have more democratic attitudes than the mass public. The conclusion that it is "good" to have large masses of apathetic people is disquieting to most reflective observers because an open, equal, polyarchical democracy requires a responsive and involved citizenry.

Many scholars have posited various models to discover how, to what extent, and with what effect the mass public affects public policy making. While most of the academic literature and many informed observers suggest little effect of public opinion on policy makers, most elected officials and public bureaucrats (and even private bureaucrats) always act as if public opinion is quite important and powerful. Ultimately any government, regardless of how totalitarian, repressive, or libertarian, rests finally on the consent of the governed — the mass public. If the masses are disturbed sufficiently, they would ultimately overthrow the government.

Historical events corroborate this point since all kinds of governments have been overthrown by the masses (with some elite help)

5

throughout recorded history. Yet the question remains — how does public opinion affect policy making? There is some indication that protests of various minority groups and the increasing feeling among scholars that voters do have general issue-oriented pictures of various candidates indicate that the situation is brighter than most of the literature suggests.

This study looks at the large picture of how opinions affect policies and then focuses on one aspect — the effect of the mass media on the policy maker, the policy process, and the feedback mechanism of opinion. The media are the catalytic agents that spotlight important policy, inform the public, and demand action from responsible officials. Some writers, like Norton Long, have suggested that the media actually set the public program priorities through their information spotlight.[4] Long suggests that the scenario happens as follows: a public official is asked what he is doing about a given problem — say pollution — by a reporter. The public official, busy with daily meetings and a host of other duties, is taken aback; he is a bit familiar with the "broad outlines" of the situation but has almost no idea what is happening in terms of specifics. As soon as possible, he finds out, forms or reforms a program, and implements an action program to show the reporter and thus the public what a dynamic problem solver he is. The action was not undertaken or even thought about seriously until the agent of the media made a direct inquiry. In many other ways such as through a story or a television special or a short editorial, the media focus attention on the problem and the public official responsible. The official responds because he fears adverse publicity and fears that the public, once it is informed, will force him to act anyway. The public opinion, then, is latent opinion waiting to be aroused on specific issues. In many cases, the media are the catalytic agents. In some cases, the media take a relatively small public outcry and give it attention which engenders even more public awareness and outcry.

While most observers might point to a few national commentators in national newspapers, the television journalist seems to have the greatest impact on the mass electorate. Roper Public Opinion Surveys have shown that most people get their news from the television news programs.[5] In addition, the surveys have indicated that, of all the media, television is most believable.[6] As table 1-1 indicates, there are only three institutions thought more highly of by the American public than television news. People believe what the newscasters say and great numbers habitually see them. If there is an effect of public opinion on public policy, it is quite certain that the media, especially the electronic media, play a central role.

Table 1-1

Percentage of Confidence in People
Running Various Institutions

	Public Total %	Leaders Total %
Medicine	57	41
Local trash collection	52	50
Higher educational institutions	44	30
Local police department	44	54
Television news	41	17
Military	40	30
Local public schools	39	46
Organized religion	36	29
Local united fund	35	45
State highway systems	34	40
U.S. Supreme Court	33	44
U.S. Senate	30	31
Press	30	19
Major companies	29	35
U.S. House of Representatives	29	26
Local government	28	50
State government	24	27
Law firms	24	20
Organized labor	20	9
Local tax assessment	19	37
Executive branch of federal government	19	17
White House	18	21

SOURCE: U.S. Congress, Senate, Committee on Government Operations, *Confidence and Concern: Citizens View American Government*, 93d Congress, 1st sess., 1974, pp. 37-38.

Books about journalism, such as Douglass Cater's *The Fourth Branch of Government*, contend it is the role of the journalist to be an antagonist with policy makers, shed any insight on complex policy matters, and insure that policy implementors do their jobs correctly.[7] Some have challenged the media's competency to do this job almost as a surrogate for the apathetic public; however, the media have done a fairly good job at getting the truth and keeping public officials working hard. One indication of this is the often repeated cliché of public officials to "never lie to reporters for eventually they will discover the truth."[8] The Nixon administration's handling of Watergate and the secret Cambodian bombings are two examples of how reporters eventually discover the truth.

Linkage Models

To assess the role the media play in the overall demand — policy-making process, we should first examine a number of linkage models posited in the literature. These models are discussed at some length in Norman Luttbeg's *Public Opinion and Public Policy*.[9] However, we shall limit the discussion to broad outlines and then suggest how the media fit into several of these models. The first model discussed is the Participant's model, in which there are no leaders and all participate in decision making. This is somewhat similar to the Marxist classless society and is usually inappropriate for most American situations. Perhaps the closest America has come to such a model revolves around the mass protests and participation of hundreds of thousands in the civil rights and Vietnam demonstrations. The model is shown graphically in figure 1.

Figure 1

Another frequently discussed model is the Rational-Activist model, which is most consistent to the polyarchical democracy espoused in much of the writing of the founding fathers and the political philosophers. This model assumes that everyone has a relatively equal influence in making public policy decisions. It also assumes that the mass public is informed, involved, and rational in its opinion and political action. Voters cast their ballots for the candidate reflecting their policy preferences.[10] The Rational-Activist model is an overt coercive model with the electorate withholding their votes if the public official fails to perform to their expectation. The model is shown in figure 2. Most of the assump-

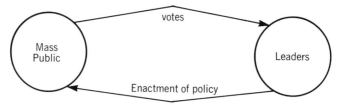

Figure 2

tions of this model are similar to those used in economic models. Just as the completely rational economic mass public is nonexistent, the rational political man is hard to find. The literature suggests that most voters fail to take the time to be informed or lack the interest to participate in party politics.

A third model often discussed in the literature linking opinion with policy is the Political Parties model.[11] This model has great impact for parliamentary democracies such as Great Britain.

The Watergate scandal best illustrates the differences between presidential and parliamentary systems, especially as they relate to this model. Many observers agree that the Nixon administration would have fallen sooner if the United States had a parliamentary government. The state-based power source of American parties and the almost complete independence of the president from political party control makes it extremely difficult to replace an American executive determined to stay in power. The impeachment process seems directly related to the intensity of public opinion pressure and the proximity of congressional elections and only indirectly related to the evidence. While scandals such as Watergate are unusual examples of the impact of public opinion on governmental decision making, they illustrate clearly the direct and immediate effects of aroused public opinion. However, it seems less satisfactory for the United States. The model assumes that (1) the political parties' candidates are a direct link between leaders and the public; (2) the model's first stage utilizes the Rational-Activist model with the citizen selecting the party having the policy platform closest to his own preference; (3) the voter chooses the party platform espousing his causes rather than voting for the individual candidate. The party and candidate are wedded as one and it should make little difference who the candidate is as long as one knows what the party program is; (4) the model assumes that the elected members of the party enact the program after they are elected. The voter is choosing the party with little regard for whoever the candidate is; and (5) that the mass public assesses the performance of the party after its term and then supports it or defeats it in the next election (see fig. 3). While most observers would suggest that

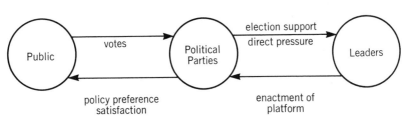

Figure 3

the political parties model is inapplicable to the American opinion-policy process, most politicians act as if public opinion is important. Presidents talk of a mandate from the people; other officials read into their elections a policy-directed mandate from the electorate. Research conducted by Warren E. Miller and Donald F. Stokes suggests that the public has little knowledge on most issues and that congressmen have even less of an idea what their electorate thinks.[12] In fact, the most predictive congressional voting model posits a low-information "cue" model in which a congressman votes with certain "cue" groups.[13] Thus, if one knows the top three cue groups of a congressman (such as state delegation, party leadership, or committee chairmen), one can predict over 90 percent of the votes in the House of Representatives.

A fourth linkage model, quite closely aligned to the Parties model, is the Pressure Groups model. In broad terms, it actually encompasses the Parties model. It is an outgrowth of group theory in political science, which suggests that all policy making can be viewed as a dynamic interaction of competing group forces. On a given issue, rival groups emerge and contest for a policy decision favoring them. The policy that emerges is directly related to the size, organization, and effectiveness of the various special interest groups involved. It includes the Parties model because political parties are considered to be another contending group interacting with other private and public interest groups (see fig. 4).

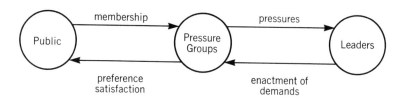

Figure 4

The model argues that very little important opinion exists within this society apart from group attitudes. It also suggests an ideal situation in which all groups compete comparatively equally and, through each partial view of the public interest, the overall public interest is served. Of course, we know that groups have differential strengths and that they represent some members of the group more than others. The elected officials simply respond to the group which eventually dominates and votes for the policies that the dominant group desires.

Two other models are also posited in some linkage discussions. Both are considered noncoercive since the electorate does not need nor desire to vote elected officials out of office. One of these, the Sharing model,[14] is presented in figure 5. This model assumes a

Figure 5

homogenous society in which there exists total consensus between the mass public and the leaders. The leaders' policy preferences, by definition, have to be representative of the public since both groups have exactly the same policy views. Ultimately, it does not matter who participates in the decision-making process or whether the leaders are unrepresentative or a closed elite because all citizens have similar preferences. Communist countries such as Russia and Eastern European regimes reflect this model. In every election, candidates of the Communist party receive nearly 100 percent of the votes. While the elections are noncompetitive, the ideologic thrust is that the leaders know what is best for all citizens since everyone believes in the same values and goals of government. There is no coercion in this model because everyone is satisfied and is, by definition, getting "correct" policies enacted.

A final model is the role model in which leaders feel they are simply representing the views of their constituents.[15] The leaders simply anticipate the preferences of their public and vote to enact policies consistent with those the mass public wants. There is little or no element of coercion since the elected official views his role as a directed delegate representing exactly the constituent views (see fig. 6).

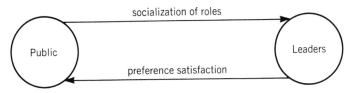

Figure 6

Both the Role model and the Sharing model break down on most issues since consensus exists only on broad general democratic principles and not on specific issues. In addition, the Role model assumes a highly informed electorate that tells its elected leaders its policy views on almost every issue. Research indicates that on all foreign policy (except Vietnam) and on most domestic policy, voters are simply uninformed and do not transmit their views to the congressmen or other elected officials.[16]

A Hybrid Linkage Model
Including the Media

How then does public opinion affect public policy? There are few case studies that look specifically at opinion formation and effect on a specific policy enactment. Election studies[17] and some preliminary linkage work[18] have been done; however, they are extremely limited in scope and make large and usually unjustified causal leaps to infer opinion effect.

Obviously, if public opinion is to have an effect on policy, the public or subpublic must be aware of the issues or, at least, have some idea of what the pros and cons are. Many studies, however, suggest an inattentive public with a very low percentage knowing even the name of their congressman and fewer still what the salient issues are. Some argue that the mass public can blissfully be ignorant while a small percentage, known as the Attentive Public, carefully watches and considers public issues. At the very outside range, Donald Devine suggests the Attentive Public consists of 25 percent of the mass public.[19] Others, like Gabriel Almond, suggest it is only 10 percent of the public.[20] The Attentive Public theorists describe the group's actions as follows. This segment of the public is relatively well-informed and watches public questions closely. When an important issue surfaces, the Attentive Public acts as a loose body of opinion that provides instant feedback to legislators through letters, discussions, editorials, petitions, and so on. When a majority of the Attentive Public proclaims itself in favor of an issue, the legislators respond fairly quickly and enact or defeat the program in question. The Attentive Public, then, is considered to directly link the mass public with the leaders and their policy enactments. The model most consistent with this would be the Pressure Groups model, with the Attentive Public being a mixture of individual and group opinion pressuring legislators to enact its policy preferences.

Devine examines the effect of opinion on policy for a number of issues — foreign aid, aid to education, medical care, extension of black rights, support for a strong foreign policy, and support for a private sector allocation.[21] Through a factor analysis of question items dealing with attentiveness to the political process, Devine differentiates four publics — the mass public together, the attentive public, the least attentive and the nonattentive. The Attentive Public by definition consists of those with the top 25 percent attentive scores. He argues that through opinion surveys we could see how, when, and to what extent these three publics affect policy. For a threshold of acceptance he used 50 percent plus 1 point. His general hypothesis is that "the more attentive a person is, the more likely he is to support a strong foreign policy, oppose extension of Negro rights, and support a private sector allocation."[22]

Devine argues that when the policy makers hear that a majority of the Attentive Public is for or against some policy, they act accordingly. Thus, he traces public opinion polls over time and compares the polls with legislative action.

Let us examine closely two public policies — one that seems to conform to Devine's hypothesis and one that does not.[23] Both represent the difficulty in inferring a causal relationship between opinion and policy (see table 1-2 and fig. 7).

While both table 1-2 and figure 7 support the hypothesis that public support for black rights coincides with legislative support, the support is generalized among all publics with the attentive public being least supportive (even though the percentage differences are quite small). Although the author believes that outputs follow Attentive Public opinion more closely than other measures of public opinion, the findings do not corroborate that. Moreover, it is extremely difficult to infer that because public opinion went over the threshold, Congress was forced to act. The votes of congressmen depend to a great extent on the type of issue-bill introduced and the direct pressure generated by protests, marches, and persuasion by other congressmen. Since it was not until 1964 that a really enforceable and meaningful bill was passed, it is hard to suggest that once opinion went over the threshold (in 1958), Congress dutifully followed. In addition, the Attentive Public was clearly indistinguishable from the other publics presented, indicating that on black rights, the other publics were as informed and as influential as the Attentive Public. Finally, the analysis ignores the structure and impact of Congress on both the opinion process and the policy process.

Table 1-2

Public Opinion Support for Federal
Negro Rights

| Support By | *Percentage of Support* | | | | |
	1952	1956	1958	1960	1964
General public	23.5	60.8	63.3	62.7	39.5
Least attentive	18.1	58.4	62.8	64.7	42.8
Nonattentive	24.1	60.4	63.5	63.9	40.3
Attentive public	21.4	61.9	62.2	59.4	37.3

Source: Donald J. Devine, *The Attentive Public: Polyarchical Democracy* (Chicago: Rand McNally, 1970), p. 85. Reprinted by permission of the publisher.

Percent of Support

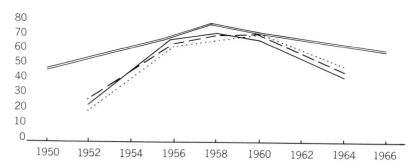

Source: Donald J. Devine, *The Attentive Public: Polyarchical Democracy* (Chicago: Rand McNally, 1970), p. 85. Reprinted by permission of the publisher.

Legend: Outputs (in percentage of support) — 1950: 44.5; 1956: 68.9; 1958: 78.5; 1960: 72.8; 1964: 66.0; 1966: 59.3.
Attentive Public ———; Nonattentive Public — —; Least Attentive Public······; Output ═══

Figure 7

Public Opinion and Policy Output:
Federal Negro Rights

Another example concerns the public opinion support for medical care. In this policy area, none of the opinion categories corresponds to the trend line for output. Devine asserts that this situation may be due to a time-lag factor between opinion and output in the medical care area. Of course, this explanation is a relatively weak one since he explicitly includes a longitudinal analysis covering a ten-year time span. Table 1-3 enables us to examine the results.

Again the Attentive Public seems to lag in support for medical care in every category. The largest support group is the least at-

Table 1-3

Public Opinion Support for Medical Care

Support by	Percentage of Support 1956	1960	1962	1964
General public	53.9	58.9	58.3	49.6
Least attentive	57.3	65.2	63.6	56.7
Nonattentive	57.1	62.7	59.4	53.6
Attentive public	44.1	47.3	54.9	37.9

SOURCE: Donald J. Devine, *The Attentive Public: Polyarchical Democracy* (Chicago: Rand McNally, 1970, p. 81. Reprinted by permission of the publisher.

tentive group (--------) and although Devine suggests that the 1965 legislation followed the 1962 finding that the Attentive Public supported medical care, it seems clear that the Attentive Public 1964 support was ineffective, especially since its 1964 percentage was well below the threshold of support (37.9 percent).[24] Thus, the data indicate almost the reverse of Devine's hypothesis. The most supportive group seemed to be the Least Attentive Public and when the legislation passed (1965), the Attentive support had diminished from a high of 54.9 percent to 37.9 percent. It was only in 1962 that the Attentive Public support exceeded 50 percent. Figure 8 demonstrates the conclusions more sharply.

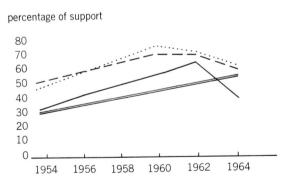

SOURCE: Donald J. Devine, *The Attentive Public: Polyarchical Democracy* (Chicago: Rand McNally, 1970), p. 81. Reprinted by permission of the publisher.

Legend: Output — 36%, 46%, 48%, 58%
Attentive Public——; Nonattentive Public__ __; Least Attentive Public----; Output ══

Figure 8

Public Opinion and Policy Output: Medical Care

Devine suggests that "it should also be mentioned that the percentage of attentive public support is closer to the percentage of system support until 1964."[25] The only problem with this statement is that the legislation was passed in 1965 when Attentive Public support had dropped considerably. Even with perfect trend lines between opinion and output, it is difficult to infer even indirect causality. Clearly, there are numerous other more immediate factors that often take precedence. While the above analysis leaves a great deal to be desired, it is probably the most thorough analysis of the possible direct linkages between opinion and system output. Besides some case studies of governmental policy making that tangentially mention the role of public opinion, there is little direct literature that explicitly studies the role of opinion on policy, especially including some longitudinal analysis. V.O. Key mentions that the Marshall Plan seemed to have broad public support.[26] He also indicates that public opinion changed markedly concerning World War II gasoline rationing after a public report by Bernard Baruch, a situation which seemed to have an effect on rationing policy. Bauer, Pool, and Dexter found that the most important opinion groups for most congressmen on reciprocal trade were those lobbyists whom they trusted and who usually had a direct interest in trade legislation.[27] There was little awareness of mass public opinion probably because most Americans were unaware of the issues concerning the policy. Sigel and Friesema studied the perceptions of 30 community leaders and over 200 citizen advisory committee members regarding education.[28] They found that community leaders had grossly inaccurate estimates of public opinion and that the magnitude, direction, and saliency of the opinion was misjudged.

Miller and Stokes examined the influence of constituent attitudes on congressmen.[29] They interviewed incumbent congressmen, their opponents, and a sample of constituents in 116 congressional districts. They examined three attitude dimensions: (1) black civil rights; (2) social welfare; and (3) foreign affairs. The correlation or agreement between the constituent attitudes and the congressman's attitude on issues was .60 on civil rights (quite high); .30 on social welfare issues (moderately high); and .09 on foreign affairs (a complete lack of agreement). This indicates that on specific important issues, the congressman has a clear perception of constituent attitudes and responds to them. However, on most social welfare issues and especially foreign affairs, the congressman has little idea what his constituents think and therefore cannot possibly attempt to represent them. In an article attempting to predict congressional votes, Matthews and Stimson suggest a lack of information model for congressmen because these representatives sometimes consider over 10,000 pieces of legislation and have to vote on 2-3,000 pieces.[30] Obviously, no individual can be completely informed on all these matters, so most specialize and are poorly informed on most legislative matters. Matthews and Stimson developed a series of "cue" groups, such as the Democratic Study Group, Republican Leadership, Democratic Leadership, Committee Chairman, State Delegations, and other discernible groups within Congress.[31] Congressmen were deciding to vote on the basis of how their fellow congressmen (more prestigious) were voting. The model suggests the impotency of both public opinion and congressional knowledge and predicts voting on the basis of informal groups in the House of Representatives.

Obviously there are times when public opinion affects public policy. Key says that, for the most part, opinion operates in a negative fashion.[32] There are certain limitations set on leaders, a kind of consensus about how much the public will tolerate. He suggests that there are boundaries of policy action set forth by public opinion and that leaders not only have a sense of what these boundaries are but also are very wary of overstepping such limits. If such parameters of public action exist, how might one discover them? Best corroborates Key's point and suggests that on most issues, leaders can do almost anything they like without fear of sanction; that is, the public attention is limited and as long as leaders stay within the fairly well-specified boundaries, policy action will seldom be questioned.[33]

To define empirically and set forth these public opinion limitations on policy action would be difficult although quite possible. One could even discover the priorities held by the public and the willingness to pay for more services and new programs. Certainly information about public attitudes such as direction, intensity, and saliency of belief could be discovered. Having gathered such information, the leaders would have some basic information concerning what the public would tolerate. The findings would present the leaders with a collective public policy preference map and would specifically set forth the negative sanctions of public opinion. When leaders transgressed those boundaries, the public would react and force a policy change.

Another point that Key raises and which must be dealt with is the manipulation of opinion by public and private leaders. Key examines the vast possibilities for manipulation present in the office of the president.[34] The public is socialized to believe that the president is always acting in the public interest and has vast amounts of information to insure correct policy development. Whenever the president has taken bold action, either in Vietnam or economic policy or with relations with China and Russia, the public has indicated extremely strong support. National public opinion polls affirm such support. In addition to the socialized support of the president, a national leader can command television and radio time at will, he can release news to reporters, and he can point a spotlight of national attention to a problem and his favored solution. Combatting the vast array of informational outlets commanded by the president is an extremely difficult task. In addition, the Executive Office has a large staff, the public relations departments of the vast federal bureaucracy, and the natural curiosity and attention of the public with which to influence public opinion.

One segment of the federal bureaucracy — the Defense Department — has been the subject of a CBS documentary, "The Selling of the Pentagon." This film shows how the powerful and well-financed Defense Department attempts to mold public opinion to support its programs. Billions of dollars are at stake as well as the president's foreign policy. Defense Department officials criticized some inaccuracies in the film but the overall picture of a vast institutional arrangement to influence public opinion was clearly conveyed.

Manipulation of opinion is the scope of both the government and the media.[35] To a large extent, the media see themselves as the natural adversaries of government, giving the alternative view or at least the opportunity for the alternative view to be expressed. The ultimate question of whether and to what extent opinion can be manipulated remains to be discovered. Experiments by Carl Hovland and others have found that the effective messages can shift a large percentage of opinion, especially when coming from a high prestige source and when the opinion is relatively uninformed and unanchored.[36] However, both mass and elite opinion seem to be more informed and responsive than opinion surveys and academic research has established. With regard to political campaigns, there is a growing body of evidence to indicate that issues are much more important than originally supposed.[37] Even if mass opinion can be manipulated, what about elite opinion? Key,[38] Devine,[39] Almond,[40] and others speak about the importance of elite opinion and suggest that it is the really relevant public for all leaders. Through a "two-step flow of information,"[41] the elites inform the masses and interpret the information for the masses. Until preference maps are established for both elites and mass public opinion, the question of whether and to what extent public opinion is manipulated remains unresolved.

The influence and manipulation of public opinion will remain unresolved simply because it is impossible to attribute a causal role to public opinion without knowing the boundaries of public attitudes. More importantly, one must know the intensity of feeling and the willingness to act on that feeling. The causal role of public opinion and attempts to investigate it will be discussed more fully later in this chapter. Mancur Olson has suggested that "individual preference maps are as distinctive as fingerprints."[42] If so, one should be able to determine the boundaries of public opinion on various issues and also how these boundaries affect governmental decision makers as these leaders enact and implement public policy.

The media's role in the opinion-policy process is even less clear. They have a powerful weapon — communications exposure. They can publish or televise events and expose them to the whole world. Elected officials, bureaucrats, and private citizens with corporate responsibility act as if the media are the "fourth branch of government."[43] Matthews shows that reporters and senators have a symbiotic relationship, with reporters helping to make the senator "look good" and the senator leaking certain specialized information to the reporter.[44] Sometimes the reporter helps keep the senator informed by telling him what others are doing or by tipping off a possible scandal. "Trial balloons," "backgrounders," and informal friendships are ways the president and other executives attempt to influence reporters and their columns. Trial balloons are ideas leaked to the press to get public reaction. Some think that President Ford's reported consideration of pardons for all Watergate defendants was a trial balloon that was quickly withdrawn and disavowed. A backgrounder is an informal, not-for-quotation discussion with reporters by some high government official. Secretary of State Kissinger uses these frequently. President Kennedy tried hard to develop strong personal friendships with key reporters;[45] every president has had favored media people to whom important stories were leaked. The relationship is still an adversary one with most reporters simply going beyond government press handouts and conferences to reveal the complete story.

The Media Influence
Model

While it is difficult to pick one model to illustrate the overall role the media play, figure 9 illustrates the relationship as fully as possible. The Pressure Groups model is employed because it is most applicable for most issues.

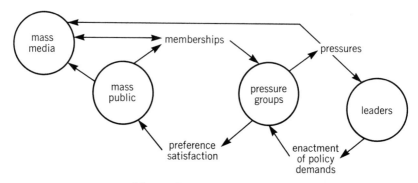

Figure 9

The model subsumes the Parties model (parties being considered just another pressure group) and argues that very little individual opinion exists within a developed society apart from group opinions. On any important issue, then, group opinions are the crucial opinions to be considered by elected officials. The model is appropriate for both major issues and day-to-day problems. While the latter issues are less observable, the decision makers are still well aware of the possibility of public attention through the mass media. The media are presented before the mass public because in many cases the media are the major input to the policy process. The public often needs considerable stimulation before it becomes sufficiently aware of issues to provoke some action. The media often interact simultaneously with each segment in the policy process, setting the agenda for the interaction of leaders with groups and the mass electorate. The arrows point both ways because all three segments often pressure the media to take part: the mass public plus pressure groups through direct action protests (sit-ins) or backgrounders and trial balloons. Thus, the media are a catalyst for action, stimulating and encouraging and even rationalizing the opinion-policy process.

If one examines carefully almost any central issue in American life, one sees a crucial role being played by the media. For example, a definite strategy of the civil rights groups, from the Congress of Racial Equality's "Freedom Rides" to Martin Luther King's Southern Christian Leadership Conference's direct demonstrations, was to incite the blind prejudices of southern whites and to attract the attention of the national press. All protests from Birmingham to Selma to Memphis were carefully planned for maximum media coverage. The outrage engendered by "Bull" Connor's cattle prods being used on black Birmingham children and police clubbing women in Selma inspired blacks and whites throughout the country to demand congressional action. With the skillful leadership of President Johnson and with mass peaceful protests being organized throughout the country, a number of major civil rights bills were enacted — the Voting Rights Act, the Fair Housing Act, the Equal Accommodations Act — and Executive Orders eliminating discrimination within the bureaucracy as well as with contractors doing business with the federal government were issued.

Another example that comes easily to mind is the protest action concerning the Vietnam War.[46] This war was the first to be telecast into the living rooms of the American people. It was a long and costly war with little apparent reward for American efforts except to "prop up" a near dictatorship in SouthVietnam which was also thoroughly corrupt. With the draft sending college students and other young Americans to die in Vietnam, a mass protest movement developed. The protest marches on Washington, the Veteran's Organization Against the War, the direct attempts to influence Congress — all were spotlighted by the mass media. However, probably the most important role the media played was in depicting the reality of Vietnam. The drug problem, the killing of thousands of civilians and especially children, the corruption and instability of South Vietnam's government, and the outright mistruths told by the American military command were indicated many times by investigative reporting of the media. Few will forget the Tet offensive of 1968 in which the Viet Cong and the North Vietnamese attacked cities throughout the South, capturing many including the Imperial Capital of Hué. This massive attack occurred almost immediately after General William Westmoreland, U.S. commander in Vietnam, had sent a report to President Johnson stating categorically that the enemy was ineffective and possessed little or no capacity for a wide-scale offensive. The ability of the media to show what was happening almost as it happened changed many minds — both elite and mass public — on the entire war situation. The results were that congressional support dissipated, President Johnson became less sure of his policies, and the mass protest gained momentum.

The Watergate scandal is the ultimate example of the crucial role of the media. Without the excellent investigative reporting of Carl Bernstein and Bob Woodward of the *Washington Post*, the story might still be unknown.

While it is difficult to pinpoint the effects of the media, most would suggest that the media played a central role in these two vital issues of the 1960s. The mass media, then, are a catalyst for latent opinion, energizing it to action; they also constitute a public lie detector test, indicating by film and commentary whether the statements of governmental leaders are true; and finally they are a quasi conscience of the American people, setting proper priorities on American policy and attempting to insure that measures are taken to correct wrongs. This latent opinion has been discussed by many, most thoroughly by David Truman.[47] He suggests that a great deal of unexpressed opinion exists in both the elite and mass public that gets expressed only after some event or crisis situation. The opinion exists, but it is disregarded by policy makers until it gets energized and then expressed.

Policy Analysis and Policy Impact

There are two kinds of policy issues being decided in America — the day-to-day decision (contracts, sewage, land use, and so on) in which public opinion appears uninvolved except for one or two special interest groups, such as the League of Women Voters, and, second, the emotional, crisis issue, in which the government must act quickly to meet the crisis. In both situations, it appears public opinion has little role to play. In both situations, the leaders have to consider the boundaries of public opinion in their decision making but there is little attempt or concern for actually finding out whether the public has an opinion and, if so, what it is. At the national level, one can see this most clearly — the crisis situation in the Cuban Missile Crisis and the day-to-day operation of the bureaucracy. There simply was insufficient time to find out whether Americans wanted to die to eliminate the missiles from Cuba. Also, there is little inclination of most bureaucrats to encourage the direct input of public opinion in the day-to-day accomplishment of the bureaucracy's task.

Thomas Dye employs six analytic models to describe, explain, and predict public policy.[48] He uses systems theory to view policy as a system output; elite theory to view policy as elite preference; group theory to view policy analysis in terms of intergroup equilibrium; rationalism to examine policy as efficient goal achievement; incrementalism to understand policy as variations on the past; and institutionalism to consider policy from the institutional activity standpoint. While all the models can be utilized almost interchangeably since most overlap but have a different focus of attention, the really important question is that of policy impact — how public policy affects the citizens and how it changes our entire political, social, and economic environment.

Since many scholars argue strongly that public opinion operates in a negative fashion in almost every case — whether with regard to everyday issues or highly emotional issues—one can argue that the public becomes involved almost always in response to governmental activity or repugnant inactivity, such as in the case of civil rights. That is, the public opinion becomes directly involved as the policy decision impacts them and as the media spotlight the policy. Bussing of school children to achieve racial integration is a typical case. Most Americans, when questioned about integration, especially in the 1970s, support the concept. However, when the Department of Health, Education, and Welfare (HEW) began suggesting strongly, with court support, that schools in a school district had to be racially balanced with the same percentage of blacks and whites as existed district-wide, the mass public began intensive protests. School boards reacted by appealing to the courts; congressmen reacted by pressuring the president; and the president reacted by issuing an Executive Order prohibiting further attempts by HEW to force large-scale bussing on school districts and by addressing the nation on the issue. Public opinion became a major factor in reaction to a public policy being implemented by a major federal bureaucracy (with power to cut off federal funds to a noncomplying school district) and the courts.

Policy impact concerns itself with the outputs of the system and how these outputs feed back into and change the system. The whole area of policy impact is relatively unexplored by most social scientists. It is a broad area that concerns itself with program evaluation, planning, and performance. Economists with their Planning, Programming, and Budgeting System (PPBS) attempted to get the federal bureaucracy a rational cost-effective, efficient, long-term planning program. As Alice Rivlin documents, the PPBS failed almost completely and has now been abandoned by the federal government.[49] Thomas Dye lists a number of policy impacts one should consider: (1) impact on the target situation or group; (2) impact on situations or groups other than the target (spillover effects); (3) impact on future as well as immediate conditions; (4) direct cost in terms of resources devoted to the program; and (5) indirect costs, including loss of opportunities to do other things.[50] In short, one has to consider the whole dynamics of policy analysis within the context of the total environment and the total policy thrusts of the government.

There are a few studies that attempt to examine the notion of policy impact. Ira Sharkansky points out that monetary expenditures for a major functional service (welfare, education, health, and the like) do not necessarily correlate with a one-to-one increase in services available.[51] In fact, in some areas, there seemed to be a quite low correlation between increased expenditures and increased services. James R. Coleman's report on education indicated that money per se may have little overall effect on the quality of education a given child receives.[52] Facilities, equipment, teacher training — all were much less impactful on a child than home environment and peer group relationships, which are determined by factors usually unrelated to public expenditures. The data developed by the report have been reanalyzed several times and all researchers reiterate the apparent lack of effect of increased expenditures — the major public input to the educational process. In an eclectic and possibly landmark study of urban systems, Jay Forrester attempted to develop a completely interacting system that analyzes, explains, predicts, and shows the impact of urban public policy over long periods of time.[53] The study predicts the eventual impact of policies enunciated at one point in time on the whole city from one to fifty years later. It is a highly technical mathematical model based on Boston city development but applicable to all cities. This model, if shown effective, could then be extended to state systems and eventually international state systems and the entire world. Its importance is that the model suggests a definite theory of urban development that has the capacity to include impact and predict impact over time. In fact, Forrester's associates have already extended their system to an analysis of the world's natural resources for the Club of Rome,[54] a group of European industrialists interested in the future of the world, which sponsors studies on world problems. Using the same analytical procedures, the associates predicted total utilization of all world resources around the beginning of the twenty-first century if countries continue their same pattern of consumption and industrial development.

The Causal Role of
Public Opinion

Many authors writing about the political and economic determinants of American state policies have suggested that the important political variables often ignored are public attitudes towards the various policies.[55] There are a number of studies that have focused on the causal role of public opinion.

Frank Munger has constructed a measure of mass public opinion for each American state using national opinion surveys.[56] While his procedure for obtaining state opinions is open to some question, he is among the first to measure public opinion toward issues and correlate them with legislative enactments. He examines 116 policy decisions and finds that 36 approximate the terms of the model (political responsiveness to the desires of the mass public) with congruence scores (a measure of the degree of agreement between opinions and laws) of 84 percent or higher. He then constructs an overall index of congruence for each state, showing a range from minimum congruence (.50 in Maryland, indicating a random relationship between opinion and policy) to a maximum score of .681 in New York and Idaho. Munger then attempts to correlate the congruence score with various political measures including party competition, malapportionment, and legislative professionalism. While Munger's study is quite innovative in attempting to measure state public opinion and also in considering a wide range of other dependent variables, it is limited in that: (1) he employs a very simple model to examine his relationships; (2) he fails to include other equally important variables — elite attitudes and elite willingness to act; and (3) he fails to put his analysis within a framework of a total theoretical system.

Another study by Philip L. Beardsley proposes to examine the causal role of public opinion on expenditure policies.[57] The project plans to compute for each state an average level of activity per capita desired by the adult population as a whole and to link opinion (X) and policy (Y) by a two-equation model:

$$Y = a_1 + a_1 X_I + u_1$$

$$X = b_1 + b_1 Y_1 + u_2$$

Since feedback processes would be included, exogenous variables (at least one) would have to be found and included in the equation system. Besides attempting to weigh the individual opinion by the salience of the issue to the respondent and measuring the respondent's willingness to pay for the level of government activity, Beardsley would try to measure the power of social groups by comparing the causal role of white opinion vs. black, or wealthy vs. poor, and so on. He notes that one problem with the measure of group "power" is how to estimate the size of the group. Another more important obstacle is that many persons are in several groups which may or may not overlap in an issue-oriented continuum. Some measure of group cohesiveness, resources, and willingness to act forcefully must be made. In any event, measuring the power of social groups would be extremely difficult but still possible.

Beardsley lists five levels of examining the effects of the democratizing process on public policies. The democratizing process is equated with various political measures — competition, participation, apportionment. At the first level, one could investigate the relationship between such factors as party competition and the level of government activity per capita. He makes a point supported by several researchers that if the deviation of the actual causal role of public opinion from its ideal were constant across all states, then the democratizing effect of party competition would be zero even if the correlation between party competition and public policy were perfect. Of course, this deviation of public opinion would never be constant; however, a number of previous investigators have suggested that party competition or any other political measure is meaningful only to the extent that it actually measures political development. An ideal causal role of public opinion (if such a role exists) and power equity among groups may not represent the political development concept that researchers are attempting to measure.

At the second level, one would focus on the degree of congruence between public opinion and public policy, something Munger attempted to do. However, Beardsley notes that a high degree of congruence could indicate either a significant impact of opinion on policy or a significant impact of policy on opinion or both. One should point out that causation can never actually be tested; it can be inferred if one assumes one-way (recursive) causation under specific conditions. The important point is *not* whether one causes the other but the nature of the interaction between public opinion and policy. How is public opinion an important legislative catalyst? When is it important and under what conditions?

Beardsley states a weakness in Munger's analysis. While Munger's study permits one to investigate the effects of democratizing factors while holding one or more variables constant, he fails to do so. A major point of the Strouse study indicated that holding one or more variables constant was an approach with little theoretical "pay off." If one is really interested in the causal role of public opinion, then one should study it within a total theoretical system.

The next three levels of inquiry involve taking larger and larger state opinion surveys (with the fifth level collecting time series data for all states) and using the states with the highest and lowest democratizing scores to estimate the equation parameters and compare those estimates with the estimates using the rest of the states. Other important problems include the diffusion process of policy adoption as indicated by Jack L. Walker,[58] Ira Sharkansky,[59] and Daniel J. Elazar.[60] Also there is the real possibility that some state policy opinions may not even exist among the majority of citizens.

Despite the number of methodological problems pointed out, Beardsley has raised a very important issue (causal role of public opinion) and made an effort both to measure the opinion structure and include it in the theoretical system of state policy analysis. In order to achieve a greater degree of sophistication, the entire question of the opinions of mass publics and their impact upon public policy needs in-depth study. Many of Elazar's observations and indirect measuring approaches could also be employed. However, the task that Munger and Beardsley have taken upon themselves is a very large and difficult one.

The important point is that if and when a causal opinion structure is identified at many points in time, it should be included within a theoretical system that explicitly posits economic, political, and output-impact theories. One should be interested in not only whether there is a causal role of public opinion but also how, why, and when the causal role becomes operative. How does it affect elite attitudes? What are elite attitudes? Is there a causal role for elite attitudes? These are equally important questions. Does elites' willingness to act really set the boundaries for socioeconomic-output interaction as Heinz Eulau and Robert Eyestone[61] and this writer suggest? Better measurement, time-series data, and complex theory modeling should offer some answers to these central questions.

Public Opinion and the
Public Choice Literature

One of the theoretical goals of the public choice literature[62] is to explain and predict governmental performance. The evaluation of governmental efficiency, social indicators and the quality of life

measures, and the application of economic theory to collective decisions at all levels of government (and private corporation bureaucracies) are central concerns of public choice theorists. One of the
most important of these theorists is Mancur Olson who establishes
the broad theoretical underpinnings for evaluation and prediction of
collective choice.[63]

A careful examination of his theory should indicate how the
causal role of public opinion can help determine these collective
choices. As most economists, Olson generally ignores the importance
of individual and group preferences even where they can be extremely useful, especially in helping solve the indivisibilities problem of governmental policies (How much is a bridge worth to the
public? What is its marginal utility when compared to other public
works or other policies such as education?). Economists generally
call this problem a "taste factor" and are unwilling to employ
attitudinal variables in their research.[64] It seems obvious that one
way to establish the worth of public projects (marginal utility) and
services is to ask people what it is worth to them in comparison to
other goods and services. Over time, then, one can establish (in
rough terms) the marginal utility of such indivisible goods as
bridges, health services, or welfare.

Although he fails to pursue the point, Olson recognizes the possible uses of public attitudes in solving the indivisibilities problem:

Like the problem of individual indivisibilities, the problem of group indivisibilities is of very great importance, and for the public problems with which this book
is predominantly concerned it is absolutely fundamental. That is primarily because of the *diversity of
preferences* that normally characterizes the real world.
We can't know for sure that this is the case, but it
is probably true that *individual indifference maps or
preference orderings are as distinctive as fingerprints*
[italics added]. In any event, whenever everyone in the
group or nation that would receive a collective good
does not have exactly the same tastes, a serious problem
emerges. ... There was, as we saw, no problem arising
out of diverse preferences where readily divisible private goods were concerned, because people with different values take different amounts of goods about which
they have different views, until because of the diminishing marginal utility of any good they all value the
marginal unit at the going market price. But the group
indivisibility inherent in collective goods makes it im-

possible for the individual independently to take more
or less of the good.[65]

The discovery of these individual and group preferences with
regard to governmental policies seem to be a relatively straightforward research project for survey research. Indeed, several studies
have been completed in this area.[66] The discovery of these public
preference maps will help solve the problem of the marginal utility
of public goods as well as offer some direct insight into the causal
role of public opinion in the general opinion-policy process.

Conclusions

We have attempted to focus on the linkages between public
opinion and public policy and to explore the specific case of the role
of the mass media in the process. A number of possible linkage
models were explored and the Media-Pressure Groups model was
found to be the best model. Devine's work attempting to link empirically the opinion-policy process was analyzed with the general
finding that it is extremely difficult to make a direct causal link
between opinion (even of the Attentive Public) and specific congressional policy action or support. Key mentions three important
concepts that one should keep in mind: (1) that boundaries exist on
policy action; if leaders go beyond those boundaries, the public
reacts strongly; (2) that opinion can be manipulated by governmental elites and that the effort is a continuous and well-founded
one; and (3) that one should explore the Attentive Public and how
they react to policy making, for this group is the one with the most
information on the issues and with the knowledge about how one can
influence and change public policy. The Watergate scandal offers the
researcher an ideal opportunity to investigate these areas.

Also, the overall question of policy impact was considered. It is
usually true that the public is rarely consulted on most issues —
whether day-to-day ones or highly emotional, crisis issues. Yet when
a policy is enunciated that goes beyond the boundaries permitted by
the mass public, the public reacts strongly. The reaction is from
more than just the Attentive Public and includes a wide representa-
tion from citizens of all backgrounds. It is in the policy impact area
that the true effect of public opinion could be noted — not only in
the formation of the policy but also, to a greater extent, in the
changing and reformation of the program after it has been adopted

by governmental leaders. One can argue that it is the absence of policy that arouses public opinion. If this is the case, the media would play a central role in exposing the lack of policy and the consequence of such inactivity of policy makers. Environmental and ecology issues are good examples of policy lacks and the process by which public opinion and the media forced action by leaders at all levels of government. Few, if any, scholars have attempted empirically to explore the policy impact-policy reformation process. But clearly public attention — with the help of the mass media — becomes an important factor in how the policy is made, changed, and implemented. Because policy impact studies are infinitely more complex than other public opinion studies, they have been ignored by most scholars. Yet interest is developing, due in part to the previous focus of the Nixon administration on program evaluation and performance, and more broadly speaking, to the entire area of social indicators.

Finally, the exciting possibilities of the public choice literature and the causal role of public opinion was examined. With the discovery of individual and group preference maps, one could determine the marginal utility of governmental goods and services to both individuals and groups. Such a determination should indicate the causal role of public opinion and, ultimately, help decision makers give the public the goods and services it wants.

NOTES

1. Perhaps the most thorough examination of what constitutes a democratic society is Christian Bay, *The Structure of Freedom* (Stanford, Calif.: Stanford University Press, 1970). Bay attempts to discover the healthy political system and reviews intensively the vast literature on democratic systems.

2. Walter Lippmann, *Public Opinion* (New York: Penguin Books, 1946).

3. V.O. Key, Jr., *Public Opinion and American Democracy* (New York: Knopf, 1963). See especially chapter 21, pp. 536-58. See also his *The Responsible Electorate* (Cambridge, Mass.: Harvard University Press, 1966). For a good discussion of the "classic" literature, see Peter Rossi, "Four Landmarks in Voting Research," in *American Voting Behavior,* ed. Eugene Burdick and Arthur J. Brodbeck (Glencoe, Ill.: The Free Press, 1959), pp. 5-54.

4. Norton Long, "The Local Community as an Ecology of Games," *American Journal of Sociology* 64 (1958): 251-61.

5. Burns W. Roper, *A Ten-Year View of Public Attitudes Towards Television and Other Mass Media 1959-1968* (New York: Television Information Office, 1969), pp. 1-8.

6. Ibid.

7. Douglass Cater, *The Fourth Branch of Government* (Boston, Mass.: Houghton Mifflin, 1959).

8. See especially David Wise, *The Politics of Lying* (New York: Random House, 1973), for a thorough treatment of this topic. Wise points out that at the federal level it seems that official lying is an intrinsic part of government action. For the most part, as Wise's book shows, the lies are exposed.

9. Norman R. Luttbeg, ed., *Public Opinion and Public Policy*, rev. ed. (Homewood, Ill.: Dorsey, 1974), pp. 1-10. Luttbeg reviews the most mentioned models concerning the opinion-policy process. The intent here is to review these models and then synthesize them into a general model with the explicit inclusion of the effect of the mass media. See also Robert S. Erikson and Norman R. Luttbeg, *American Public Opinion: Its Origins, Content, and Impact* (New York: Wiley, 1973), pp. 289-310.

10. For the most elaborate use of this model, see Anthony Downs, *An Economic Theory of Democracy* (New York: Harper and Row, 1957). Downs attempts to apply the economist's rational man model to voting and governmental decision making. See especially pp. 36-77. The public choice literature of James M. Buchanan and Gordon Tullock, *The Calculus of Consent* (Ann Arbor: University of Michigan Press, 1965), develops this model more fully. See also Mancur Olson, *The Logic of Collective Action* (Cambridge, Mass.: Harvard University Press, 1971).

11. For an elaboration of this model and an attempt to develop a theory of political parties, see Frank J. Sorauf, *Party Politics in America*, 2d ed. (Boston, Mass.: Little, Brown, 1972). See especially part one, pp. 1-28 and chapter 18, pp. 408-21. For a discussion of the relationship between public opinion and party realignment and disintegration, see Walter Dean Burnham, *Critical Elections and the Mainsprings of American Politics* (New York: Norton, 1970).

12. Warren E. Miller and Donald E. Stokes, "Constituency Influence in Congress," *American Political Science Review* 57 (1963): 45-56. See also Charles E. Cnudde and Donald J. McCrone, "The Linkage Between Constituency Attitudes and Congressional Voting Behavior: A Causal Model," *American Political Science Review* 60 (1966): 66-72.

13. Donald R. Matthews and James A. Stimson, "Decision-Making by U.S. Representatives: A Preliminary Model" (Paper presented at the Conference on Political Decision-Making, University of Kentucky, April 10-11, 1968).

14. Joyce M. and William C. Mitchell, *Political Analysis and Public Policy* (Chicago. Ill.: Rand McNally, 1969). See especially chapter 9, pp. 391-410.

15. For a complete examination on the role model as it relates to predictive legislative behavior, see John C. Wahlke et al., *The Legislative System: Explorations in Legislative Behavior* (New York: Wiley, 1962).

16. Miller and Stokes, "Constituency Influence in Congress."

17. Among others, see Angus Campbell et al., *The American Voter: An Abridgement* (New York: Wiley, 1964) and *Elections and the Political Order* (New York: Wiley, 1967).

18. Luttbeg, *Public Opinion and Public Policy*, and Donald J. Devine, *The Attentive Public: Polyarchical Democracy* (Chicago: Rand McNally, 1970).

19. Devine, ibid., pp. 31-64.

20. Gabriel A. Almond, *The American People and Foreign Policy* (New York: Praeger, 1960, originally published 1950). The Almond and Devine model of influence will be compared in later chapters with Elihu Katz and

Paul F. Lazarsfeld's *Personal Influence*, 2d ed. rev. (New York: Free Press of Glencoe, 1964), among many others.

21. Devine, *The Attentive Public*, pp. 65-93. For an earlier attempt to link opinions and policy, see V.O. Key, *Public Opinion and American Democracy* (New York: Knopf, 1963), pp. 398-404.

22. Devine, ibid., p. 75.

23. While the analysis stops between 1964 and 1966, an update would be useful but unnecessary, since Devine concerns himself strictly with the time periods before and immediately after the congressional decision making.

24. Luttbeg, *Public Opinion and Public Policy*, and Devine, *The Attentive Public*, p. 80.

25. Devine, ibid.

26. Key, *Public Opinion and American Democracy*, p. 420.

27. Raymond A. Bauer, Ithiel de Sola Pool, and Louis Anthony Dexter, *American Business and Public Policy* (New York: Atherton Press, 1968).

28. Roberta Sigel and H. Paul Friesema, "Urban Community Leaders' Knowledge of Public Opinion," *Western Political Quarterly* 18 (December 1965). For a good review of the community leadership literature, see M. Margaret Conway and Frank B. Feigert, *Political Analyses: An Introduction* (Boston, Mass.: Allyn and Bacon, 1972), pp. 169-92.

29. Miller and Stokes, "Constituency Influence in Congress."

30. Matthews and Stimson, "Decision-making by U.S. Representatives."

31. Ibid.

32. Key, *Public Opinion and American Democracy*, pp. 535-57.

33. James J. Best, *Public Opinion: Micro and Macro* (Homewood, Ill.: Dorsey Press, 1973), p. 221.

34. Key, *Public Opinion and American Democracy*, pp. 414-18.

35. For a thorough account of television information manipulation see Edward Jay Epstein, *News From Nowhere: Television and the News* (New York: Random House, 1973). Also see William Small, *To Kill a Messenger: Television News and the Real World* (New York: Hastings House, 1970). The best account of government news manipulation is Wise, *The Politics of Lying*.

36. Carl Hovland was one of the most prolific investigators of factors causing attitude change. Among his more important works are: *The Order of Presentation in Persuasion* (New Haven, Conn.: Yale University Press, 1957); with others, *Communication and Persuasion* (New Haven, Conn.: Yale University Press, 1953); and, with others, *Experiments on Mass Communication* (New York: Wiley, 1949).

37. For an excellent review of the vast literature concerning issue voting with special attention given to popular control of public policy see Gerald M. Pomper, Richard W. Boyd, Richard A. Brody, Benjamin I. Page, and John H. Kessel in a series of articles on "Issue Voting," *American Political Science Review* 66, no. 2 (June 1972): 429-71.

38. Key, *Public Opinion and American Democracy*.

39. Devine, *The Attentive Public*.

40. Almond, *American People and Foreign Policy*.

41. Katz and Lazersfeld, *Personal Influence*.

42. Mancur Olson, "The Evaluation of Collective Performance," forthcoming, part I, chapter III, p. 67.

43. Cater, *Fourth Branch of Government.*

44. Donald R. Matthews, *U.S. Senators and Their World* (Chapel Hill: University of North Carolina Press, 1960).

45. The relationships between the press and the president will be explored more fully in chapter 5. Lyndon Johnson attempted to control the press by tightly controlling information. In fact, several times he changed a decision simply because it had leaked to the press. President Nixon's relations with the press were considerably strained with Nixon believing the media were generally against him personally as well as against his policies. His attempts to intimidate the press are well known and his overall relationships with the mass media bordered on mutual hostility and distrust. The handling of Watergate and the resulting scandal were a reflection of this hostile atmosphere.

46. Michael J. Arlen, *The Living Room War* (New York: Tower Publications, 1966).

47. David B. Truman, *The Governmental Process* (New York: Knopf, 1955). See also Key, *Public Opinion and American Democracy*, pp. 262-86.

48. Thomas R. Dye, *Understanding Public Policy* (Englewood Cliffs, N.J.: Prentice-Hall, 1972).

49. Alice M. Rivlin, *Systematic Thinking for Social Action* (Washington, D.C.: The Brookings Institution, 1971). For a more complete review of PPBS, see Harold A. Hovey, *The Planning-Programming-Budgeting Approach to Government Decision-Making* (New York: Praeger, 1968); Charles L. Schultze, *The Politics and Economics of Public Spending* (Washington, D.C.: The Brookings Institution, 1968); Charles J. Hitch, *Decision Making for Defense* (Berkeley: The University of California Press, 1965); Murray Weidenbaum, *The Modern Public Sector* (New York: Basic Books, 1969); and finally, U.S. Congress, Joint Economic Committee, Subcommittee on Economy in Government, *The Analysis and Evaluation of Public Expenditures: The PPB System, A Compendium of Papers*, 91st Cong., 1st sess. (1969, 3 vols.). For a good case study see Robert J. Art, *The TFX Decision* (Boston, Mass.: Little, Brown, 1968).

50. Dye, *Understanding Public Policy,* pp. 291-99.

51. Ira Sharkansky, "Government Expenditures and Public Services in the American States," *American Political Science Review* 61 (December 1967): 1066-77.

52. James R. Coleman, *Equality of Educational Opportunity* (Washington, D.C.: Government Printing Office, 1966).

53. Jay W. Forrester, *Urban Dynamics* (Cambridge, Mass.: The M.I.T. Press, 1969).

54. Bonella H. Meadows et al., *The Limits of Growth* (Secaucus, N.J.: Universe Books, 1972).

55. For a complete literature review, see James C. Strouse, "Politics, Economics, Elite Attitudes, and Public Policies: A Dynamic Analysis Using a Block Recursive Causal Model" (Ph.D. diss., University of North Carolina at Chapel Hill, 1970). A more complete discussion of the causal role of public opinion is included on pages 168-76.

56. Frank Munger, "Opinions, Elections, Parties, and Policies: A Cross State Analysis" (Paper presented at the American Political Science Association meeting, New York, September, 1969). For a more elaborate presentation of the methodology for estimating the policy preferences of the public in comparative state research, see Ronald E. Weber, *Public Policy Preferences in the States* (Bloomington, Ind.: Institute of Public Administration, 1971).

See also Anne L. Schneider, "The Use of National Survey Data to Estimate Aggregate Opinion in Small Political Units: A Computer Simulation Approach," mimeographed (Indiana University, 1972), and Ronald E. Weber and William R. Shaffer, "Public Opinion and American State Policy-Making," *Midwest Journal of Political Science* 16 (November 1972).

57. Philip L. Beardsley, "The Determinants of Public Policies in the American States: A Critique of Recent Studies" (Ph.D. diss., University of North Carolina at Chapel Hill, 1970).

58. Jack L. Walker, "The Diffusion of Innovations among the American States," *American Political Science Review* 63 (September 1969): 880-900.

59. Ira Sharkansky, *Regionalism in American Politics* (Indianapolis: Bobbs-Merrill, 1970).

60. Daniel J. Elazar, *American Federalism: A View From the States* (New York: Crowell, 1966).

61. Heinz Eulau and Robert Eyestone, "Policy Maps of City Councils and Policy Outcomes: A Developmental Analysis," *American Political Science Review* 62 (March 1968): 124-44.

62. While the entire literature is too vast to cite here, some of the more important books are: Olson, *The Logic of Collective Action*; Buchanan and Tullock, *Calculus of Consent*; James M. Buchanan and Robert D. Tollison, eds., *The Theory of Public Choice* (Ann Arbor: University of Michigan Press, 1972); James M. Buchanan, *Public Finance in Democratic Process* (Chapel Hill: University of North Carolina Press, 1967); Gordon Tullock, *Private Wants, Public Means* (New York: Basic Books, 1970); and *Papers on Non-Market Decision Making* (Charlottesville: University of Virginia Press, 1966).

63. Mancur Olson, "The Evaluation of Collective Performance," forthcoming.

64. Economists' extreme distrust of attitudinal data seems to be a result of their preference for "hard" economic statistics and their graduate training. Although the point about graduate training is hearsay evidence from economist friends, most of them indicate a distrust of attitudinal data. Since attitudinal data has been used successfully by political scientists, sociologists, and psychologists for decades, this pervasive mistrust by economists seems overdone and theoretically limiting. This is especially true because the federal government commissions a quarterly attitude survey that measures consumer confidence and spending inclinations of the public. These attitudes have been used to predict successfully consumer spending and saving habits for future quarters. In addition, stock market economists are always explaining their predictions in terms of business attitudes towards investment and public attitudes towards business growth. The famous prediction of former Secretary of the Treasury George P. Schultz of a gross national product of $1065 billions was based in part on the predictions of public attitudes by stock market analysts. I suspect the reluctance of economists to use attitudinal measures is based directly upon their lack of training in the development and measurement of attitudes.

65. Olson, "Evaluation of Collective Performance," part I, chapter III, p. 67. Used by permission of the author.

66. See Munger, "Opinions, Elections, Parties, and Policies"; Weber, *Public Policy Preferences*; Beardsley, "Determinants of Public Policies"; and Strouse, "Politics, Economics, Elite Attitudes, and Public Policies."

2 Professional
Public Relations and Political
Power

We will now explore the impact of professional public relations firms on the political process, especially political campaigning. Most congressmen and senators either employ a full-time public relations man or have a semipermanent relationship with an experienced firm. Politicians feel the need to put forth the best image and have speeches and presentations received in the most advantageous manner possible. Among the areas to be discussed are a historical inquiry into public relations firms in the political process; the successes and failures of the firms in recent elections; and the hypothesis of Walter DeVries concerning the ticket-splitter (the behavioral independent) and the problems of image building.[1]

The Media Culture and Politics

Marshall McLuhan has suggested, "Voting in the traditional sense is through as we leave the age of political parties, political issues, and political goals and enter an age where the collective tribal image and the iconic image of the tribal chieftains is the overriding political reality."[2] Hal Evry of the Public Relations Center in Los Angeles states he can elect anyone to any office if the candidate has: (1) sufficient money to wage a good media campaign ($60,000 for a state senator; $100,000 for a seat in the United States Congress); (2) an appearance that is relatively normal and from a middle-class background; (3) a better-than-average intelligence quotient (Evry suggests 120); (4) the ability to make no speeches, attend no rallies, kiss no babies and generally take a restful vacation while Evry wages an intensive media campaign with slogans on billboards, radio, and television.

While both McLuhan and Evry take rather radical approaches to the "New Politics," few would deny that the media — especially television — and the image, style-conscious candidate now dominate political campaigning. One only has to look at the multi-million dollar campaigns of many statewide candidates in 1970 to note the increasing dominance of public relations firms in politicking. The outcome of those 1970 elections, however, would suggest that both men are overstating their case.

Examining the records of some of the major political campaign firms,[3] one finds:

1. Harry Treleaven, considered the mastermind behind the "New Nixon" image, losing four of five races.

2. Robert Goodman, who successfully sold the electorate on Spiro Agnew as governor of Maryland and then vice-president, winning only two of four contests. And in Ohio, where he handled Robert Taft, Jr., Goodman stated that television only neutralized the media blitz for the Democrat Metzenbaum.

3. Charles Guggenheim, an Oscar-winning documentary film-maker, found things a bit tougher in the political marketplace. Of the eight major candidates he handled, four lost.

4. David Garth, a campaign director for John Lindsay, was one of the few clear winners with four victories in five contests. However, even Garth was doubtful about his overall effectiveness since his sole loser, Richard Ottinger, outspent his rivals and still failed to defeat the Conservative Party's James Buckley.

Given these conflicting statements and results, just what are the effects of the media on changing voters' minds? Are voters simply mesmerized by the new TV culture and mere lambs in the grasp of voracious public relations men? The eminent political scientist V. O. Key thinks not. He states that ". . . voters are not fools. To be sure, many individual voters act in odd ways indeed; yet by and large the electorate behaves as rationally and responsibly as we should expect, given the clarity of the alternatives presented to it."[4] Key then argues that the electorate is clearly moved by central concerns of public policy and governmental performance. In the 1952 presidential election, Key relates that the data show voters were rejecting a distasteful Democratic administration as much as accepting a war hero. More recent work by Richard M. Scammon and Ben J. Wattenberg states that the social issue was to dominate the 1970 state and national elections, with the voters deciding primarily on how the opposing candidates stood on crime, pollution, urban disorders, bussing, drugs, race.[5] They also mention the importance of the economic issue and its adverse reflection on the party in power, but they believe that voters did have basic perceptions of important policy-related issues and voted upon these perceptions.

Whether or not the American electorate[6] is swayed by social determinates or moved by devilishly skillful propagandists, it is quite clear that American politics in general and political campaigning specifically has been changed by the mass media and the public relations experts. It was no accident that President Nixon's personal staff was dominated by former advertising executives from California's J. Walter Thompson agency. Nixon, who many contend was defeated by his performance in the famous Nixon-Kennedy television debates, was recently considered one of the most consummate political television performers.

As early as 1952, James Reston commented: "The modern campaign is leaning more and more to use of the television and other forms of rapid communication . . . to put — [forth] arguments without giving the people much chance to answer back."[7] Reston was repulsed by the idea that one could merchandise candidates for high office as if they were breakfast cereals, an idea which seemed the ultimate indignity to the democratic process.[8]

Early Professional
Public Relations Campaigns

No discussion of the impact of public relations on politics would be complete without some discussion of the pioneers of the art — Whitaker and Baxter.[9] Since associating professionally in the 1930s, they claimed victory in seventy-four of eighty campaigns.[10] Some significant and far-reaching victories were the ones over the gubernatorial candidacy of Upton Sinclair and their nationwide victory over the Medicare proposal of the Truman administration.

The great majority of their victories involved contests in California, a state noted for its heavy influx of citizens and its lack of effective political organizations. Until the 1950s when candidates were identified by party, a candidate could run in both the Democratic and Republican primaries. Many times, in spite of a registration disadvantage (three-to-two Democratic), the Republican candidate was able to get both the Republican and Democratic nominations because of the cross-filing and voting. Former Governor Earl Warren (a Whitaker and Baxter client) consistently did this when a candidate for governor in California. California with its cross-primaries (voters, regardless of party identification, could vote in either the Democratic or Republican primary), lack of patronage, and constant influx of new citizens was a good climate for the mass-appeal campaign.

The design of each campaign was different, but all were really the same with certain basic similarities in strategy and tactics. Timing was very important. A cardinal Whitaker and Baxter rule was to allocate 75 percent of their budget to the final three to four weeks of the campaign. "Repetition is the only way to get someone to grow from neutral to affirmative."[11] Every campaign had a dominant theme, emphasizing simplicity and clarity. The key to their strategy was to put on a fight or put on a show, both of which were approaches that they claimed the American public loves.

The firm's success was credited to shrewd strategy utilizing thorough organization and to the imaginative exploitation of all the media of communications. By the time one of their campaigns was over, the unwary citizenry had been engulfed in propaganda — 10 million pamphlets, 50,000 letters to leaders in the community, 70,000 inches of ads in 700 newspapers, 3,000 spot announcements on 109 radio stations, theater slides and trailers in 160 theaters, 1,000 large billboards, and 18-20,000 small posters.[12]

Whitaker and Baxter believed that what they were doing was only a refined approach of what the old style politician did. Others would point out that the old-timers did not have the domination of the mass media and had to stick to some facts — at least they did not manufacture reality. The old politician had to let the public engineer its own consent, while today's public relations firms attempt to engineer what they want to be the public consent.[13]

The Tydings-Butler
Campaign

Stanley Kelley in his discussion of the "star" system in politics points out that, in the future, "the public relations man may be expected to affect the people's choice of candidates as a manager and a coach — perhaps even as a talent scout."[14] In the Butler campaign for the Maryland Senate, Jon Jonkel, a Chicago public relations man, was not a recruiter, but he did run the entire campaign for John Marshall Butler — so much so that Butler was reported seen in his campaign headquarters only three days in the entire effort.

The Butler-Tydings conflict has become a classic example of the power of propaganda and slogans. To get some idea of the odds against the Republican Butler winning, one should consider that Maryland has a three-to-one Democratic registration edge; Senator Millard Tydings was a veteran of eighteen years in the Senate and considered one of the most powerful political leaders in the country; and Tydings won by substantial margins in his two previous re-elections (200,000 in 1938, 134,000 in 1944). In his 1938 effort, Tydings defeated President Roosevelt's efforts to unseat him.

Tydings was a war hero, chairman of the Senate Foreign Relations Committee, and a product of a state that was over 70 percent Democratic. Butler was a lawyer and a socialite but his race for the Senate was to be his first elective office. He was married to the daughter of the family which published the *Baltimore Sunpapers*, but even the *Sunpapers* supported Tydings. The state had had no Republican senator since 1928. Butler had money but little organizational support.

Since Jonkel could not hope to equal the well-oiled political machinery of the Democrats, his strategy became one of publicizing Butler's name, creating an illusion of victory for his candidate and concentrating on winning the primary. An advertising schedule was set up. One inch, one column "Be for Butler" ads were placed on each page of Maryland weeklies. Direct mail was sent to group leaders. About 200,000 postcards were sent to Republicans asking for help and support.[15]

After Butler won the Republican primary, Jonkel concentrated on Tydings and tried to associate the senator with a whitewash of suspected Communists since the Foreign Relations Committee, which Tydings chaired, had just conducted an investigation of Communists in the State Department and concluded that the much-suspected department was free of subversive influence. Since the 1950s were the heyday of the McCarthy charges about communism in government, the effect of the Tydings-communism link was significant. Along with this approach, the newspaper advertising was continued. On radio and television, the stress was on spot announcements — to gain name familiarization with the same themes phrased and rephrased, interwoven and reiterated until the public was inundated by them.

Throughout the six weeks of campaigning, Jonkel hammered on Tydings and communism since he felt it was a big issue. "The Democratic party has to resolve the issue of communism. It is a big issue. The doubt exists. All you have to do is to go against it."[16] He kept it up with the slogan. In the last three and one-half days of the campaign Jonkel used 465 spot announcements for Butler in an attempt to give the name of Butler as much exposure as possible.

In the final week, a photo appeared showing Senator Tydings shaking hands with the Communist Browder. While Tydings and Butler disavowed the picture, many political observers felt this did substantial damage to the Tydings candidacy. The final results were Tydings, 283,258; Butler, 326,286. Tydings reported spending $35,840 while Butler's reported expenditure had been $82,913. The seemingly invincible Tydings, conqueror of President Roosevelt, had been beaten by a political unknown with a perceptive public relations man.

Public Relations Center, Inc.

William Miller has warned, "If present trends continue, we may get political campaigns tailored to fit the requirements of public relations and then government tailored to fit the requirements of the campaign."[17] In California at least the trends have continued, and now there is the Public Relations Center, Inc., which promises any candidate victory if he has money, makes no speeches, does nothing, and allows the firm to have complete control over his campaign. The whole campaign is waged by getting the public to recognize the candidate's name through the mass media. If this can be done, perhaps Marshall McLuhan's thesis that the medium itself is the message is true.

For those who doubt the effect of the new scientific way of politicking, consider the case of Jerry Pettis who came to the Public Relations Center and asked for help in running for Congress. Pettis was completely unknown; the campaign was based entirely on cartoons of a little boy and a little girl lying on their backs with warm folksy words ballooning out of their mouths saying: "I like Jerry Pettis. He likes us kids." Pettis' vote count was greater than any candidate in either the Democratic or Republican primary. But because of pressure to campaign more by traditional methods, Pettis decided to employ a bigger, more sophisticated public relations firm. This firm provided him with issues, statements, and speeches. He was defeated in the November election by an opponent whose public relations firm was none other than Hal Ervy's.[18]

To observers who charge that an Evry type of campaign degrades the level of politics by making possible the election of unqualified candidates, Evry replies that unqualified candidates are being elected all the time under the old methods. The new methods may actually improve the level of politics by allowing qualified candidates to run who would never have tried to in the unsophisticated days because the political leaders would have convinced them that they did not have a chance without the backing of the organization.

How valid is the Evry technique? Since he claims to have won in thirty of thirty-four political elections, perhaps the technique has already been meaningfully tested. Survey research indicates that he is correct in the assumption that the great majority of the electorate is uninformed and uninterested in politics. Converse showed that party identification only counts as the decisive influence on the vote choice when there is a lack of information or when mass media campaigns cancel out each other's influence.[19] Since the great majority of political candidates still rely on organization support and the backing of key leaders, they are not waging a total communications campaign like the one indicated by Evry. From the literature surveyed, this technique of campaigning seems to have great merit.

The ideal campaign for Evry and his associates is one similar to Senator Ted Kennedy's who waged his campaign from his hospital bed.[20] Without making one speech or going to one political rally, he received the biggest vote in the history of Massachusetts.

The mass of clichés about the clubhouse organization, the precinct workers, the volunteer workers, and the grass roots are just self-serving terms to describe the tiny percentage of the public which takes an active interest in politics. Most candidates will listen to the suggestions of friends, relatives, party workers, and old-fashioned party leaders. But the candidates who win nowadays are invariably those who have taken advice from research analysts who have thoroughly examined the attitudes of the mass of voters and have communicated with them in terms of their common frames of reference. The communications experts of this new generation of political strategists translate the information about the public into meaningful and useful ideas which can be relayed to the voters in words, pictures, and music that have a profound impact on voter attitudes and behavior. For this public relations firm, aiming the campaign at the politically active and interested makes about as much sense as it would be for General Motors to aim all its advertising communications at racing-car drivers.

The Evry strategy is straightforward: figure out what the people want, then hit them early and hit them hard — with advertising, posters, bumper strips, letters, publicity stories, television spots — anything at all but speeches. If the strategy is effective the candidate gains, first, recognition; second, favorable recognition; and, finally, the political office the candidate desires. In this type of campaign, issues are not nearly as important as the job of conveying the issues in a simple way to capture the disinterested people who make up the great bulk of the voters.

Recent Elections

During the 1966 contest, Milton Shapp in Pennsylvania and Nelson Rockefeller in New York had effective media campaigns. At the start of Shapp's campaign, he was familiar to 5.2 percent of Pennsylvanian voters.[21] In July, a few weeks after the primary media blitz directed by new politics expert Joe Napolitan, the recognition figure leaped to 65.5 percent. Governor Rockefeller was trailing Democrat O'Connor by a wide margin in early polls. Through an intensive media barrage aimed at changing the negative aspects of his image, Rockefeller was able to overcome this initial disadvantage. Both candidates were wealthy and waged campaigns primarily through the media and especially through television. In comparing the two campaigns, Robert MacNeil comments, "Whereas Milton Shapp's primary campaign in Pennsylvania showed the extraordinary potency of a last minute [television] blitz for a candidate who is unknown, Rockefeller's demonstrates the power of a long, low-keyed saturation of opinion. A comparison of these two campaigns suggests that where there is something unfavorable in the established image of a candidate [Shapp's arrogance, Rockefeller's tax increase], the slow treatment dispels it more efficiently, like irradication of a cancer."[22] Perhaps the Rockefeller campaign experts used a modified version of the "Sleeper Effect" that Hovland's studies showed. This hypothesis states that over time people forget the source of the message but retain the message itself. Many other campaigns could be recounted that indicate the potential effects of a sophisticated media campaign. One of the more interesting and crucial elections was the 1968 presidential election in which President Nixon's advisers devoted a great deal of money and effort to negate the "Old Nixon" and create the "New Nixon."

Joe McGinniss relates the influence of the media in the Nixon campaign: "Politics, in a sense, has always been a con game. The American voter, insisting on his belief in a higher order, clings to his religion which promises another, better life; and defends passionately the illusion that the men he chooses to lead him are of finer nature than he."[23] Of course, the purpose of the media campaign is to convince the voter of the ultimate truth of his illusion. "Style becomes substance. The medium is the massage, and the masseur gets the voters."[24] In dealing with the negative image of the voters, Nixon's advisers believed the negative response was to the image, not the man. "It's not what's there that counts, its what he projects — and carrying it one step further, it's not what he projects but rather what the voter receives."[25] However, in spite of Nixon's heavy investment in image reformation, the later polls indicated that his campaign was losing its appeal to the American electorate, and Humphrey, in spite of Vietnam and his poor television appearances, was catching up.

It is interesting to note the attitudes of Nixon's managers toward the end of the campaign. "A candidate can't be too smooth. There have to be some rough edges that cling to the surface of the country. . . . Nixon is hiding behind his communications effort. Humphrey, because he doesn't have one, is out front. In the end, communications skills alone can't do it. . . . I don't think it's possible to merchandise a vegetable."[26] Nixon would not have been pleased with his adviser's analogy, but the "New Nixon" was slipping rapidly and the campaign "that was to rewrite the textbooks" seemed in danger of disaster.[27] The results of the election saved Nixon's public relations men and practically willed them the White House. Of course, media campaigns are but one factor in the mass of causal factors determining the vote decision. If used properly they can be an effective weapon, but they are very seldom the ultimate weapon.

One of the most effective uses of the media is to create group approval. Group influence was crucial in determining one's reaction to the test. Harry Treleaven, one of Nixon's chief media experts, comments, "No advertising will ever have the influence that friend's opinion has. Fifty million dollars worth of Ford advertising can't convince you like a neighbor's comment, 'Best car I ever owned.' This is the 'prior approval' factor at work; he likes it, so maybe I would (or should) too. One should recall that many of the Nixon programs had 'average Americans' of all races and ethnic groups asking questions directly to the candidates and receiving homey, seemingly unrehearsed answers. The feeling supposed to be transmitted was, if they like him maybe I should also."[28]

This group or sociocultural model of persuasion follows from the idea that media effects in general are influenced by the social interactions a group member has. Melvin DeFleur inquires into how social and cultural variables affect the persuasion process.[29] He comments on the dearth of research in this area while noting that such appeals are used in mass advertising with regularity. "Existing theories of persuasion see group or interactional phenomena largely in terms of possible tools to be used in achieving the desired effects."[30] The model for the influence process is shown in figure 10.

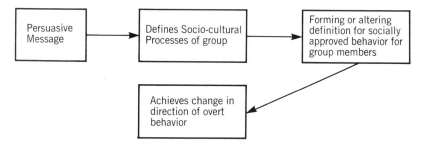

SOURCE: Copyright © 1966 and 1970 by David McKay Co. Inc. From the book *Theories of Mass Communication* by Melvin DeFleur, p. 135. Published by the David McKay Company Inc. Used with permission of the publishers.

Figure 10
A Socio-Cultural Model of Persuasion

The persuasive message presented via the mass media should provide the appearance of consensus with respect to a given object or goal. It can be suggested that: (1) the nonadopter is a deviant, with implications of possible social sanctions; (2) at the same time, one can show social rewards and approval for the adoption of the communication; and (3) the adoption achieves group integration consistent with group-approved values. Thus the persuasive message becomes an integral part of the group process. Of course, public relations experts have attempted to integrate group appeals with their political advertisements and often have been quite successful. Whitaker and Baxter, in their prime days as America's preeminent political public relations firm, used to concentrate on all kinds of groups throughout California. The point that DeFleur is making is that the group norms and sanctions should be an integral part of the persuasive message. Thus, even accepting the two-step flow of information and influence, one can readily see that this two-step flow, rather than being an obstacle in potential influence of a persuasive message, can be the message's most important component.

DeFleur gives an example of how the process works regarding cigarette advertising.[31] The goal of much of this advertising is to increase the rate and quantity of cigarette consumption among young adults. First, the peer group includes the use of cigarettes. Then, cigarettes are presented to relate to important group norms. Adoption thus becomes normative and nonadopters appear by implication to be deviants. Finally, the young adult is shown that social disapproval is a well-deserved fate for the nonconformist and that most sophisticates smoke. The overall purpose of the communication is to provide social realities where none actually exist.

Public Relations and Political Power
in the Agnew-Mahoney 1966 Contest

In a partial test of the Evry thesis, we will study the 1966 gubernatorial election in Maryland. One candidate used Evry as a part-time consultant for both the primary and the general election. The Republican candidate was a well-regarded Republican elected four years previously as county executive of the largest county in Maryland. He was Spiro "Ted" Agnew, whom the *Washington Post* and the *Baltimore Sun* called the liberal, concerned candidate in the election.[32] In fact the *Washington Post* and its television subsidiary was accused, and many observers reported quite fairly, of staging a Ku Klux Klan rally purported to endorse George P. Mahoney, the Democratic candidate. WTOP-TV just happened to be at a Montgomery County farm one evening where the rebuilding Klan organization was staging a massive rally attended by more TV personnel than KKK followers. The interview featured the hooded leader extolling the candidacy of Mahoney.

The primary contest was the most appropriate test of Evry's ideas, for Mahoney, the perennial candidate, was running against two formidable foes — Thomas Finan, the state's attorney general and the organization's candidate, and Carlton Sickles, a Washington suburban congressman with considerable liberal, labor, and suburban support. Mahoney ran a heavily media-oriented campaign saying little more than "Your home is your castle," since open housing was an important issue, both locally and nationally. However, Mahoney refused to stay at home, and since he enjoyed "shoeleathering," meeting the people, and talking to his political allies, he also waged a more traditional campaign based primarily in Baltimore. Nonetheless, almost all the party organization and liberal reformers were backing either Finan or Sickles. Mahoney, with few people even willing to listen to him, ran on his anti-open housing slogan. In a very close election, Mahoney won, polling just over a third of the votes cast. Many political analysts, attempting to construct some ex post facto reasoning, stated that Mahoney (who was running for his sixth time for statewide office) always received that many votes (approximately 135,000) and people in Baltimore City and Baltimore County were simply continuing a habit established over the many Mahoney campaigns. However, most of these same analysts refused to even consider the Mahoney candidacy seriously and virtually ignored his campaign.

The general election was harder to analyze even though the Democrats outnumbered Republicans in the state almost three to one. Spiro Agnew, the hero of the liberal press, had an excellent public relations firm, the Robert Goodman Agency of Baltimore. Agnew was a better speaker, younger, more liberal, less racist, and gave a much more impressive appearance than Mahoney.

Campaign Strategies

To determine the campaign strategies of the two gubernatorial candidates, the writer interviewed Paul Reed, Jr., campaign manager for Mahoney, and Ronald Wilner, the individual who handled all publicity for the Agnew campaign. (Wilner related that Agnew's objective in the primary was to gain name familiarization since he was not well known outside the Baltimore metropolitan area and would have only token opposition in the Republican primary.) A song entitled "My Kind of Man" was adapted for this purpose and played continually over the radio. Agnew gave this agency complete control of his publicity and, according to Wilner, never changed or "second-guessed" the agency's decisions. "He was the perfect client."[33] When asked about the Evry technique, Wilner claimed to know something about it and said that it oversimplified the whole campaign process. He felt that Mahoney's refusal to debate or discuss other issues actually helped Agnew since it placed a mantle of incompetence on Mahoney.

When asked about the complete editorial support of the major newspapers, the advertising specialist claimed that the *Baltimore*

Sun would have supported Agnew regardless of the Republican's opposition since Agnew was the type of "middle road" politician that the *Sun's* editors liked. To avoid the registration disadvantage, Agnew's strategy was to discuss his bipartisan approach to problems. His advertisements never mentioned that Agnew was the Republican candidate — they simply stressed that he was the candidate of all the people. Although Wilner felt that employing a simple name familiarization campaign was an oversimplification, especially in a statewide campaign, he was impressed with the power of sloganism. In this backhanded way, the publicity expert paid tribute to the power and impact of the Mahoney slogan, "Your home is your castle." The slogan seemed to be effective in reaching the electorate, yet Mahoney's complete reliance on it gave Agnew the opportunity to charge him with incompetence and racism.

While bitter because he felt that the press did not treat Mahoney fairly, Reed related that the Democratic nominee's campaign strategy was to use a timely issue effectively (presumable, open-housing) and meet the people. Reed felt that the papers and their editors were against Mahoney because they "knew they couldn't control him." Also, Reed mentioned that the people with money in the state probably put pressure on the editors and might have used their advertising as a threat if the editors did not agree to oppose Mahoney. The conspiracy theory advocated by Reed seemed to pose the traditional view of the Democrat representing the people while the Republican was controlled by the monied interests.

When asked about Hal Evry and his political campaign techniques (no speeches, no debates, sloganism to gain recognition), he did deny that Evry was in any manner connected with the Democrat's campaign. In fact, Reed was quite emphatic in his belief that voters will not accept this type of campaign. "People won't buy just slogans; they will think you are crazy. You need timely issues and a saleable product. A candidate has to be quick and photogenic like Ronald Reagan and be able to convey his thoughts to the people."[34]

While admitting that open housing was a timely issue, Reed emphasized that the issue was only part of the Mahoney message. He listed twenty other issues that Mahoney mentioned but were ignored by the press. He thought that Agnew's attacks on Mahoney's incompetence and racist beliefs were groundless. He instead pointed to Mahoney's record of accomplishments in business and charity drives; however, Reed admitted that the attacks were effective. When asked about Mahoney's tendency to slur words and appear incoherent at times, Reed pointed out that the Irishman was no orator and because he had just switched dental plates, he tended to slur his words much more than he ever did and gave the impression of being incoherent. Reed also felt that if anyone was a racist, it was Agnew for bringing up the subject constantly. The turning point in the campaign was the point at which religious leaders throughout the state attacked Mahoney's campaign for its racist quality. Reed pointedly referred to Monsignor Gallagher's editorial in the *Catholic Review*, a statement which strongly condemned the racial overtones of Mahoney's campaign.

While commenting about campaign strategy, Reed mentioned that radio and television should constitute about 75 percent of a campaign. He thought that the organization was still important, its main function being to get you "off the ground." "For example, there are 580 precincts in Baltimore and in each there are four workers; if there are four factions working together, each having four workers and each worker talking to four different people, then there are almost 41,000 people talking about the candidate and his qualifications for office. Usually the factions are not cooperating but supporting five different candidates. In any case, though, the organization gets you started — you must do the rest."[35]

Hal Evry commented on Mahoney's campaign:

"A Man's Home Is His Castle" is a slogan widely used in last year's election. It was used successfully by Kirk, new Governor of Florida, newly elected Assemblyman Wakefield in South Gate, California and of course in the primary by Mr. Mahoney.

We did have a number of conversations with Mr. Mahoney but his campaign was steered by other people.

Mr. Mahoney is a classic example of our philosophies in action. Not only was he an ineffective and unarticulate speaker, he was also ill equipped in experience to serve as Governor of that state. Consequently, he made few public appearances and communicated through mass media.

I point out also that despite party hostility he was able to whallop the Democratic supported candidate in the primary. This sort of thing happened all over America — Rolwag in Minnesota, Morrison in Louisiana, Shapp in Pennsylvania and Samuelson in Idaho — all good examples of winning without party support and actually in the face of party hostility.

You asked my opinion as to why Mahoney lost in the final election. My only answer is that his TV techniques were pretty deplorable. Professional TV direction, I think, would have made him a shoo-in.[36]

According to Evry, Mahoney did seek advice from the Public Relations Center, contrary to what Reed suggested. However, as both Reed and Evry stated, Mahoney's own advisors ran his campaign.

Issues and Results

The important issues in the campaign seemed to be racism and incompetence. On both issues, Mahoney came out behind Agnew. Mahoney's public speaking performances were atrocious with Mahoney's slight speech impediment giving the sound of moderate inebriation. Tables 2-1, 2-2, and 2-3 report the findings of a random sample taken from Baltimore County (Agnew's home county) and indicate strongly that Mahoney was considered to be a racist and an incompetent individual.

Table 2-1

Comparison[a] Between the Vote and Whether the Voter Believed Any Candidate a Racist

Vote	Any Candidate Racist [b]	
	Yes $(N = 66)$	No $(N = 177)$
Agnew	71% $(N = 47)$	42% $(N = 74)$
Mahoney	29% $(N = 19)$	58% $(N = 103)$

$X^2 = 16.62$; d.f. $= 1$; $p < .001$

[a]Chi square (X^2) values help indicate whether the relationship posited in the table is statistically significant; that is, whether one is justified in generalizing the relationship to the population-at-large. A $p < .05$ or lower ($p < .01$; $p < .001$) indicates statistical significance and means that only five times in one hundred possible surveys would this relationship happen by chance. Because the table indicates a $p < .001$ (one chance in a thousand possible surveys would this happen by chance), one can say that there is a significant relationship between the vote and whether voters thought one candidate to be a racist. N is the number of voters.

[b]Do you think any of the candidates for governor was a racist?

If the voter perceived any candidate as a racist, it had a significant effect on his vote. As table 2-1 indicates, 71 percent of those who thought one candidate was bigoted voted for Agnew while only 42 percent voted for the Republican if the voter saw no candidate with racial prejudgements. Thus, racism was a key factor in changing the direction of the vote from Democratic to Republican.

To further test the hypothesis that Agnew's accusations were the most important factor in the voter's decision, the voters' choice was compared with whom they thought was the prejudiced candidate (table 2-2). Again there is a significant relationship between the voters' perception of which candidate was a racist and their vote choice.

Table 2-2

Comparison Between the Voters' Choice and Who the Voters Thought Was the Racist Candidate

Vote	Who Racist[a]	
	Agnew ($N = 8$)	Mahoney ($N = 51$)
Agnew	38% ($N = 3$)	78% ($N = 40$)
Mahoney	62% ($N = 5$)	22% ($N = 11$)

$X^2 = 5.68$; df = 1; p < .05
[a]Who did you think was the racist candidate?

Another charge that Agnew leveled at Mahoney was that the Democrat was incompetent. Agnew said that Mahoney had no governmental experience, that Mahoney could not speak and that he was old and perhaps ill. To test the effectiveness of the incompetence charge, the respondents were asked to identify whether they thought any candidate was incompetent. These answers were compared with the vote (table 2-3). Chi square of 36.0 is significant at the .001 level. This means that there is less than one chance in one thousand that we would obtain these results by chance. The measure of associations, gamma, indicates that the voters felt that competency was an issue in the election. This strong positive relationship does not tell who the voters thought incompetent. Two controls were applied to determine the breakdown of voter attitudes. One control was race; the other was age. Three measures of association were obtained for three race subdivisions. The gamma for white voters was a positive .54, for black voters it was positive

Table 2-3

Comparison Between Voters' Choice and
Whether the Voters Thought Any
Candidate Incompetent

Voted for:	Yes (N = 122)	No (N = 122)	Totals
Agnew	69% (84)	29% (33)	117
Mahoney	31% (38)	71% (79)	117

Gamma = +.48
$p < .001$ level   Chi Square = +36.0   df = 1

.67, and for oriental, it was positive .33. These positive measures indicate that blacks considered Mahoney incompetent. The white voters were close and the oriental voters were third. However, it is important to notice that no group considered the Republican candidate incompetent.

Another finding that supports the notion that racism and Mahoney's slogan "Your home is your castle" were very important in the campaign is the voters' awareness of the issue and their understanding of it. Surveys show that most Americans are unaware of issues and unable to describe most issues except at the most general level, yet questions from this campaign concerning open housing indicated a widespread awareness of the issue and an understanding of its meaning (table 2-4). It is true that race has always been an explosive and emotional issue; however, neither Agnew nor Mahoney had a racist background and race had almost never been a central issue in Maryland politics, at least in recent decades.

Table 2-4

Results of Questions Concerning
Open Housing (in percent)

	Yes	No
Was open housing important?	74% (N = 194)	26% (N = 67)
	Know	Did not know
What is open housing?	81% (N = 213)	19% (N = 48)

Because of the high percentage of persons perceiving the issue as being important and the even more impressive percentage of persons who understood what the issue meant, one would think that it would have a substantial impact upon the electorate. We have already tested whether the vote of a given individual was statistically related to remembering Mahoney's slogan and found no significant relationship. We will now examine what effect the voters' perception of open housing as being important had on the vote. From table 2-5 we can see that there is no significant difference be-

Table 2-5

Comparison Between the Vote and
Whether the Voter Believed
Open Housing To Be Important

Vote	Open housing important[a]	
	Yes (N = 192)	No (N = 55)
Agnew	50% (N = 96)	51% (N = 28)
Mahoney	50% (N = 96)	49% (N = 27)

X^2 = .01; df = 1; p > .05
[a]Do you think that open housing was an important issue in the election?

tween how one voted and whether he did or did not consider open housing to be important. One might conclude, then, that open housing and Mahoney's slogan had no effect on the voter's choice.

While table 2-5 shows no significant results, one should not discount the high percentage of respondents who thought the issue important (74 percent) or the high percentage who could explain what open housing meant (81 percent). The 81 percent who could explain the issue is quite surprising since other survey research indicates that the public's issue familiarity is very low. Angus Campbell relates the example of the Democrats choosing the Taft-Hartley Act as a major point of attack during the 1948 election.[37] In spite of acrimonious and widespread debate on the issue, survey research showed that seven out of ten adult Americans saw the election end not understanding the meaning and intent of the act. However, one might speculate that this question affected the election indirectly, reinforcing some other variable influencing the election.

While the Agnew victory tends to discount the effect of Evry's public relations philosophy, Mahoney made an impressive showing, especially in the primaries. Mahoney was a perennial candidate lightly regarded in the primaries by Thomas Finan, the Democratic old-line organization's candidate. Mahoney's primary victory seemed directly related to his slogan while his general election loss seemed related to his general inabilities as a public speaker and as a man incapable of being an effective governor. The public relations techniques worked well in the primaries but were ineffective in the general election. This has been the experience of many candidates handled by slick public relations firms. In the primaries, where voter interest and attention are low, name familiarization and skillful use of slogans appear to be extremely important. In the general election,[38] where public scrutiny is much closer and in much greater depth, issues and candidate image (ability to do the job, appearance) appear to outweigh and overwhelm slogans and name familiarization campaigns. The ultimate strategy is to meld the image with the slogan and sell it to a more interested and informed electorate. Recent elections showing major public relations firms failing 50 percent of the time indicate that the selling job in the general election is very difficult. In fact, the candidate would probably do as well (certainly with less expense) without the public relations effort in the general election.

The Ticket-Splitters

Walter DeVries and V. Lance Tarrance distinguish between an independent (self-perceived) and a behavioral independent (based on ticket-splitting voting behavior).[39] The group they focus on is the group that consistently splits its votes between the major parties in election after election. While over 30 percent of the American electorate perceive themselves as being political independents, DeVries and Tarrance indicate a much larger behavioral independent group. In a 1967 national survey, 25.7 percent perceive themselves as Republicans; 44.9 percent say they are Democrats; and 25.1 percent call themselves Independents. Of those who called themselves Republicans, 19.3 percent say they vote a split ticket; that is, they are behavioral independents. Of the Democrats, 32.7 percent vote a split ticket. The Independents vote split tickets

43.7 percent of the time. With the increase in Independent registration, one would expect the split ticket voting to be even higher.

DeVries and Tarrance assess the causal factors in the vote decision differently than most academicians. They suggest that candidate image and then issues are the paramount factors. The thrust of the public relations effort is to meld the image with the crucial issues. Their findings are shown in figure 11.

TODAY_ _ _ _ _ _ _ _ _ _ _ _ _ _ and_ _ _ _ _ NOT SO LONG AGO

1. *Candidates*
   ability to handle the job
   personality

1. *Party*

2. *Issues*
   candidates' stands
   candidates' and party's ability
   to handle problems

2. *Group Affiliations*

3. *Party*
   identification
   membership

3. *Candidates*

4. *Group Affiliations*
   religious
   ethnic
   occupational

4. *Issues*

SOURCE: Walter DeVries and V. Lance Tarrance, *The Ticket Splitter: A New Force in American Politics* (Grand Rapids, Mich.: Eerdmans, 1972), p. 74. Used by permission of the publisher.

Figure 11
Factors Causing Voter Choice

In this figure, DeVries and Tarrance point out that the crucial causal variable is no longer party identification but the voters' perception of a candidate's ability to handle the job, of his image, and of his personality. Both party and group affiliation are relegated in importance behind candidates and issues. Of course, issues are closely related to the projected image of a candidate. This finding agrees substantially with the Converse finding concerning the influence of short-term factors such as information.[40] Converse found that as information becomes more readily available to the general population, party impact declines in importance as a major determinant of the election decision. With more and more candidates gearing their campaigns to the media, especially at the statewide and national levels, the importance of party identification will continue to diminish.

Table 3-6 serves to substantiate the general conclusions in figure 11. When asked: "As you make up your mind about political matters, what were the most important things that come to mind?", voters answered heavily in terms of candidate — especially image-related factors — and issue-oriented responses.

Table 2-6

Most Important Things in Deciding Political Matters: Michigan*   (May, 1970; n=809)

Candidate-oriented responses:	
Personality and background	48.1%
Ability to do the job	28.0
Stand on issues	19.9
Issue-oriented responses:	36.8
Party-oriented responses:	11.9
Media-oriented responses:	9.5
Others/Don't know	15.2
(multiple responses)	

* = The question asked was: "As you make up your mind about political matters, What are the most important things that come to mind?"

SOURCE: Ray E. Hiebert et al., *The Political Image Merchants* (Washington, D.C.: Acropolis Books, 1971), p. 67. Used by permission of the publisher.

Concentrating on an intensive analysis of the undecided vote, DeVries and Tarrance asked a sample of 809 undecided voters throughout Michigan how important to their vote decision was the list of factors indicated in table 2-7. The respondents were asked to indicate how important each factor was on a scale of 1, not important, to 7, very important. Table 2-7 indicates the results. In the very important category were five items directly involving television, a total of nine items related to media (of eleven considered very important), only one item concerning primary or secondary group influence, one party item, and one person-to-person contact item. From this, it seems that the undecided voter is getting most of his important political information and interpretation from the media, especially television. DeVries commented on the importance of television news and editorials and related a basic campaign strategy in the Milliken campaign.[41] He concentrated most of his short political advertisements right before and after the news programs and formated these spots to be very similar to actual news broadcasts. The mass media, and especially television, dominate the very important category. Personal contacts and social relationships seem to dominate the important category.

Table 2-7

Relative Importance of Factors that Influence the Voting Decisions of 1970 Gubernatorial Undecideds   (May, 1970; n = 809)

Very Important (5.0 and over)	Important (3.0–4.9)	Not Important (1.0–2.9)
Television newscasts	Talks with friends	Magazine advertisements
Television documentaries and specials	Radio talk shows	Television entertainers
Newspaper editorials	Magazine editorials	Billboards
Television editorials	Talks with political party workers	Telephone campaign messages
Television talk shows	Talks with work associates	Movies
Television educational programs	Radio editorials	Stage plays
Radio newscasts	Political brochures	Phonograph records
Radio educational programs	Talks with neighbors	
Talk with family	Magazine stories	
The Democratic party	Newspaper advertisements	
Contacts with candidates	The Republican party	
	Television advertisements	
	Books	
	Political mailings	
	Membership in religious organizations	
	Membership in professional or business organizations	
	Radio advertisements	

Source: Walter DeVries and V. Lance Tarrance, *The Ticket Splitter: A New Force in American Politics* (Grand Rapids, Mich.: Eerdmans, 1972), p. 76. Used by permission of the publisher.

The last table in this study reflects responses of 206 interviewees surveyed immediately after the election (table 2-8). As noted before, the switch from one candidate to another was very small — almost nonexistent (3 percent). However, if one includes those who were undecided in the change category, then the majority of voters were in this category — almost 60 percent of the voters sampled. The undecided to Levin category, the Democratic opponent, decided mostly on the basis of issues. The undecided to Milliken voters seemed to make their decision on the basis of candidate-oriented reasons. The candidate-oriented reasons are directly related to image and personality factors which are most clearly presented to most voters via television campaign spots. The authors concluded that Milliken's superior image actually won the election for him in a state that is heavily Democratic and which gave strong majorities to most Democratic candidates in the 1970 election.

Table 2-8

1970 Michigan *After-Election Study:*
Most Important Things in Deciding How
to Vote for Governor[1]   (n = 206)

Voting Decision[2]	Candi-date Oriented	Issue Oriented	Media Oriented	Party Oriented	Inter-personal Oriented	Don't Know/ Other	Number of Respond-ents
Milliken to Levin	—	—	—	—	—	100.0%	1
Levin—Levin	17.4%	19.6%	2.2%	15.2%	2.2%	43.4	46
Undecided to Levin	16.3	27.9	6.9	16.3	—	32.6	43
All Levin voters	16.7	23.3	4.4	15.6	1.1	38.9	90
Levin to Milliken	20.0	40.0	—	20.0	0.0	20.0	5
Milliken—Milliken	32.5	15.0	10.0	5.0	2.5	35.0	40
Undecided to Milliken	33.8	11.3	5.6	4.2	—	45.1	71
All Milliken voters	32.8	13.8	6.9	5.2	0.9	40.4	116
TOTAL ALL VOTERS	25.7	18.0	5.8	9.7	1.0	40.8	206

[1]The question asked was: "As you think about how you made up your mind to vote for governor, what are the most important things that helped you to decide?"
All of the responses were grouped into six categories related to candidates, issues, media, party, inter-personal and "other" which included "Don't knows."

[2]These categories represent behavior shifts (where appropriate) that occurred between October 27 and November 16.

Source: Ray E. Hiebert et al., *The Political Image Merchants* (Washington, D.C.: Acropolis Books, 1971), p. 77. Used by permission of the publisher.

While the data just presented are some of the most comprehensive available on the undecided voter, data at several time points indicating the most important influence on the final decision are still needed. The impact of television specifically and the media in general is shown quite clearly by these results.

Given all this information about the American voter and how he is likely to make his electoral decision, what implications can be drawn from future elections and future campaign managers? What are the effects of media on the electoral process and what implications are there for American participatory democracy?

Effects and
Implications

Comments by Public Relations Managers

Robert Bonitati, author of a recent book of campaign management and former president of Robert-Lynn Associates, Inc., relates a number of ideas concerning the New Politics.[42] First, few politicians really understand the media. Only the marginal candidates (those elected with less than 55 percent of the vote) are likely to lose and most politicians direct their media on petty public relations such as handouts, letters at the time of high school graduation, and so on, rather than on the real vote getter, the media on the 6 o'clock news. Because of money problems most candidates never have a chance. It takes a great deal of money to wage a sophisticated media campaign and most candidates are unwilling to pay the price. But even with enough money, the real keys are style and personality; "he must come on as a real person." To get rid of an incumbent, one must find something wrong with him. People do not like to change for the sake of change and are generally fearful even at the mention of change. So, the keys to success are: a believable candidate; money; effective use of media; and something wrong with the incumbent.

Paul Lutzker attempted to survey political generalists to find out their method of operation and their collective beliefs about the American voter.[43] He found that they basically agreed on the type of help given to the clients. Polling and effective interpretation of the polls was an essential ingredient. Establishing proper political organization and effective use of volunteers was another key aid. Getting the best possible use of the candidates' resources was particularly appealing since most public relations firms argue, "you can't afford not to have me." Finally they bring a wealth of experience in running campaigns. As for specific strategies, most replied it depends on the candidate and the specific campaign.

Television versus Newspaper Effects

According to a series of Roper Public Opinion Surveys, television had begun to displace all other media as a "primary" news source for the majority of the public (51 percent) as early as 1959. By 1967, the Roper surveys indicated that 64 percent of the American public cited television as its primary news source. This trend is expected to continue, as youth is particularly addicted to television. When asked what is the most believable medium (among television, radio, newspapers, and magazines), 36 percent of those over fifty said television. It is this potential domination by television and other electronic media that McLuhan believes will transform politics.[44] Television has created the electronic man who sees things in totality. He sees government not as a series of checks and balances but as a centralized mass governing all. He is basically antiscience, a situation which is reflected by the popularity of mysticism and the feeling that one does not have to dissect everything but can really know the totality of knowledge in one grasp. He perceives himself as what he does. The electronic politician is an image politician who appears to look and sound like a leader. It is a sort of "fill in the blank" politician who gives different auras to different people.

There is little question that technology helps to shape and, in some respects, determines a society's culture. However, McLuhan is not saying that substance makes no difference, just that the substance is somewhat ephemeral while the impact of television on politics is pervasive, spreading throughout the entire political process.

In a comparison of the effects of newspapers versus TV during a New York mayoralty campaign, Wychoff states:

> In summary, then, the influence of candidate images conveyed by newspapers is probably less than TV image of the same candidates because: 1. readers derive candidate character from descriptions of deeds and reputation whereas viewers judge character from directly perceived appearance and demeanor (on television); 2. the most intense descriptions of a candidate's character reach the fewest reader-voters; and 3. the surviving mass circulation newspapers tend to be bland about candidate character, describing candidates in terms of non-offending shades of gray rather than the black and white literary fiction characterization of yesterday's newspapers.[45]

Newspapers probably influence the result of an election more than television when there is little personal contrast between the TV images of major candidates and when there is a contrast in their reputation or position on important issues. Therefore, in bland, strifeless campaigns newspapers are probably more influential on the voter. However, in most elections, if we are to believe McLuhan, the images, of necessity, will contrast and will be directly related to issue positions as perceived by the voter. The voter accepts a candidate on image and then attributes to the candidate the issue position he (the voter) thinks important.

In a survey that examined the effect of media bias in the 1968 election, John Robinson offers some different conclusions than Wychoff.[46] He indicates that while the public ranked television as its most important and relatively unbiased source of campaign news in 1968, its voting behavior seemed more linked with newspaper endorsements than any other media. With other variables controlled, a newspaper's perceived support of one candidate rather than another resulted in a 6 percent increase in vote for the endorsed candidate.

In a new series of studies, Robinson suggests that newspapers played an important role in both the 1968 and 1972 elections.[47] He found that Nixon was the overwhelming favorite of the nation's newspapers in the last two presidential campaigns—approximately eight of every ten newspapers endorsed him in 1968, nine out of ten in 1972. While the votes of Republicans did not appear to be influenced by newspaper endorsements, both the Independents and Democrats voted differently depending on what candidate was endorsed by the newspaper they most often read. Independents exposed to pro-McGovern newspapers were almost twice as likely to vote for McGovern (50 percent) as Independent voters exposed to pro-Nixon newspapers (26 percent).

Robinson concludes that even in an age of television, newspapers persuade voters because "the newspaper endorsement is perceived as a non-partisan message which appears to cut through the confusing arguments of the campaign and reduce them to a single conclusion."[48] His study specifically attempts to account for twelve other factors that cause voter choice such as party identification, interest, age, and education. Thus, it seems as though the print media may be as influential as television and the radio on voter choice.

Campaign Electoral Process Effects

1. The crystallization effect—the most important influence of television is the crystallization of attitudes. The latent leaning toward one candidate is stimulated to decide for a politician.

2. The slow constant impregnation—effective propaganda via the media should create convictions and compliance through imperceptible influences that are effective only by continuous repeti-

tion. It should create a complete environment for the individual voter by allowing him to add to the candidate whatever qualities he (the voter) would like.

3. The possible massive conversion — one should remember that examples of massive conversion largely due to a sharp contrast in competing image candidates are becoming more common. The election of Eisenhower in 1952 and 1956 involved the conversion of many Democrats for whom the sentiment generated by the soldier-hero-father image of Ike was stronger than their party identification and Stevenson's intellectual image.

4. The image conscious candidate — "the real combined effects of polls and television have been to make obsolete the traditional style of American politics and to substitute a "cool," corporate-executive style. The new politics is purposefully analytic, empirically opportunistic, and administratively manipulative.

5. The preconvention effects — by virtue of the media reports, the public learns early who the outstanding candidates are. Also, the media indicate the relative standing of these hopefuls.

6. The entire political process—(a) the media and the polls have altered the manner in which candidates are first selected; (b) they have modified and reshaped our expectations of political candidates; (c) they have changed the national election conventions from the exclusive privilege of a few political bosses to a more popular will-oriented selection; (d) they are making fundamental changes in the traditional national political party structures and functions. Protest politics and bringing the people in are ideas popularized by the media and forced by the new politics. It may be a "cool" medium in the parlance of McLuhan, but television invites, structures, and demands either psychic or real participation by the electorate.

7. Theory of Perceptual Effects — involves the reinforcement, neutralization, crystallization, or activation of attitudes. The purpose of persuasion is not to change the attitude of the committed but to shift the perception of voters with low involvement.

While the above catalogue is useful, it should be applied to political campaign effort. In the following discussion, we will attempt to set forth the best ways to win elective office. As mentioned before, the media, especially television, have changed the electoral process as described in earlier years and offer political candidates a weapon of immense potential.

Some general guidelines are as follows:

1. First, remember issues count. Voters are not fools; they perceive and vote on the basis of overriding political issues such as

Vietnam, unemployment, urban riots and crime. This was the point of Scammon and Wattenberg's *The Real Majority*, and, except for a general ignorance of the economic issue, was a most perceptive review of important issues in American politics. Polls should indicate what the entire American public is thinking at any one point in time. The aspiring candidate should be on the right side of any overriding issues and emphasize his answers to specified problems of his future constituents.

2. Remember the candidate counts. He must be an acceptable candidate; he must look like a senator or congressman, be intelligent, be willing to work hard to become well informed, and he should speak well. To some extent, good television shorts or commentaries can overcome special handicaps of the candidate; however, given a choice, the candidate should reflect the above characterizations.

3. Merge important issues with the candidate. Use the sociocultural method of persuasion indicating group approval and possible group sanctions for deviants. As mentioned earlier, Evry uses the issue-candidate technique: first, he finds out what issue is important to the local voters and then he emphasizes that issue in his media campaign, indicating that his candidate has the answer or at least understands the problem. The candidate can be identified with any number of groups, and advertisements should indicate general approval of the entire community.

4. Have both a short-range and long-range media blitz. The media campaign should be well financed and should attempt to crystallize opinion early in the campaign when expenditures for other candidates are relatively low. The short-range media program should be centered around concerns of the undecided voter.

5. Insure that the campaign is well financed and have a good party organization. The party organization can be built with proper funds and good volunteer organizing, but the money is crucial.

6. Look at past voting patterns and socioeconomic data, pick the districts most likely to give the candidate the most votes, and concentrate all organization efforts there.

7. Remember the sleeper effect. Even if voters hear something from a biased source, they will tend to forget the source and remember the message if it is repeated enough.

8. Poll, poll, poll with a reputable firm or in-house experts devoted to doing a good job and knowing how to do it. The undecided vote should command all the analysis time since how his vote perceptions are crystallized will determine the election. It is important

to use the panel technique and reinterview the undecided voter repeatedly.

9. Make television and radio spots look and sound similar to news programs. Recruit a good organization (can be helpful in polling and getting out the votes). Do not underestimate the power of some poorly used techniques such as direct mailing.

The above guidelines attempt to list only effective techniques of reaching the electorate. The issue-oriented candidate with clear policy stands will likely offer a better image to the voters; that is, the voter must have some substance to take hold of (even those whose perceptual screen will interpret whatever the candidate says). It is important that one stay away from issues which are extremely emotional except to offer a reasonable and moderate attitude on them. Thus, if one had come out strongly for bussing during the 1972 campaign, he would have surely lost the nomination and certainly the general election. There are a whole range of less emotional but still important issues on which one should take a forthright stand such as health, welfare, or defense spending, so that voters have a policy picture of the candidate.

Conclusion

The media never determine the outcome of an election, but they can influence it greatly. This is especially true in primary elections. At the general election level, there will normally be competition from equally qualified and experienced media experts. To a great extent their efforts will cancel each other out, and simply bombarding the voter with larger and larger doses of political advertisements will lead to a quick mental "tuning out" by the electorate. Ultimately, then, the election will be decided on the issues of the campaign unless one candidate is clearly incompetent or senile.

NOTES

1. Walter DeVries and V. Lance Tarrance, *The Ticket-Splitter: A New Force in American Politics* (Grand Rapids, Mich.: Eerdmans, 1972).

2. Marshall McLuhan, "Interview," *Playboy*, March 1969, pp. 71-72. Also see Marshall McLuhan and Quentin Fiore, *The Medium is the Massage* (New York: Random House, 1967).

3. For a complete listing of campaign firms, see Dan Nimmo, *The Political Persuaders* (Englewood Cliffs, N.J.: Prentice-Hall, 1970).

4. V. O. Key, Jr., *The Responsible Electorate* (Cambridge, Mass.: Harvard University Press, 1966), pp. 7-8.

5. Richard M. Scammon and Ben J. Wattenberg, *The Real Majority* (New York: Coward McCann and Geoghegan, 1970). See also Kevin P. Phillips, *The Emerging Republican Majority* (Garden City, N.Y.: Anchor Books, 1970).

6. One of the more important segments of the voting population is the newly enfranchised eighteen- to twenty-one-year-old and the youth vote in general (usually below thirty). While Scammon has commented in several interviews that the party identification of the new voters and the young voters is almost identical to that of the young in 1940, several commentators have suggested a far more pervasive influence. Louis Harris, in *The Anguish of Change* (New York: W. W. Norton, 1973), says that the youth thought more positively towards Nixon than McGovern, even though McGovern's policies seemed closer to those espoused by youth. However, Harris suggests that the young did cast a decisive vote in 1972 as they did in 1970. While Nixon won by a landslide, the young vote allowed the Democrats to control the House of Representatives. He states "the 30 and over vote went Republican by a narrow 45% to 43%. But the young voted Democrat by a lopsided 53% to 32% count" (p. 226).

In his book, *The Changing Sources of Power* (New York: McGraw-Hill, 1971), Frederick Dutton sees the young as a major new force in American politics. He sees the willingness of the young to get involved in politics and their increasing emphasis on quality of life issues to be the force that will transform American society. Further, he argues that the growth in Independent party identification and the possible demise or critical realignment of the political parties is due to the influence of the young. See especially his chapters on "The New Voters and the Numbers Game" and "The Politics of the New Generation."

7. James Reston, "Our Campaign Techniques Re-Examined," *The New York Times Magazine*, 9 November 1952, p. 62.

8. In 1964, John G. Schneider wrote an almost prescient book, *The Golden Kazoo* (New York: Signet Books, 1962), in which he presented the concept of merchandising politicians. He depicted the 1968 presidential election as one which would ban speeches as being too dull for a citizenry accustomed to the eye-catching, slogan-engendering television commercial. Instead he saw the candidate being given a "walk-on spectacular" carefully designed to drive home a big point with political campaigns degenerating into a sales promotion job and the electorate simply becoming a market to exploit. Anyone reading Joe McGinniss' *The Selling of the President* (New York: Trident Press, 1969) knows that Schneider's predictions were almost exactly Nixon's tactics.

9. Stanley Kelley, Jr., *Professional Public Relations and Political Power* (Baltimore, Md.: Johns Hopkins Press, 1956).

10. Irwin Ross, "The Super Salesmen of California Politics: Whitaker and Baxter," *Harper's Magazine* 219 (July 1959): 15.

11. Kelley, *Professional Public Relations*, p. 58.

12. Ibid., p. 57.

13. William Lee Miller, "Can Government Be Merchandised?" *The Reporter Magazine* 9 (October 27, 1953): 12.

14. Kelley, *Professional Public Relations*, p. 225.

15. Ibid., pp. 114-15.

16. Ibid., p. 122.

17. Miller, "Can Government Be Merchandised?"

18. Letter from Hal Evry, Public Relations Center, Inc., Los Angeles, California, 28 June 1956. This entire discussion is based upon the materials enclosed with that letter.

19. Philip E. Converse, "Information Flow and the Stability of Partisan Attitudes," in *Elections and the Political Order*, ed. Angus Campbell et al. (New York: Wiley, 1965), pp. 136-57.

20. Ibid. See also Murray B. Levin, *Kennedy Campaigning* (Boston, Mass.: Beacon Press, 1966), especially chapter 1 and chapter 6.

21. Robert MacNeil, *The People Machine: The Influence of Television on American Politics* (New York: Harper and Row, 1968), p. 153. For an insider's view of Shapp's campaign, see Joe Napolitan, *The Election Game and How to Win It* (Garden City, N.Y.: Doubleday, 1972).

22. Ibid., p. 219.

23. McGinniss, *The Selling of the President*.

24. Ibid., p. 30.

25. Ibid., p. 37.

26. Ibid., p. 130.

27. Ibid., p. 161.

28. Ibid., p. 177.

29. Melvin L. DeFleur, *Theories of Mass Communication* (New York: David McKay, 1966).

30. Ibid., p. 135.

31. Ibid., p. 137.

32. Of course, Agnew's career after beating Mahoney was meteoric with his election to the vice-presidency only two years later in 1968. Agnew seemed to be overwhelmed with the national election and made a number of media "faux pas." Later, the Nixon administration used Agnew to attack the media, especially the television commentators. We will deal with these speeches in depth in chapter 5.

33. Interview with Ronald Wilner, 28 April 1967.

34. Interview with Paul Reed, Jr., 28 April 1967.

35. Ibid.

36. Letter from Hal Evry, 1 May 1967.

37. Angus Campbell et al., *The American Voter: An Abridgement* (New York: John Wiley, 1964), p. 99.

38. For a dated but still fairly complete account of Maryland politics, see John H. Fenton, *Politics in the Border States* (New Orleans, La.: Chauser Press, 1957). While Mahoney's primary victory was surprising since he had little "old-line" organization support and almost no liberal Democratic support, his vote total (146,000) was very close to his average primary vote total in the previous election. Some have suggested that Mahoney voters just don't switch. While Mahoney's votes came primarily from the Baltimore metropolitan area, he received strong support from the eastern shore counties and other counties that gave George Wallace 43 percent of the vote in the 1964 presidential primary. Thus, his slogan "Your home is your castle" played a

crucial role in his ultimate victory in the primary. For a more complete discussion of the campaign and Maryland politics, see James C. Strouse, "Name Familiarization: Its Importance in a Political Campaign" (Master's thesis, University of Maryland, 1967).

39. DeVries and Tarrance, *The Ticket-Splitter*, p. 53.

40. Philip E. Converse, "Information Flow and the Stability of Partisan Attitudes," *Elections and Political Order*, ed. Angus Campbell et al. (New York: Wiley, 1966), pp. 136-59.

41. A related account supporting DeVries is Gary Hart, *Right from the Start* (New York: Quadrangle Books, 1973). The book reviews Senator McGovern's 1972 presidential campaign, which was an issue- and volunteer-oriented campaign.

42. Interview with Robert Bonitati, April 1972.

43. Paul Lutzker, "The Cognitive Framework of Campaign Decision-Makers, the Case of Electoral Generalists" (Paper presented at the Annual Meeting of the American Political Science Association, Washington, D.C., September 1968).

44. Burns W. Roper, "Emerging Profiles of Television and Other Mass Media," *Public Attitudes* (New York: Random House, 1967), p. 24.

45. Gene Wychoff, *The Image Candidate* (New York: Macmillan, 1968), p. 107. His comments apply to all the candidates, but primarily to Lindsay, Wagner, and Buckley, the major mayoralty candidates.

46. John P. Robinson, "Perceived Media Bias and the 1968 Election," *Journalism Quarterly* 49 (Summer 1972): 239-46.

47. John P. Robinson, "Newspaper Endorsements — Do They Play a Role in Electing American Presidents?" *Institute for Social Research Newsletter* (Ann Arbor: University of Michigan, 1974).

48. Ibid., p. 4. For an interesting series of papers investigating the effects of television advertising and television news, see Thomas E. Patterson and Robert D. McClure, "Political Advertising, Voter Reaction" (Paper presented at the Annual Meeting of the American Association for Public Opinion Research, Asheville, North Carolina, May, 1973). Among their preliminary findings are: (1) political commercials are more effective when they convey issue information to the voter than when they project a candidate image; (2) TV spots effectively reach the low political interest voters and those who get very little information from other sources; and (3) the spots can reach supporters of the candidate's opponent, but the effect may be a "backlash" strengthening of the voters' intention to support the opponents. Among other working papers are "Television News and Voter Behavior in the 1972 Presidential Election" where Patterson and McClure find the independent effects of television news is minimal, and "Voter Information Change in the 1972 General Election" by Thomas Patterson and Robert A. Milne who find no relationship between the level of political interest and information gain during the 1972 general election. Papers are available by writing to Patterson or McClure at the Department of Political Science, Syracuse University.

3

Causal Factors and Media Influence in Voters' Choice

The Voting Environment

In a democracy, one is taught that voters should choose their representatives on the basis of good information about competing candidates, public policy preferences, and the citizens' collective ability to hold their representatives accountable for legislative actions. The citizenry should possess an interest in public affairs and a willingness to participate actively in influencing public policy. Most studies of the voters would indicate this is an inaccurate characterization of most American citizens. Angus Campbell suggests that the voter has a low information level on most public issues, that only 12 percent could identify ideologies with the two major parties, that few people participate in public affairs, that they know little about the policy preferences of their elected representatives, and that they normally participate at a very low level in elections.[1] In addition, they should be informed on both alternative public policies and the stands of their candidates on these policies. Most polls and studies indicate a very low level of information by the American public especially on foreign matters and most domestic matters.[2] Survey research in congressional districts indicates that few voters (less than a majority) could give even the name of their congressman.[3] Studies indicate that the agreement between voters' attitudes towards various issues, both domestic and foreign, and their congressmen's perceptions of those attitudes is very low, ranging from a minus correlation (no perception) on foreign affairs to a highly positive correlation on civil rights issues.[4] However, on the broad range of issues such as civil rights legislation or the Vietnam War, representatives have knowledge of what their constituents think—and even more importantly, the voters have pretty clear perceptions of where those representatives stand on the issue. However, it is still true that most American voters are ill informed and will probably continue to be so. Finally, the voters should engage in political discussions and perceive political realities. Studies show that only one in five Americans engages in political discussions.[5] Whether or not one perceives political realities is partly a function of his information level. Given a low information level most voters probably are incapable of perceiving political realities or acting upon their perceptions.

The low information level of the American electorate is well documented. In a Detroit study, only 38 percent of Detroit residents knew the term of service for congressmen; only 16 percent knew that senators are elected for six years.[6] Another information survey asked citizens about the Electoral College. The Gallup poll, which for years had been questioning the public about the merits of the Electoral College, asked repondents to explain the concept. Only 32 percent were able to do so. As the 1960 presidential campaign got under way, Elmo Roper and Associates reported only 20 percent of the public could name the Democratic vice-presidential nominee. Six percent did not even know the name of any candidate.[7]

Some would argue that democracy is best served by the generally low participation and information rate of the American citizenry. (One should note that even though the American rates are low, they are among the highest participation, information, and political interest rates of the Western democracies and developing countries studied.) The passive, uninterested citizen is more prejudiced and more likely to be antidemocratic in basic ideas than those who participate. Yet we know that the majority of those who do participate — even at a minimal level — have little good information on candidates and policy preferences. It would seem that these citizens could be manipulated by catchy slogans, image candidates, and fancy public relations firms well endowed with money from rich candidates and their friends.

Decline of the
Urban Machine

Many academicians and journalists have noted the decline of the urban political machine. The welfare state and the various city, state, and federal civil service commissions have largely replaced the once vast patronage system that enabled many political leaders to control the nominations and elections of most candidates and the implementation of public politics. Frank Sorauf, in a study of a segment of Pennsylvania's still large patronage system, noted that highway workers — all political appointees — were not very loyal to the party which gave them their jobs.[8] A sizable minority had not even voted for the party's candidate. Certainly most political jobs pay too little to be worthwhile or are too few in number to reward all the industrious party faithful who contributed to victory. And every politician understands well the tired cliché, "You give one supporter a job, and you make ten enemies."

With the population increasingly mobile and voters better educated and at least aware of the issues involved in the campaign, party leaders are less able to control elections. Electoral laws that call for primaries and candidates rich enough to afford an expensive public relations firm are able to win the nomination despite the wishes of the political leadership. One only has to look at Milton Shapp's 1966 gubernatorial primary campaign to get some idea of the lessening power of the urban and state party machines. Shapp was a comparative unknown in Pennsylvania politics and encountered the almost unanimous opposition of the party organization. Yet, through a skillful media campaign he was able to win the nomination.

There is considerable evidence that the organization is failing to accomplish the basic party functions of contacting the voters, getting them to the polls or at least trying to persuade them to vote for the party's candidate. One study in Detroit noted that only 20 percent of the Detroit precinct leaders had at their disposal such an elementary tool as a cardfile of their party's supporters.[9] Less than 33 percent had conducted door-to-door canvassing or called a meeting of their precinct workers during the 1956 campaign. In city after city, reform groups are defeating the machine candidates and new coalitions of voters are electing their own candidates. This is not to say that urban machines are dead. Obviously, Mayor Daley's well-oiled organization indicates that the old ways are still effective. Yet, recent elections show that even Mayor Daley's organization is quite vulnerable. At least one of the more notable campaign firms, Matt Reese Associates, bases its entire effort on organizing volunteer efforts in precincts regarded as favorable to its candidate. These precincts are inundated by volunteer workers who do all the traditional party functions of contacting voters and helping them get to the polls.

However, many political scientists and public relations experts point out that the party controls at the most 5 to 10 percent of the electorate. Given only a moderate turnout of 20 to 45 percent for a local election, most of the voters are going to be unaware of or at least unaffected by the virtue of the party's candidate. With the power of the mass media to contact, inform, and possibly persuade the masses of voters, it is likely that nonparty chosen candidates have a good chance of winning the primaries and even the general election. The media are one weapon that can effectively bypass the political boss.

V. O. Key has argued that the party organization remains, with workers in almost every precinct who seek to build up person-to-person relationships with the electorate, but the radio, the newspaper, and the mass media are the most important channels for dissemination of appeals calculated to manipulate the attitudes of the electorate.[10] The representative and opinion-managerial function of the party machine is becoming less important than before since leaders (and nonorganization people) have available devices and methods for appealing directly to the great mass of the people. There seems to be little question that the organization's complete control of nominations, elections, and policy making is gone; however, formal studies still indicate that the party machine remains a potent force. Studies by Phillips Cutright and Peter H. Rossi,[11] Raymond E. Wolfinger,[12] and William J. Crotty[13] show that the party effort can have an important positive effect on a candidate's vote. Crotty examined the effect of party effort on five different offices — the president, governor, state senator, state representative, and local sheriff — and found that party activity made an important difference in all the contests. Nevertheless, the media have changed the control of the party machine. Candidates with enough money to mount an extensive media campaign and hire political campaign experts can bypass the party leaders. Unknown candidates are most successful in the party primaries where voters are unable to choose their candidates on the basis of party preference. The effect of the media campaigns on changing voter attitudes is not clear; however, one should note that primaries attract less than normal voter turnout and interest and are traditionally very susceptible to machine control. Also, experience has indicated that it is in these very primaries that media campaigns seem most effective. Rich candidates such as Milton Shapp and Howard Metzenbaum have won their party nominations on slick, name-familiarization media campaigns. Without benefit of party labels (all Democrats in a Democratic primary), the voters appear to vote for a candidate whose name they can rememeber, along with possibly a slogan.

Nonpartisan Elections

One attempt to eliminate boss control of elections is through non-partisan elections. If candidates are not identified by party, then the citizen should make his decision on important factors such as issue positions and qualifications. Reformers throughout the country have attempted to use nonpartisan elections as one device to eliminate the usually corrupt political party machine.

In nonpartisan elections the candidates on the ballot are not labeled. Usually there are a number of candidates for each office since there were no primaries to eliminate any. Most voters find themselves choosing between lists of unfamiliar names; consequently, anything that makes a candidate stand out on the ballot is to his advantage. Adrian reports that celebrities are likely to have a political advantage and reports a successful candidate for Detroit's nonpartisan city council who "stood on the implicit platform that he had been a shortstop for the Detroit Tigers."[14]

There are several elections which confirm the political advantage of a famous name — and most would consider a voting decision based on name recognition to be irrational. Both cases that will be cited involve the Kennedy name, but not the famous family. In the primarly election for Massachusetts state treasurer in 1954, John Francis Kennedy won. Kennedy's chief qualification for office was eighteen years' service in the stockroom of a razor company. Since primary campaigns are essentially nonpartisan, Adrian's finding that well-known names count in nonpartisan elections is substantiated.[15] In 1962, another unknown Kennedy (Richard) won the nomination for Ohio's congressman-at-large seat by 2,582 of 530,404 votes cast in an eleven-man field. Civil rights-minded Democrats were mortified to learn that this Kennedy — who spent a total of $10.50 on his entire campaign — was an ardent and outspoken segregationist. This Kennedy, unlike the state treasurer, was beaten in the general election by a man with a name very famous in its own right — Robert A. Taft, Jr.

Primary elections seem even more volatile when in a nonpartisan atmosphere, where many candidates run and little party organization exists. Voters are appealed to on general slogans and name-familiarization campaigns. Recent campaigns offer some additional evidence that puts the mass electorate in a different focus.

In 1970, Prince George's County, Maryland, had its first election run in a nonpartisan fashion, and several major candidates emerged. Steny Hoyer, a state senator, was the Democratic organization's (informal) candidate. His campaign was well financed (he spent by far the most money), supported by a strong and active Democratic governor (Marvin Mandel), and employed the services of a nationally known public relations man, Joe Napolitan. Arrayed against Hoyer were William Gullett, the candidate of the Charter organization (Citizens for the New Charter), and Carlton Beall, a postmaster with some electoral experience (no relation to U. S. Senator Beall or to the prosecutor of former Vice-President Agnew). Beall had the backing of much of the regular Republican organization in the county. There were several other minor candidates also. Both Gullett and Beall were Republican in a county with a two and one-half to one registration edge for the Democrats. In addition, Hoyer was a young, handsome, energetic candidate with good speaking talents while both Gullett and Beall were much older, not very handsome, and just adequate speakers. In terms of party identification, media campaign effect, and candidate orientation, Hoyer should have overwhelmed his opposition. The results, however, showed Gullett the victor, Beall second, and Hoyer a poor third.

How do we explain these results? An ill-informed electorate should have been swayed by Hoyer's professional media campaign. Gullett had almost no media campaign and relied on handouts, rallies and some radio spots. It appears that Prince George's voters were disgusted with the previous Democratic domination of the county with corrupt commissioners and unplanned growth engulfing the Washington, D.C., suburbs. Gullett was known to be an honest administrator in his job as mayor of College Park, Maryland and was a professional engineer. His support of the Citizens for the New Charter and his ideas to clean up the county appeared to be effective campaign weapons, enough to overcome the Democratic registration advantage and the slick, media-oriented campaign of a young, ambitious Democrat. The voters saw the issues in the campaign rather clearly and voted on those perceptions. This would imply that voters do have quite a bit more information and rationality than most politicians and academicians would ascribe to them.

Mass Society and
Mass Culture

Writers such as Erich Fromm[16] and David Reisman[17] tell us that the masses of citizens are other-directed, afraid to have and espouse independent views, and generally follow what they think is the "crowd view." Few would argue that primary and secondary groups have important influence. Studies indicate that the family is the basic political and cultural socialization agent for most people. Friends, work, and peer groups exercise an important influence on one's political judgments. In advertising one often finds a distinct group appeal. Group approval is an important part of the advertisement's message.

The mass society develops a mass culture, in which cultural and political values tend to be homogeneous and fluid. In the middle and at the bottom people think and feel alike. Since thoughts and feelings are not anchored anywhere, they are susceptible to fads and fashions. Like the traditional theorists from de Tocqueville to Mannheim, commentators such as Reisman,[18] Fromm,[19] C. Wright Mills,[20] and Seymour Martin Lipset[21] see indications that the mobility, heterogeneity, and centralization of modern society is weakening and destroying the ties that bind men to the common life, rendering the mass susceptible to manipulation — especially by the mass media.

C. Wright Mills describes the individual's life in the mass society. "He loses his independence and more importantly, he loses the desire to be independent. Life in a society of masses implants insecurity and furthers impotence; it makes men uneasy and vaguely anxious."[22] David Reisman sees man moving from self-reliance on the masses toward other-directedness.[23] He sees society slowly becoming undifferentiated and undistinguished, marked by a drab sameness of literature, art, politics, and people. In an insightful analysis of modern society, Erich Fromm points out that "modern society has developed the marketing personality, of which the main theme is the experience of oneself as a commodity, and of one's value as an exchange value." To be a success as a commodity, Fromm says that one must be an "empty vessel" into which one can "pour in the right trait at the right time."[24] For these writers, at least, the Orwellian world of 1984 is not far off.

Elihu Katz and Paul F. Lazarsfeld report a very interesting study which was undertaken by Muzafer Sherif.[25] Basically, his study concerned group influence on opinions, attitudes, and actions. His experiment utilized the autokinetic effect, which is the name given to the illusion of movement created by an actually stationary pinpoint of light when flashed on in a totally darkened room. First, he tested his subjects singly and let them develop norms of movement perception. Then he tested them in twos and threes and found that all altered their judgments somewhat to conform to the group norm. He was able to show how the effect of judgment of others resulted in the convergence of substantially different private standards.

Sherif's experiment can be legitimized only to situations where individuals are forced to make decisions without sufficient information or interest. Katz and Lazarsfeld point out, "For very large numbers of people the presidential voting situation (or really any voting situation) can be characterized as a situation where social pressures (1) force people to make decisions they would not otherwise make, (2) between candidates about whom they probably know nothing, and (3) about whom they may not care at all. In such a situation, one may expect informal groups to play a large part in defining the situation, and in influencing decisions."[26]

Since survey data show that only one in three[27] belong to groups taking political stands, the only real basis for the electoral decision for most people would be party identification. If party identification were shown to be a weak influencer, then other influences such as information campaigns could have a sizable effect on the electorate.

There are some advantageous social implications of conformity. The implicit trust in the opinions of the masses makes for stable government since there is a tendency for those in the minority to be influenced by majority opinion. Many scholars have pointed to the bandwagon appeal in the American electorate. Thus, Americans who vote against the winner tend to change their opinion after the victory because of their desire to be in the "mainstream of public opinion."[28] Since compromise is necessary to placate opposing interests, this type of conformity tends to make democracy more viable. However, C. Wright Mills sees ominous clouds. He notes that "in a mass society, the dominant type of communication is the formal media, and the public becomes mere media markets. Our standards of reality tend to be set by these media rather than by our fragmentary experience."[29] In this kind of atmosphere there is little discussion, and like a herd of cattle, they move at the prod of the mass media.

Vance Packard has popularized some of the notions mentioned above.[30] He has documented the susceptibility of Americans to advertising and manipulation as well as America's changing value structure based on its high mobility rates and nuclear family relationships. Old ties based on extended families and long neighbor-hood acquaintances seem lost in mindless suburban development and constant transfers from one city to another. Personal contact and communication are almost nonexistent because of this new pattern of living.

It would appear that tendencies to conformity, the break-up of the nuclear family and friendship groups, the high mobility of America's population, and the capitalists' "sell yourself" orienta-tion contribute to a manipulatable, nonparticipatory American electorate. This is exactly the theory of several political public rela-tions firms. If the electorate has few "anchor points" political ad-vertising can create some to influence the voter to support a given candidate. In terms of linkage models, the mass culture-mass society literature would suggest very little impact of opinion on policy even in elections where some choice-action is systematically forced. While other literature supports many of the conclusions of mass culture theorists, there is some evidence to the contrary.

The Voting Studies versus
Experimental Attitude Change Studies

About thirty years ago, social scientists started to empirically uncover the causal factors in the vote decision. Important findings of the first major voting study were: (1) people have brand loyal-ties (party identification); (2) they make up their minds very early in the campaign; (3) the campaign's effects were not clearly discernible; and (4) the personality measures employed were in-effective measures.

An Erie County, Pennsylvania, study by Paul Lazarsfeld, Bernard Berelson, and Hazel Gaudet was one of the first to employ the panel technique interviewing the same voters at two points in time. Generally, the findings indicated that few voters changed from one candidate to another, that most had made up their minds before the campaign or early in the campaign, and that "brand loyalties" or party identification was the most important factor in the vote decision.[31] In addition to this study,[32] other early voting studies were made by Berelson, Lazarsfeld, and McPhee,[33] and by Angus Campbell, Gerald Gurin, and Warren E. Miller.[34] Again their find-ings generally were consistent in that they found few change voters (narrowly defined) and most deciding before or early in the cam-paign. Campbell's study introduced new attitudinal variables such as issue-orientation and candidate orientation.[35] The previous studies had concentrated more on sociological influences such as group affiliation, income, education, religion, and so on.

In a study of the 1952 election, Morris Janowitz and Dwaine Marvick[36] were among the first to explicitly consider the influence of the mass media on the vote decision. They employed two measures of the media, one of simple media-exposure and the other of media-involvement. The exposure variable showed the number of media used to follow the campaign. The involvement measure distinguished TV, radio, and press "fans" from ordinary users and nonusers. Media fans were defined as those persons using the media to follow the campaign closely and who thought the media to be the most important source of political information. Ordinary users were those who said the media were important but did not use them regularly to follow the campaign. The nonusers did not use any media regularly. Although the authors committed a heinous sin in this McLuhan world by not distinguishing between television, radio, and the newspapers, they argued that "by combining the media involvement measure it was possible to make a summary comparison of media fans, ordinary users, and nonusers."[37]

Table 3-1 examines the influence of the media while controlling the group influence. A careful reading of the table indicates that media fans were more likely to be Eisenhower voters. Under concerted Stevenson group pressure, almost 8 percent of the media fans voted for Eisenhower; when group pressure conflicted, the plurality chose Ike; and when the media fans were under concerted Eisenhower pressure, they voted over 94 percent for the Republican. With the ordinary users, Stevenson received almost 13 percent of the vote even when the primary group pressure was for Eisenhower. When the pressure was for Stevenson, the General received less than 4 percent of the ordinary user vote. The above evidence is far from conclusive; however, those voters following the campaign closely through the media seemed more likely to vote for Eisenhower while those voters who were ordinary users were more likely to vote for Stevenson or likely not to vote at all.

Janowitz and Marvick stated, "the data indicated that concerted primary group pressure did not isolate the citizen from the impact of the mass media. In fact, it worked to reinforce the effects of the mass media rather than counter balance them."[38] This conclusion would lend support to the crystallizing effect of the media and the broader definition of change voters to include the changers from one candidate to another *and* those who are undecided and then choose a candidate. Overall they concluded that the media: (1) stimulated

Table 3-1

Primary Group Pressure and Mass
Media Involvement

	PRIMARY GROUP PRESSURE		
	Concerted Eisenhower	Conflict	Concerted Stevenson
	$N = 240$	$N = 596$	$N = 102$
Mass Media Fans			
Eisenhower Voters	94.1%	40.4%	7.9%
Stevenson Voters	2.1	37.7	82.3
Nonvoters	3.8	21.9	9.8
	$N = 78$	$N = 338$	$N = 54$
Ordinary Voters			
Eisenhower Voters	77.0	28.4	3.7
Stevenson Voters	12.8	29.6	66.7
Nonvoters	10.2	42.0	29.6
	$N = 4$	$N = 87$	$N = 11$
Nonusers			
Eisenhower	—	10.4	—
Stevenson	—	13.8	—
Nonvoter	—	75.8	—

SOURCE: Morris Janowitz and Dwaine Marvick, *Competitive Pressure and Democratic Consent* (Ann Arbor, Mich.: Bureau of Government, 1956), p. 84. Used by permission of the publisher and the authors.

the activation and participation of nonvoters; (2) assisted the Republicans in mobilizing their partisans; and (3) helped Stevenson to become better known, thereby preventing a larger defection from the Democratic party.

Two-Step Flow of
Influence

After reviewing the voting studies, Katz and Lazarsfeld formulated the two-step flow of influence.[39] Briefly, this proposition states that information about elections (and most other things such as products or movies) flows from primary sources and the mass media to opinion leaders. Opinion leaders then interpret this information to their followers. Since everyone is a member of primary and secondary groups, the masses of the electorate get their information interpreted by their opinion leaders. The problems with such a hypothesis are obvious. What if a person has a number of opinion leaders — one in the family, one at work, one at social gatherings? What happens when the interpretations of the leaders conflict? What happens when the information is interpreted for the voter by commentators? What happens when opinion leaders do not get the information in the first place?

Katz and Lazarsfeld state, "the image of an audience as a mass of disconnected individuals hooked up to the media but not to each other could not be reconciled with the two-step hypothesis that ideas flow from the media to opinion leaders and from these to less active sections of the population."[40] In their examination of this hypothesis they studied public affairs, product advertising, movies selection, and the like. Of all the areas studied, they found that "there is least opinion leadership of all in public affairs." They attempted to explain the difference between merchandising commodities and merchandising good citizenship by suggesting that there is no direct social mechanism for public affairs so the listener must erect his own. This suggestion would seem to compromise their two-step flow for public affairs in that it indicated that opinion leadership is less operative in public affairs (especially in vote decision) than in other areas. However, their basic hypothesis seemed substantiated by the consistent voting study finding of little change by voters during the campaign (of course, changers were defined to include only those who, after deciding on a candidate, actually switched to another candidate).

In a study of diffusion, Everett Rogers indicated the following failings with the Katz and Lazarsfeld hypothesis: (1) it lacks integration with the idea of stages in the adoption process; it does not take into account the relative importance of communication sources at different stages in the adoption process; (2) most persons use the mass media at the awareness stage. At the evaluation stage, personal communications are important for adoption; (3) opinion leaders are hard to define and research indicates that there is a multistep flow of influence with opinion leaders influencing other opinion leaders who then influence followers.[41] At any one point in time there are two steps, but the whole process is infinitely more complex.

In another study, Herbert Hamilton examines influence models and suggests that public opinion leadership has a self-concept dimension and a functional dimension.[42] The flow of influence is not a perfect flow and to study influence one must examine the different dimensions of opinion leadership and the separate impact of each of them.

In any case, it is clear that the two-step hypothesis has been modified and attacked as a basic influence conduit. It still remains as the primary explanation of why there is not much change in the voters during the campaign. Of course, if the definition of change voters were broadened to include those who change from undecided to one candidate, then other more direct influences could be posited as causal change agents.

Attitude
Change

Philip Converse has done an intriguing study on information flow and the stability of partisan attitudes.[43] He notes that the low level of public information about politics has been documented ever since the survey technique was developed and, also, that it is the least informed member within the electorate who seems to hold the critical balance of power in the sense that alternatives in the governing body depend disproportionately on shifts in their sentiments. The shifting or floating voters tend to be those whose information about politics is low.

He finds that the same theory which predicts that the less involved are more susceptible to party change suggests that the less involved will also give less accurate accounts of past political behavior. For simple psychological reasons one would expect them to distort past behavior in the direction of current preference. Such distortions build a false impression of stability; if their distortions are more frequent among the less involved, then they act to weaken empirical results.

In discussing why people shift parties, Converse argues that if no other factors intervene in a systematic way, the two party divisions of the popular vote at the national level would remain constant from election to election, reflecting nothing more than an underlying division of loyalties.[44] Usually, however, oscillations of the actual vote are fashioned by forces associated with the immediate election — Eisenhower's personal attractiveness or Kennedy's Catholicism. Thus, party identification may be seen as an inertia or momentum component which determines the partisan direction of any individual decision unless there are short-term forces in the immediate situation acting with sufficient strength in an opposite partisan direction to deflect the momentum and shift the behavior. Table 3-2 indicates that those with low information levels are more susceptible to changing their vote to the other party or to nonvoting.

Table 3-2

Association Between Stability or Change
in Presidential Voting Over Time and
Political Information Level, 1965-60
(in percent)

Information Level	Voted Twice for Same Party ($N = 712$)	Voted Twice Shifted Parties ($N = 207$)	Failed to Vote in One of Two Elections ($N = 220$)	Twice a Nonvoter ($N = 201$)
High	49	33	19	11
Medium	32	32	35	17
Low	19	35	46	72
Total	100	100	100	100

SOURCE: Philip E. Converse, "Information Flow and the Stability of Partisan Attitudes," *Elections and the Political Order*, ed. Angus Campbell et al. (New York: Wiley, 1965), p. 139. Used by permission of the publisher.

On the basis of the previous discussion, Converse hypothesized that the probability that any given voter will be sufficiently deflected in his partisan momentum to cross party lines in a specified election varies directly as a function of the strength of short-term forces toward the opposing party and varies inversely as a function of the mass of stored information about politics.

Other things being equal, both the individual rates of defections and the rate of vote changes will be limited if the flow of information is weak. If information is available in quantity and intensity, the outcome depends on how strong the information flow is on either side. If there is no new information input at all, there will be no defection and no oscillation; the vote will be a pure party vote. Thus, in the presidential election year of 1956, many normal Democrats voted for Eisenhower and other Republicans on his ticket. Then, in the congressional election of 1958 when information was limited, the voters reverted back to their normal patterns and elected many more Democratic congressmen.

To measure the stability of partisan attitudes, Converse employed two indices.[45] The first had to do with the rate of turnover between the statement of vote intentions prior to the election and actual vote behavior. A high correlation would indicate high stability; a lower correlation, relative instability. The second index dealt with the correlation between party identification and the final vote. A low rate of defection from party identification (a high party-vote correlation) should reflect high attitude stability whereas a low correlation should reflect relative instability, reflecting the power of the short-term forces (one of which was the debates on television) of the 1960 election.

A 3 x 3 table was constructed also and a rank-order (tau-beta) correlation computed for it within subsets of the population, according to whether no media were used or some higher number (see fig. 12). Since there might be some question as to the effect of differences in proportion of nonvoters upon the correlation, a comparable coefficient was also calculated for the 2 x 2 (two rows and two columns) table reflecting constancy or change in choice of candidates.

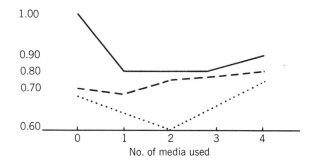

Key: Solid rep. 2 x 2 table, party intention by party choice
    Dashed rep. 3 x 3 table, vote intention by vote
    Dotted rep. party intent by vote

Source: Philip E. Converse, "Information Flow and Stability of Partisan Attitudes," *Elections and the Political Order*, ed. Angus Campbell et al. (New York: Wiley, 1965), p. 146. Used by permission of the publisher.

Figure 12
Information and Party Choice

The rank-order correlations between vote intention and vote for nonwatchers was .96; for watchers, it was .89 (2 x 2 case). In the 3 x 3 case, taking into account intention to vote or not, the correlation was .88 among nonwatchers but only .64 among watchers. For the watchers, there was an important reduction in the correlation which indicates watching the debates changed a number of votes.

Thus, watching the television debates between Nixon and Kennedy in the 1960 presidential election led to substantial increases in the Kennedy vote. Almost all the switches came from the undecided vote. The Kennedy performance tended to disprove the Nixon charge about Kennedy's inexperience, especially in foreign affairs. Almost all the studies investigating the effects of the debates on the election concluded that they helped Kennedy significantly.[46] Since Nixon had a substantial lead at the beginning of the campaign, the TV debates were a significant short-term force in the ultimate Kennedy victory.

The latter comparison is relatively weak, but one subset of nonwatchers did not watch because they could not (work, TV broken) and some listened to the radio. Among remaining nonwatchers (who were too uninterested) the correlation was a perfect 1.00 in the 2 x 2 case ($N = 52$). For the nonwatchers, 100 percent voted for the individual they intended to originally.

The more remote the respondent was from information, the more stable was the vote. This was true except for those that used all four of the media. Since these persons would be highly informed, media use may have had less of an impact.

The study indicates that party identification is strongest when little information is available and used. A corollary hypothesis might be that the more information available in an election, the less stable the party identification. Reflecting on previous elections, when information is greatest and all parties involved wage vigorous media-oriented campaigns, party voting is much less stable than in state or local elections. In local elections where information, interest, and party efforts are usually less organized, party voting seems to be strongest. Therefore, attitude change or crystallization is partly a function of information available.

Table 3-3

Relation of Degree of Attitude Development to Direction in Which Conflict of Party Identification and Partisan Evaluation Is Resolved in Voting

	Well developed evaluation	Poorly developed evaluation	No evaluation
Vote with PID	20%	47%	75%
Vote no PID	80%	53%	25%
N =	143	164	36

SOURCE: Angus Campbell et al., *The American Voter* (New York: Wiley, 1960), p. 142. Used by permission of the publisher.

Another finding, as described by Campbell, adds evidence to the above discussion.[47] He looked at the degree to which there is conflict between party identification and partisan evaluation with the vote decision. As table 3-3 shows, if there was conflict, the vote was heavily inconsistent with party identification. When the voter had formed no evaluation, he voted 75 percent for his party, indicating that the influence of party identification is compromised by information causing a negative partisan evaluation.

Controlled
Experimental Studies

In their review of the findings of the voting studies, Muzafer Sherif and Carl I. Hovland relate experiments showing that on issues that are highly emotional, attitude conversion based on exposure to adverse communication is relatively ineffective.[48] However, they found that on less vital, more superficial issues, of the type normally dealt with in many opinion surveys, the role of the media in changing attitudes may be great. With issues that are not deeply involving, distinct changes may be expected, particularly when the source is an expert or well-known figure. The media would be most effective on the independent voter who typically is not highly involved or informed and has few ego-involved positions to protect.

Other major findings by Hovland and his colleagues in their numerous communication experiments are: (1) Law of Primacy — when two sides of an issue are presented the first does not have the advantage necessarily; (2) Order of Communication — when contradictory information is presented in a single communication by a single communicator, there is a pronounced tendency for those segments presented first to dominate the impression received; (3) Order of Presentation (first or last) — is a more significant factor in influencing opinion for subjects with relatively weak desire for understanding than for those with "high" cognitive need; (4) Repetition — repetition does not influence the retention of information content of a communication in any simple manner. While the usual effect is to increase retention under some circumstances, too frequent repetition without any reward leads to loss of attention, boredom, and disregard of the communication; and (5) Sleeper Effect — when a communication is repeated over a long period of time, even by someone or a group not highly regarded by the receiver, the communicator tends to be forgotten but the message lingers on.[49]

Voting Studies and
Experiments Compared

Hovland notes that in the voting studies, the authors estimate that the political positions of only about 5 percent of their respondents were changed by the electoral campaign — and even this small change was attributed to personal influence.[50] However, a number of experimental studies have been discussed in which the opinions of a third to a half or more of the audience are changed. Hovland attributes the difference to research design and naturalistic conditions in which the audience is limited to those who expose themselves to the communication. To test this hypothesis, Hovland set up an experiment which measured the desirability of prohibition in Oklahoma and Texas, where the local option can be exercised. He tested a wet and dry communication on three groups — those with dry opinions, those with wet opinions, and those who did not care. He found that individuals whose position was only slightly discrepant from the communicator's were influenced to a greater extent than those whose positions deviated to a larger extent. When the wet issue was advocated, 28 percent of the middle-of-the-road subjects were changed in the direction of the communication as compared with only 4 percent of the dry group. With the dry communication, 14 percent of the middle group were changed, while only 4 percent of the wet group were changed.

He concludes that the magnitude of effects was directly related to type of attitude involved. Since the types of issues most often utilized in survey studies are ones which involve deep commitments, small changes in opinion due to communications could be expected. Where the attitude was not deeply entrenched, the change caused by mass communications could be great. The point at issue is whether the attitude involved was or was not deeply entrenched. It seems that most of the literature dealing with voting suggests an electorate without deeply entrenched attitudes except for party identification.

The Polls, Bandwagon Effects, and
Election Night Broadcasts

Polls have become an important part of the political process. They legitimize the candidacies of relatively unknown candidates;

they attempt to take the pulse of the American electorate for incumbents and candidates both during and after the elections at all levels of government. They are one of the most effective measures of the impact of a candidate's campaign.

In spite of the debacle of the *Literary Digest* and the experience in 1948, opinion polls are still believed by most citizens and politicians to be accurate reflections of public opinion at any one point in time. The *Literary Digest* suspended operations soon after it predicted a Landon victory in the 1936 Landon-Roosevelt presidential election. In 1948, all the pollsters predicted a Dewey victory and stopped polling three weeks before the election. Truman's victory over Dewey was one of the great upsets in our political history. The *Digest* poll was wrong because it sampled persons with telephones at the height of the Depression. The 1948 polls were wrong because they failed to account for last-minute voter shifts. The Kennedy-Nixon campaign brought the political survey to its influential height. The Kennedy campaign used various opinion polls and attempted to find out what campaign appeals would most affect regional and local voting decisions. One of the polls employed was the Simulmatics Corporation,[51] which was established by a group of political scientists to predict the ultimate vote decision of voters throughout the country. Polls were taken at many points during and before the election and almost 500 voter types were recognized by the simulation. Then, on the basis of past voting patterns, background socioeconomic and political variables, a prediction was made of voters in a given state, locality, or region. Unfortunately the accuracy and impact of these predictions are subject to some dispute.

Polls are used for many purposes during a campaign. Favorable results are often leaked to the press or to key politicians and contributors. Candidates, whether running for election or not, are constantly assessed by the public and other politicians, and political campaigning becomes a never-ending process. Mendelsohn and Crespi[52] note two general categories of poll effects. First, they affect candidate preferences by both political leaders and the public. Second, they affect voters. Voter turnout is a function of the closeness of the election as well as perceived issue differences between candidates.

Many politicians and academicians believe that a bandwagon effect influences the American electorate. Thus, a voter seeing that one candidate is a sure winner via the polls will attempt to get on the side of the winner by voting for him. Polls taken shortly after the Kennedy election indicated a winning percentage margin of almost 60 to 40 rather than the real margin of less than one-half of

a percentage point. Joseph T. Klapper, in his review of the literature concerning the bandwagon effect, notes, "there is absolutely
no conclusive evidence that ... the publication of poll results does
or does not affect the subsequent vote. The bandwagon influence
has to fight party identification, family influence, friends, etc."[53]
In a recent experiment attempting to simulate bandwagon conditions, Daniel Fleitas found that "mere poll results are insufficient
to impel would-be bandwagon or underdog identifiers to switch
their vote. Rather, the voting behavior that results from these
identifications does not occur until sensitized or cued by a strong
qualitative stimulus."[54] Moreover, he noted that polls had an important effect until party label was introduced.

Of more interest to politicians and political scientists is the
effect of the television broadcasts of winners before some sections
of the country had finished voting. Thus, early predictions by the
sophisticated Vote Profile Analysis and similar predictive models
used by the major networks is reported to influence the ultimate
turnout and voter decision in the western states. At least four
major studies were carried out during the 1964 presidential election
to test the early broadcast effects. Harold Mendelsohn interviewed
1,212 voters before and after the election and found that only 14
persons had actually switched their votes (1 percent) and 97 percent voted for candidates of their original choice. He did report
that "of the 70 who, as last minute deciders, made the vote decision
in the last day, 39 or 56 percent said it was because of the last day
television broadcast."[55] One should note that in the first wave of
interviews, almost 20 percent refused to state their vote intention.
Many of those who refused could have been simply undecided and
their ultimate choice should have been explored at some length.

The Lang and Lang study had fewer respondents (364 California
voters and a control group of 116 Ohio voters).[56] However, their
findings agreed with the Mendelsohn study in that it showed that
television broadcasts had little impact on the California voter.
Other studies corroborated both the Mendelsohn and the Lang and
Lang studies.

Mendelsohn and Crespi sum up the potential impact of the media
by stating: (1) most people, from 90 to 95 percent, have made up
their minds before the election day; (2) last-minute switching is
very small; and (3) all the studies indicated that the broadcasts
had no effect on voter turnout.[57] Further, they indicate that the
American electorate tolerates a certain amount of exhortation and
directed communication during the three nonelection years, then

during an election, the voter receives an overload of stimuli and attempts to "tune-out." The political campaign offers a whole new set of symbols very incongruous with the normal mass communications situation. Also the media plunge the voter into a serious matter, a situation which has some built-in anxiety for him. Where he previously received entertainment, he now gets work. Ultimately, the anxiety translates itself into resentment that is directed against both the media and the candidates. In addition, it is clear that effective mass persuasion must be both intense and long-term.

Many writers have contended that the effect of the mass media is much more subtle than forcing the voter to change his vote choice. The media have changed the way the United States goes about electing its representatives. The nomination process can no longer be controlled by the political bosses because the media can appeal directly to the voters without the leaders' endorsement. The long speeches and technical arguments have changed into short, pithy slogans or well-made television documentaries. The nominating conventions rearrange their whole pattern of operation to get prime-time coverage of the keynote address, the balloting, the acceptance speeches, and so on. The television is the major source of political news for most voters, and the styles and personalities of major candidates are a primary consideration. Some political campaign experts suggest that style is paramount — how you say it, not what you are saying. McLuhan suggests that the media utilized have a message all by themselves.[58] Not that the message itself is of no importance, but that it gets received and translated differently depending upon the medium used. The contrast between opinions of those listening to the first Nixon-Kennedy debate via radio and those watching their televisions illustrates this point.

However, the contention here is that the media — especially television — have an important effect on the voter decision. If properly used, they can have a critical effect. This is not to argue that voters are fools and can be swayed like herds of cattle. Voters do perceive critical issues and react to them. Vietnam was a critical issue for Johnson as most observers will substantiate and the economy was among the critical issues for 1972. Effective use of the media is compromised somewhat by both candidates having excellent media programs. But there are a number of classic elections indicating that effective media campaigning defeated well-known, party-backed candidates using a more traditional approach in both primaries and general elections.

Party Identification, Issue-Orientation, Candidate Orientation, and the Independent Voter

In this section we will consider the effect of the three major proximate factors in the electoral decision — party, issues, and candidate orientation. Also we will explore the changing nature and impact of the independent voter and the implications for party realignment and critical elections. Much of the literature points to the 70 percent party identification of the American electorate as the chief anchor for their attitudes towards issues and candidates. In addition, more recent literature would suggest a public with much stronger issue positions than previously thought possible. Finally, the effect of charisma and media-induced image will be explored carefully.

In a recent collection of articles by six major scholars discussing the impact of issue voting, Gerald Pomper concluded:

Perhaps the major fault of the Michigan studies has been the comparative neglect of the political environment as an independent variable. The methodology of survey research has brought an over-emphasis on the individual behavior of isolated respondents. The influence upon these respondents has been studied only indirectly, through the voters' personal perceptions and actions. But voters are in fact not isolated, for they are affected by their environment, the mass media, the economic system, and the prevailing ideology.[59]

Pomper is suggesting an overemphasis on individual attitudes and perceptions (although even these are poorly studied) and a complete neglect of environmental factors including the mass media. The presentations concerning the American electorate have been misleading. Voters are not fools and they do have issue pictures of both candidates and parties. These issue pictures are a primary determinant of their eventual electoral choice. To some extent the overemphasis on party identification as a causal factor in the voters' choice can be integrated into the discussion above. Party identification, critical realignments, and party voting are usually tied to issue positions. Over time the original issues become less meaningful and the habit of supporting one party becomes ingrained. However, strong identifiers are not simply robots doing what daddy did but individuals who have some definite issue base to their straight party voting. As Walter Dean Burnham has pointed out, when these issue-based party habits get challenged strongly, a critical realignment can occur. Scammon and Wattenberg[60] along with Burnham[61] see the American electorate at one of these realigment junctures today. The social issue discussed by Scammon and Wattenberg and the increasing issue awareness of the general public as indicated by Burnham are clear signs that realignment can occur. Some catalytic issue is needed to force the change; however, this has not occurred. The strong issues of the economy, war in southeast Asia, and the social issue appear to be unable to force the change. Of course, the whole concept of critical elections suggests an American electorate with issue information and issue voting habits. It is the critical issues that will force a re-identification of the American electorate. In part, issue awareness is limited in America because of poor information sources. The media tend to spotlight a given number of simple issues and ignore equally important but more complicated ones. Cable television is one issue that has received very little in-depth press coverage, yet is potentially the most explosive and pervasive technological revolution in this century.[62] The problem is one of conflict-of-interest (all the major media are attempting to establish their own cable systems) and of complications. The potential impact on America is great; however, all such discussions are clearly speculative. Government control of information, governmental spying via cable, free channel access, the elimination of mail and telephones, living room originated programming, new teaching techniques — all are real possibilities with an extensive cable system.

First let us examine the effects of party identification. Many scholars attempting to explain voter choice have suggested that party identification is the primary factor in the decision making of most American voters. Approximately 70 percent of the electorate identifies with one of the parties and many voters seemingly vote for a candidate simply because he is a Democrat or Republican. As mentioned above, the party identification factor cannot be totally separated from issue-oriented voting; however, it seems clear that the issues that forced the last critical realignment (depression and social reform) are much less potent today.

If one examines the distribution of party identification over the last decade or so, one sees that party identification has been relatively stable although the independent voter percentage is increasing steadily. An increasing independent voter percentage can be viewed (as Burnham does) as an indication of widespread dissatisfaction with the present parties.

Table 3-4 clearly shows that the independent category has grown strongly (increasing by 50 percent) while the Democrats and Republicans have both lost between 5 and 10 percent of their partisans. While we will discuss the question of independents at some length, it appears that a good deal of the increase in that category is due to highly informed citizens losing confidence in the present major parties.

Table 3-4

Perceived Party Identification
University of Michigan

	Oct 1952	Oct 1956	Oct 1960	Nov 1962	Oct 1964	Nov 1966	Nov 1968	Nov 1970	Trend 1952-1970
Strong/Weak Republicans	27	29	27	28	24	25	24	25	−2
Strong/Weak Democrats	47	44	46	46	51	45	45	43	−4
All Independents	22	24	23	22	23	28	30	31	+9
Don't Know	4	3	4	4	2	2	1	1	−3

SOURCE: Walter DeVries and V. Lance Tarrance, *The Ticket Splitter: A New Force in American Politics* (Grand Rapids, Mich.: Eerdmans, 1972), p. 24. Used by permission of the publisher.

An even more revealing table is offered by Burnham (see table 3-5).[63] He starts in 1940 and looks at *strong* identifiers exclusively. This is an important distinction since only strong identifiers can resist short-term influences (such as special issues or media campaigns) and can be expected to vote an almost straight party ticket. Since 1966, less than one-third of the American electorate could be defined as strongly identified with one party or the other.

The table indicates that strong identifiers — those most likely to vote a straight party ticket — constitute only one-third of the voters. If one adds the weak identifiers, those voting mostly for Democrats or mostly for Republicans, the percentage rises to almost 75 percent. In political science, as in most social sciences, predicting 70 percent of anything is considered something short of phenomenal. The prediction is not true for the majority of the identifiers since the majority are weak identifiers. A full 25 percent of the voters cannot be predicted at all; therefore, even if one accepts that 70 percent of the vote can be predicted, he can only

Table 3-5

The Decline of Party: Movements in Party
Identification, 1940-1969

Year	Independent	Strong Democrat	Strong Republican	Total Strong Identifiers
1940	20			
1944	20			
1948	19			
1952	23	23	14	37
1956	20	23	16	39
1960	23	21	16	37
1962	22	24	13	37
1964	23	27	11	38
1965	23			
1966	29	18	10	28
1967	31			
1968	28	23	9	32
1969	30			

SOURCE: Reprinted from *Critical Election and the Mainsprings of American Politics* by Walter Dean Burnham, p. 120. By permission of W. W. Norton & Company, Inc. Copyright © 1970 by W. W. Norton & Company, Inc.

say that short-term forces — forces that influence the completely unpredictable one-fourth — will determine the election. The point of the discussion is that while party affiliation is important, it does not seem to be the determining factor in most elections, especially in national and statewide elections.

Philip Converse looks at the vote in two components, the long-term and the short-term vote. "The long term component is a simple reflection of the distribution of underlying party loyalties, a distribution that is stable over substantial periods of time. In any specific election the population may be influenced by short term forces associated with peculiarities of that election."[64] Of course, one of the more important short-term variables that influences voting is the impact of the candidate's media campaign. One sees clear evidence of media effect where one candidate has a well-financed media campaign and the other has little money and little media exposure. The effect is particularly noticeable in primary elections.

The Independent Voter

The independent voter constitutes at least one-quarter of the electorate and, if one includes the weak identifiers, this voter really constitutes 60 to 70 percent of the electorate. This means that the political campaign decides the election for most of the voters. This conclusion runs counter to much of the literature which suggests that very few minds are actually changed during a campaign. However, the definition of the changers for most researchers is that group which decides on one candidate and then changes to another. Because most studies look at attitudes of the voters at only one or two points in time, it is probably true that the campaign changes few voters already committed to a candidate. If one expands the change category to those who have not yet made up their minds, then the category is clearly the majority of the electorate. This broader change categorization is the most appropriate group to examine when one studies the effects of political campaigns on the electorate.

The independent voter is that part of the electorate most likely to be undecided during the campaign, more likely to actually change from one candidate to another, and most susceptible to short-term forces including the impact of the mass media. Also, he is less likely to participate in the elections or have good information or interest in the campaign, and less likely to vote than the strong identifiers. How the independent voter thinks and decides is still a comparatively unstudied phenomenon in spite of the great interest among political scientists, politicians, and journalists in voting studies.

The situation that was described by Samuel J. Eldersveld over twenty years ago still prevails. He said, "We still know very little about the political behavior of that segment of the electorate which presumably is highly irregular in party allegiance. . . . The truth is that the strategic significance of the independents have never been carefully studied, although we are quick to say they may hold the balance of power. . . . Our objectives presumably are to determine the extent, characteristics, relevant factors, and effects of independent voting."[65] But the theory basic to such research has been nonexistent or ill-defined, and as a consequence we have mere fragments of information.

Some would say that this increase in Independents means a further erosion in the impact of party identification, thus allowing short-term forces to be more important. The increase in this category probably reflects the increasing mobility of the American population and the general diminishing importance of the party machine. However, the independent category should really include those who are only weak identifiers and are also susceptible to short-term influences. Part of the problem in studying the importance of the Independent voter — now narrowly defined — is that these voters tend to vote infrequently and have very little interest or information about the campaign. Of course, their ultimate influence on the election is relative to whether or not they vote.

Campbell describes them succinctly: "Far from being more attentive, interested, and informed, Independents tend as a group to be somewhat less involved in politics. They have somewhat poorer knowledge of the issues, their image of the candidates is fainter, their interest in the campaign is less, their concern over the outcome is relatively slight, . . ."[66]

More recent studies of the Independent voter suggest that the category is expanding and that the new Independents and the "behavioral" Independents are at least as informed and participatory as the strongly identified citizen. Burnham suggests that there appears to be a bimodal distribution of Independents with regard to their political information and participation rates.[67] He presents three very interesting tables that suggest the Independent voter is at least the equal in most respects with the party-identified stratum. Burnham goes on to argue that the increase in Independents and their characteristics portend a possible critical realignment of parties for the future. He states:

The significant point is that none of the groups among which independents have the largest share . . . is the kind of group associated with low political participation or efficacy. . . . The problem is further complicated when one examines certain ranges of political opinion among our party-identified groups. If the Survey Research Center's involvement index is studied, the result is quite clear: independents are indeed disproportionately concentrated at the lowest end of the scale, particularly by contrast with strong identifiers of either party. On the other hand, a study of the efficacy index—a measure of the individual's sense of political competence — reveals an entirely different picture. Among 1964 independents, 36 percent scored high to very high on this efficacy index, a proportion exceeded only by the 50 percent strong Republican identifiers who also had a high to very high score. Of the independents, 37 percent of strong Democratic identifiers also registered low to very low, while only the Republican identifiers had a share of low efficacy individuals (28 percent) which was significantly below that of the independents.[68]

Table 3-6

The Structure of Party Identification
(in percent) 1964

Category	Number	Strong Dem	Weak Dem	Ind	Weak Rep	Strong Rep
Occupation						
Professional-manager	245	20%	21%	30%	13%	16%
Clerical-sales	172	24%	25%	23%	16%	12%
Skilled, semi-skilled	271	31%	24%	27%	10%	8%
Unskilled, service	147	41%	28%	22%	8%	2%
Farmers	44	32%	32%	9%	16%	11%
Retired, not head of household	631	26%	26%	20%	16%	12%
Income						
$10,000 and over	309	20%	20%	26%	19%	15%
$7,500 – 9,999	235	23%	22%	26%	18%	11%
$6,000 – 7,999	216	27%	30%	24%	12%	7%
$4,000 – 5,999	305	20%	28%	21%	11%	11%
Under $4,000	471	33%	26%	20%	11%	10%
Education						
Grades 0–8	373	39%	27%	17%	11%	7%
9–11 +	302	30%	28%	23%	10%	8%
High school grad	329	23%	28%	23%	16%	10%
High school grad + training	156	21%	19%	29%	16%	15%
Some college	195	19%	21%	30%	14%	16%
College graduate	172	19%	21%	23%	17%	20%

SOURCE: Reprinted from *Critical Elections and the Mainsprings of American Politics* by Walter Dean Burnham, p. 124. By permission of W. W. Norton & Company, Inc. Copyright © 1970 by W. W. Norton & Company, Inc.

With regard to party identification and issue questions, Burnham presents a table that indicates very little difference between the Independents and any of the other four categories of identifiers, with the exception of strong Republicans (table 3-6). The Independents appear to be as informed as all the other categories when one compares the "don't know" percentages for the three issue questions (again excepting the strong Republicans). In addition, for the higher categories of occupation, income, and education, there are consistently higher proportions of Independent voters. While 30 percent of professional-managers are Independents, only 20 percent are strong Democrats and only 16 percent are strong Republicans. For the college graduates, 23 percent are Independents while 19 percent are strong Democrats and 20 percent are strong Republicans.

On issue questions, Independents appear to be as informed or at least as willing to give a definite opinion as the Democrats or the

Republicans (see table 3-7). On these three major issue questions, the Independents appear both informed, interested, and willing to assert a definite opinion. This new view of the Independent differs strongly with that espoused by Campbell and suggests an informed electorate that is abandoning the traditional two parties. As table 3-8 shows, the trend is increasing, especially with the higher education, higher income, and white-collar groups. Table 3-8 focuses on the demographics of Independents and the changes in the last five years.

What is clear from this discussion is that more and more Americans are becoming Independents and that this category seems to be about the same as the strong identifiers for both major parties in terms of participation and attitudes toward the political system.

Issue
Voting

There has been considerable discussion recently in both academic and practical politics about the extent of issue voting. One of the central themes in Scammon and Wattenberg's work was that Americans were not only aware of the key issues (the social issue) but also were ready to change their party affiliation or at least their voting habits because of it.[69] As stated before, the literature and conventional wisdom of politicians present an ill-informed, unattentive American electorate. Yet, if one examines some recent elections at all levels of government, one gets a different impression.

George McGovern's candidacy was born and nourished on specific issue stands. While he inherited some of the McCarthy-Kennedy legacy, McGovern had little money and less media exposure than almost any other candidate.[70] He was almost unknown by the general public. With the skillful use of volunteers and good organization and an ability to project issues of concern, McGovern made some excellent primary showings and finally won the Wisconsin primary. Until Wisconsin, McGovern was almost ignored by the major media and complained bitterly about it. One should remember that McGovern is from South Dakota, is uncharismatic, and is an average speaker — all qualities that should have eliminated him from serious consideration. His major strategy was to organize well and hit issue positions clearly and forcefully. Instead of the usual equivocation, McGovern stated his positions concisely on welfare, defense, crime, foreign policy, taxation, and others. While he backed away from some of his more radical proposals, he nonetheless

Table 3-7

Party Identification and Issue Questions, 1964

Response	Number	Strong Dem	Weak Dem	Ind	Weak Rep	Strong Rep
A. Is the (federal) government getting too powerful?						
Yes	468	16%	24%	30%	43%	66%
Depends	49	3	3	5	2	2
No	554	49	39	35	25	15
Don't know, No Interest	465	32	34	30	30	17
B. Do you favor Medicare?						
Yes	763	66%	54%	47%	35%	22%
Depends	94	6	4	6	7	8
No	435	12	24	30	39	62
Don't know, No Interest	244	15	17	17	19	8
C. Do you favor government help to Negroes who can't find jobs?						
Yes, favor	596	50%	35%	43%	31%	19%
Depends	114	6	6	7	11	9
Leave to states	618	33	41	36	44	63
Don't know, No interest	205	11	18	13	15	9

SOURCE: Reprinted from *Critical Elections and the Mainsprings of American Politics* by Walter Dean Burnham, p. 124. By permission of W. W. Norton & Company, Inc. Copyright © 1970 by W. W. Norton & Company, Inc.

Table 3-8

Growth of the "New Independent":
Shifts in Proportion of Independents by Social
Category, June 1965 — September 1967

Category	Increase
Age	
Highest income ($7,000 and over)	11
College educated	10
Nonwhite	10
Age 21–29	10
White-collar occupations	10
U.S.	8
Age 50 and over	6
Women	6
Grade school education	5
Middle-income ($5,000–6,999)	5
Low income (under $3,000)	3
Farmers	2

SOURCE: Reprinted from *Critical Elections and the Mainsprings of American Politics* by Walter Dean Burnham, p. 128. By permission of W. W. Norton & Company, Inc. Copyright © 1970 by W. W. Norton & Company, Inc.

focused his campaign efforts on policy changes he would make. It was the most issue-oriented campaign effort since Goldwater, and one of the few times a candidate for the nomination of a major party was willing to commit himself so clearly to a whole array of issue positions. His upset victory astounded those interested in politics and some of his radical positions later were responsible for his defeat. Still, his effort was an issue-oriented one and the electorate responded to those issue positions.

Scammon and Wattenberg, while suggesting that it is normal for the American electorate to be unattentive and uninformed, document the impact of issue voting at both the national and local levels.[71] From their studies of Los Angeles, Pittsburgh, New York, and the presidential primaries, they believe that people are deeply concerned about rioting, crime, marijuana, pornography, civil disorder, and so on and are expressing this discontent at election time. Issues — both social and economic — are the crucial factors determining present-day elections. They go on to suggest that American voters are "up for grabs" and the party that appeals to the issues of concern will win the new majority's allegiance. The possibility of a major realignment of party identification was continually alluded to and discussed. The elections in 1970, immediately after their study, seemed to offer some corroboration to the Scammon and Wattenberg thesis; however, since candidates of both parties started to say approximately the same thing with regard to the "social issue," it was difficult to analyze the importance of that issue.

The presidential election of 1972 seemed clearer. The issue positions that attracted volunteers and money to McGovern's primary campaign were seen to be "too radical" by most Americans and even most Democrats. McGovern's positions were explicit and explained in great detail. Nixon's positions were much more general and more ambiguous. He would seem to agree with some McGovern ideas about tax reform, welfare reform, and reduction of defense expenditures, but he was generally vague and indeterminate about how to solve the problems. The thrust was "trust Nixon and he'll do the best he can, but he won't do anything too different from the past." Even without Nixon's "Department of Dirty Tricks," it appears McGovern would have lost. McGovern's positions were seen as radical ones; Nixon's were moderate and addressed directly some of the worries of the mass electorate.[72]

Pomper examines the relationship between issue preferences and three partisan variables from 1956–1968.[73] The variables are party identification, the awareness of differences between the parties on the six issues examined, and the consensus among the electorate on the positions of the parties on these issues. In each, he found a definite trend showing an increase in voter consciousness during the 1956–1968 period. The six policy issues were: federal air to education; government provision of medical care; government guarantee of full employment; federal enforcement of fair employment and fair housing; federal enforcement of school integration; and foreign aid. Pomper derives three implications from his data and findings. His first implication is that the 1964 campaign was a critical election rather than just an aberrant event because it led to heightened issue awareness. While his data do show more issue awareness, it is a bit farfetched to suggest that 1964 was a critical election. Certainly the 1966, 1968, and 1970 national elections indicated that no major realignment of party identification or power emanated from the 1964 Goldwater emphasis on issue positions. A second implication also seems to read more into the data than is apparent. Pomper suggests that "the clarification and realignment of the parties' policy positions leads to . . . the possible development of a responsible two-party system in the United States."[74] While party platforms seem to be getting more issue explicit, the state-based party system in the U.S. really prevents any possibility of responsible parties similar to those in a parliamentary system. The national party simply does not have sufficient power to control or to even substantially influence the votes of congressmen.

A final implication relates to the study of American voting behavior and the conclusions of Campbell's work. Pomper suggests that the findings of data from the 1950s are no longer relevant and that the Michigan Survey Research Center scholars failed to note the increasing importance of ideological conflict and the total environment that affects the voters' choice, such as the mass media, the economic system, and the prevailing ideology. Further, he states, "most critically, we must emphasize . . . the stimuli they receive from the parties and other electoral actions. If these stimuli are more ideological and dynamic, we are likely to see different perceptions and behavior, such as that evidenced in the 1964 and 1968 elections."[75]

Richard Boyd examines the popular control of public policy by employing Converse's concept of the normal vote.[76] Converse was interested in the impact of the religious issue on the 1960 election and used the normal vote as a baseline, with the impact of religion being measured as a deviation from the normal vote. The logic of the normal vote presumes that the force of issues constantly changes and their impact varies. His data indicate clearly that beliefs about

Vietnam, race and urban unrest, and Johnson's performance as president were all highly related to the vote in 1968. Boyd notes the relationship between parties and issues and suggests one should expect issues to be more important in times of party realignment or disintegration than in periods of stability in party strength.[77]

In a more speculative vein (one which directly relates to the linkage model chapter), Boyd suggests that issues having a similar impact on voting preferences can pose very different restrictions on the discretion of leaders in policy making. "On some issues the electorate exercises no effective constraints on leaders' policy choice. On others, the electorate permits political leaders a wide array of options at the time of the adoption of policy, while passing a retrospective judgment on such choices in subsequent elections. It is argued that the issues of Vietnam and Johnson's performance as president are examples of this type of public control of policy."[78] This discussion tends to substantiate the need to develop public preference maps so that leaders know what the public wants. In addition, it indicates direct public control over policy in some instances, a control based on information primarily received through the mass media.

Candidate Orientation, Charisma, and Image

While it appears that charisma is not a major factor in most presidential elections (certainly not in 1972 with the bland McGovern and the neuter Nixon), many observers point to candidate-orientation as an important factor in the vote decision. The public relations specialists prefer to use the whole category image; however, the impact of image was dealt with extensively in the last chapter. Ever since James C. Davies' work there have been few attempts to really measure the impact of candidate-orientation.[79] Davies found that, among the few voters he could identify as being charismatic, their votes were heavily influenced by their devotion to the war hero Eisenhower or the intellectual Stevenson. Most of the charismatics were for Eisenhower since he was the war hero and possible savior from future wars. However, the thrust of Davies' study was that very few voters could be judged charismatic (something less than 5 percent even in 1952).

Candidate-orientation does get intermingled with issues to some extent, and image-building is almost an entirely different orientation. DeVries and Tarrance deal most thoroughly with efforts to build images for candidates.[80] They look at the behavioral independent and attempt to discover what influences the individual who says he is a Democrat or Republican but who frequently switches to the other party. DeVries is both an academician and a practical politician, being campaign manager for several statewide Michigan candidates. He suggests that image is becoming more important than party identification and uses telephone polling to test some interesting hypotheses about voting behavior. His data and conclusion about the behavioral independent and the impact of image in a campaign have been presented in the previous chapter where the entire question of public relations firms is examined closely.

Conclusions

We have examined the voting environment, the voting studies compared with attitude change research, and the effects of party, issue, and candidate orientation upon the voters' choice. Among the findings presented were:

1. Studies indicate that most Americans are ill-informed about issues and generally inattentive to the political process.

2. The party machine that traditionally gave many voters information on the election seems to be almost extinct, with the Daley machine in Chicago being the last major big-city political machine still operating effectively.

3. Election law reform such as nonpartisan elections and the highly mobile population has left even greater numbers of people poorly informed and unable to make a rational choice in politics. All this would suggest an unanchored population that could easily be manipulated by the effective use of the media during a campaign.

4. Voting studies have indicated that few people change their minds during a campaign and that most are influenced by opinion leaders.

5. Experimental psychologists found that persons forced to make a choice (such as voters) who have little information with which to make a choice could be influenced and manipulated through the skillful use of the media and propaganda.

6. The two-step flow of influence was suggested as the cause of the apparent minor effect of the media. Messages and information get filtered through opinion leaders, who explain it to the mass public.

7. Polls and bandwagon effects seem to be minimal.

8. While the great majority of Americans are party identified, the trend is away from the parties.

9. Independents are no longer the most uninformed group, and more and more interested voters are becoming Independents.

10. The Independent voter appears to be bimodal in distribution with a large portion uninformed and an equally large portion very participatory and interested in the political process.

11. Issue voting appears to be increasing rapidly; some researchers suggest that party realignment and critical elections are now occurring in American politics.

12. Candidate-orientation and charisma appear to have little effect on the voters except in the area of image where issues and candidates' quality are combined for total effect. One issue is the ability of the man to do the job. However, the hero worshipping of the American electorate seems to affect its voting habits very minimally.

NOTES

1. Angus Campbell et al., *The American Voter: An Abridgement* (New York: Wiley, 1960), p. 144. See also Fred I. Greenstein, *The American Party System and the American People* (Englewood Cliffs, N.J.: Prentice-Hall, 1964), p. 33.

2. Campbell, ibid.

3. Greenstein, ibid.

4. Warren E. Miller and Donald E. Stokes, "Constituency Influence on Congress," *American Political Science Review* 57 (1963): 45-56.

5. Lester W. Milbrath, *Political Participation* (Chicago: Rand McNally, 1963), p. 21. Poll results indicate that new voters, eighteen to twenty-one, have approximately the same information levels and political activities as other young voters twenty-one to thirty. Later in the chapter, the independent voter and the possibility of a much better-informed citizenry due in large part to the television news programs will be discussed.

6. Daniel Katz and Samuel J. Eldersveld, "The Impact of Local Party Activity upon the Electorate," *Public Opinion Quarterly* 25 (Spring 1961): 1-24.

7. Greenstein, *American Party System* p. 14.

8. Frank J. Sorauf, "State Patronage in a Rural County," *American Political Science Review* 50 (December 1956): 1046-56. For a general discussion of the decline of the urban political machines, see his *Party Politics in America*, 2d ed. (Boston: Little, Brown, 1972), pp. 106-12. For a more elaborate treatment, see Warren Moscow, "The Machines," in *Political Parties and Pressure Groups*, ed. Frank Munger and H. Douglas Price (New York:

Crowell, 1964). For an outstanding novel on old-time political leaders and machines, see Edwin O'Connor, *The Last Hurrah* (Boston: Little, Brown, 1946).

9. Katz and Eldersveld, "Impact of Local Party Activity," pp. 16-17. More recent studies have indicated greater party effects. See William J. Crotty, "Party Effort and Its Impact on the Vote," *American Political Science Review* 65 (1971): 439-50; Raymond E. Wolfinger, "The Influence of Precinct Work on Voting Behavior," *Public Opinion Quarterly* 27 (1963): 387-98; and Gerald H. Kramer, "The Effects of Precinct-Level Canvassing on Voter Behavior," *Public Opinion Quarterly* 34 (1970): 560-72.

10. V. O. Key, *Public Opinion and American Democracy* (New York: Knopf, 1963), pp. 344-70. Key spends two chapters examining the effects of the media on individual citizen attitudes and party organization. While he concludes that the media appear to reinforce attitudes rather than change them, he calls for studies over time concerning specific issues to examine carefully the effects of the mass media on the opinion-policy process.

11. Phillips Cutright and Peter H. Rossi, "Grass Roots Politicians and the Vote," *American Sociological Review* 23 (1958): 171-79.

12. Wolfinger, "Influence of Precinct Work."

13. Crotty, "Party Effort and Its Impact."

14. Charles R. Adrian, "Some General Characteristics of Non-partisan Elections," *Democracy in Urban America,* ed. Oliver P. Williams and Charles Press (Chicago: Rand McNally, 1961), p. 263.

15. Greenstein, *American Party System,* p. 58.

16. Erich Fromm, *Man for Himself* (New York: Avon Books, 1941), and his *Escape from Freedom* (New York: Holt, Rinehart and Winston, 1947).

17. David Reisman et al., *The Lonely Crowd* (New Haven, Conn.: Yale University Press, 1950).

18. Ibid.

19. Fromm, *Man for Himself.*

20. C. Wright Mills, *The Power Elite* (New York: Oxford University Press, 1956).

21. Seymour Martin Lipset, *Political Man: The Social Bases of Politics* (New York: Anchor Books, 1963).

22. Mills, *The Power Elite,* p. 311.

23. Reisman, *The Lonely Crowd,* p. 84.

24. Fromm, *Man for Himself,* pp. 68, 76.

25. Elihu Katz and Paul F. Lazarsfeld, *Personal Influence,* 2d ed. (New York: Free Press of Glencoe, 1964), p. 55.

26. Ibid., p. 56.

27. Lilian L. Woodward and Elmo Roper, "Political Activity of American Citizens," *American Political Science Review* 44 (December 1950): 874. For a more complete discussion of the effects of groups on electoral choice, see H. T. Reynolds, *Politics and the Common Man* (Homewood, Ill.: Dorsey, 1974), pp. 149-57. See also Lester W. Milbrath, *Political Participation* (Chicago, Ill.: Rand McNally, 1965). Of course, similar questions are asked on each of the Michigan Survey Research Center's national surveys. Results continue to be similar to those found by Woodward and Roper.

28. For a complete and recent discussion of the "bandwagon effect" literature with a special focus on public opinion polls and television electronic predictions, see Harold Mendelsohn and Irving Crespi, *Polls, Television and the*

New Politics (Scranton, Pa.: Chandler, 1970), pp. 17-25. Generally, the literature indicates little if any effects of either polls or television predictions on turnout or voter choice. However, after the election is won, many more people perceive themselves to have voted for the winner than the actual election results indicate. See also Daniel W. Fleitas, "Bandwagon and Underdog Effects in Minimal-Information Elections," *American Political Science Review* 65 (June 1971): 434-38.

29. Mills, *The Power Elite*, p. 311.

30. Vance Packard, *The Hidden Persuaders* (New York: David McKay, 1957).

31. See, for example, Herbert Blumer, "Suggestions for the Study of Mass-Media Effects," *American Voting Behavior*, ed. E. Burdick and A. J. Brodbeck (Glencoe: Free Press, 1959); Herbert A. Simon and Frederick Stern, "The Effects of Television upon Voting Behavior in Iowa in the 1952 Presidential Election," *American Political Science Review* 49 (June 1955): 470-77; Mendelsohn and Crespi, *Polls, Television and the New Politics*; and Dan Nimmo, *The Political Persuaders* (Englewood Cliffs, N.J.: Prentice-Hall, 1970). See also James C. Strouse, "Name Familiarization: Its Importance in a Political Campaign" (Master's thesis, University of Maryland, 1967), pp. 19-37.

32. Paul F. Lazarsfeld, Bernard Berelson, and Hazel Gaudet, *The People's Choice* (New York: Columbia University Press, 1948).

33. Bernard Berelson, Paul F. Lazarsfeld, and William McPhee, *Voting* (Chicago: University of Chicago Press, 1954).

34. Angus Campbell, Gerald Gurin, and Warren E. Miller, *The Voter Decides* (Evanston, Ill.: Row, Peterson, 1954).

35. Ibid.

36. Morris Janowitz and Dwaine Marvick, *Competitive Pressure and Democratic Consent*, Michigan Government Studies, no. 32 (Ann Arbor: Bureau of Government, 1956). Perhaps the most complete investigation of media influence on the undecided voter is Walter DeVries and V. Lance Tarrance, *The Ticket-Splitter: A New Force in American Politics* (Grand Rapids, Mich.: Eerdmans, 1972). The findings of this book are examined closely later in the chapter.

37. Janowitz and Marvick, ibid., p. 114.

38. Ibid., p. 109.

39. Katz and Lazarsfeld, *Personal Influence*.

40. Elihu Katz and Paul F. Lazarsfeld, "The Two-Step Flow of Communication: An Up-to-Date Report on an Hypothesis," *Public Opinion Quarterly* 21 (Spring 1957): 61. For a more recent elaboration on the two-step flow of information and the many studies on the subject, see Melvin DeFleur, *Theories of Mass Communications* (New York: David McKay, 1966). DeFleur's book and his sociocultural model of persuasion will be examined in detail later in the book.

41. Everett Rogers, *The Diffusion of Innovations* (New York: Free Press, 1962), p. 223. The diffusion of innovation literature is a vast one and is reviewed in some depth in Rogers' book. For a study on state policy diffusion see Jack L. Walker, "The Diffusion of Innovations Among the American States," *American Political Science Review* 63 (September 1969): 880-900. On p. 881, Walker reviews some of the major diffusion studies.

42. Herbert Hamilton, "Dimensions of Self-Designated Opinions, Leadership, and Their Correlates," *Public Opinion Quarterly* 35, no. 2 (Summer 1971): 266-79.

43. Philip Converse, "Information Flow and the Stability of Partisan Attitudes," *Elections and the Political Order*, ed. Angus Campbell et al. (New York: Wiley, 1965), pp. 136-58.

44. Ibid.

45. Ibid., p. 146.

46. For a good review of the debate studies, see Sidney Kraus, ed., *The Great Debates* (Bloomington: Indiana University Press, 1962).

47. Campbell, *The American Voter*, p. 142.

48. Muzafer Sherif and Carl I. Hovland, *Social Judgment* (New Haven, Conn.: Yale University Press, 1961), p. 198.

49. Carl I. Hovland, *The Order of Presentation in Persuasion* (New Haven, Conn.: Yale University Press, 1957).

50. Carl I. Hovland, "Results from Studies of Attitude Change," *Public Opinion and Communications,* ed. Bernard Berelson and Morris Janowitz New York: Free Press, 1966), p. 655.

51. For a complete discussion of the simulation process, see Ithiel de Sola Pool, Robert P. Obelson, and Samuel L. Popkin, *Candidates, Issues, and Strategies* (Cambridge, Mass.: MIT Press, 1964).

52. Mendelsohn and Crespi, *Polls, Television and the New Politics.*

53. Joseph T. Klapper, *The Effects of Mass Communication* (Glencoe, Ill.: Free Press, 1960). See particularly "Bandwagon: A Review of the Literature," mimeographed (Office of Social Research, Columbia Broadcasting System, Inc., June 17, 1964), cited in Mendelsohn and Crespi, p. 18.

54. Fleitas, "Bandwagon and Underdog Effects."

55. Harold Mendelsohn, *Ballots and Broadcasts* (Denver: University of Denver Press, 1965), p. 15.

56. Kurt and Gladys Engel Lang, *Voting and Non-voting* (Waltham, Mass.: Blaisdell, 1968).

57. Mendelsohn and Crespi, *Polls, Television and the New Politics*, pp. 234-36.

58. Marshall McLuhan, *Understanding Media* (New York: McGraw-Hill, 1964).

59. Gerald M. Pomper, "Issue Voting: Rejoinder," *American Political Science Review* 66 (June 1972): 427. See also the series of articles in the same issue included on pages 415-70. They represent a definitive discussion of this area.

60. Richard M. Scammon and Ben J. Wattenberg, *The Real Majority* (New York: Coward, McCann, and Geoghegan, 1970).

61. Walter Dean Burnham, *Critical Elections and the Mainsprings of American Politics* (New York: Norton, 1970).

62. We will examine cable television in greater detail in chapter 9. An excellent overview of the possible impact of CATV is in Ralph Lee Smith, *The Wired Nation* (New York: Harper Colophon Books, 1972).

63. Burnham, *Critical Elections*, p. 120.

64. Philip E. Converse, "The Concept of a Normal Vote," *Elections and the Political Order*, ed. Angus Campbell et al. (New York: Wiley, 1966), p. 14.

65. Samuel J. Eldersveld, "The Independent Vote: Measurement, Characteristics, and Implications for Party Strategy," *American Political Science Review* 46 (September 1952): pp. 732-35.

66. Campbell et al., *The American Voter*, p. 83.

67. Burnham, *Critical Elections*, pp. 123-26. Used by permission of the publisher.

68. Ibid., p. 123.

69. Scammon and Wattenberg, *The Real Majority*. For an extensive insider's view of the future of American politics, see Frederick G. Dutton, *Changing Sources of Power: American Politics in the 1970's* (New York: McGraw-Hill, 1971). Louis Harris looks at change among blacks, youth, women, and many other groups and issues in his *The Anguish of Change* (New York: Norton, 1973). Of course, one of the definitive works on the 1972 election is Theodore White, *The Making of the President 1972* (New York: Atheneum, 1973).

70. While McGovern did generate a substantial amount of funds through direct mailings, his financing was certainly much inferior to Senator Edmund Muskie's.

71. Scammon and Wattenberg, *The Real Majority*.

72. While Theodore White and others suggested that McGovern was simply ahead of his time, like Stevenson or Wilson, the overall point still holds. In the 1972 election, citizens focused on issue difference between McGovern and Nixon and made their choices on those issues. For labor groups and many ethnic groups, the social issue as described by Scammon and Wattenberg seemed to be extremely important as they abandoned decades of Democratic support to vote for Nixon.

73. Pomper, "Issue Voting." See also his *Elections in America: Control and Influence in Democratic Politics* (New York: Dodd, Mead, 1968).

74. Ibid., p. 426.

75. Ibid., p. 428.

76. Richard W. Boyd, "Popular Control of Public Policy: A Normal Vote Analysis of the 1968 Election," *American Political Science Review* 66 (June 1972): 429-49.

77. Ibid.

78. Ibid., p. 446.

79. James C. Davies, "Charisma in the 1952 Campaign," *American Political Science Review* 48 (December 1954): 1083-1102.

80. DeVries and Tarrance, *The Ticket-Splitter*.

4 Presidential Manipulation and Reporters' Bias: The Eternal Conflict

The Press as the Fourth Branch of Government

The role of the media in our society is a vital one. The reporters and commentators are charged with informing the American public, watching the lawmakers so that they do their job properly, and generally being an indispensable weapon of the American democratic constitutional government. While political leaders, especially national ones, reinforce the notion that the media are always probing the actions of lawmakers, the record of investigative reporting is a poor one by any man's measure.

Jack Anderson puts the situation most succinctly: "The pressures for conformity, the preference for entertainment over information, the intolerance for certain points of view — suppress controversy. Radio and television producers shy away from controversy as if it were unpatriotic. ... Even the great networks take care not to offend sponsors who might withdraw a multi-million dollar account over a political comment not to their liking."[1] There are many, many examples that substantiate Anderson's charge. For example, Howard K. Smith's documentary on the "Political Obituary of Richard Nixon" enraged politicians and others because Smith interviewed Alger Hiss.[2] Right-wing sponsors forced ABC to stop airing the film.

The story of the Nixon fund received very little attention until the national newspapers started belated investigations. The *St. Louis Post-Dispatch* was the only paper to demonstrate what the seventy-six contributors were getting for their money. The Howard Hughes loan to President Nixon's brother was also hushed up and ignored by most reporters and commentators in America. William Rivers reports that Senator Clark asked Washington reporters during the *Bobby Baker* case: "Where have all you guys been all this time?"[3] The prestigious *New York Times* is as guilty as any publication in the country. It covered up for the Bay of Pigs invasion of Cuba, knew about the U-2 flights long before Powers' crash, and let John McCone, former director of the Central Intelligence Agency, pre-view everything the *Times* published about the Pentagon papers. One might argue that the *Times* and other newspapers were simply doing a patriotic duty by taking precautions to protect the national interest. While that argument does hold in a very few instances, the real truth is that reporters and newspapers do not do their job. They are afraid that their sources and/or advertisers will shun them, and they are unwilling to follow Anderson-Pearson's example of developing a maze of independent overlapping sources of information that are far better and certainly more accurate than government spokesmen.

The media people are easily scared into inaction. One only has to look at the results of the Agnew attacks on television commentators. Almost immediately after the Agnew speeches the TV commentators refused to say almost anything other than quote what the president said. One had to wait until the next morning's *Times* to find Tom Wicker's reflections on the alternative views to the ones in the Nixon speech.

If it is true that reporters and commentators are frightened by the president, one might ask, why does the president always seem to criticize them? Any president, especially those such as LBJ and Nixon with their desire for a place in history, is supersensitive to the press. Any criticism, regardless of how petty, becomes a major source of irritation. Even President Kennedy, who had excellent relations with the media and who carefully cultivated them, once sent Secret Service personnel to call on reporters late one night so that the reporters could be informed how inaccurate their columns were.

Donald Matthews provides some insight into the media-government interaction.[4] Matthews centered his attention on the interaction of the press with U. S. senators. However, most of his analysis is germane to the larger discussion of media-national government relations. He reports that the interaction between reporters and senators shapes much of a senator's behavior in Washington and also shapes the news itself. In a sense, reporters are engaged in manufacturing the news. The reporters promise to give favorable publicity so that they can get inside information on what goes on. The reporters themselves give tips and information about legislative matters to the senator. They help start investigations and let the senator know how some of his friends and enemies feel about him and his legislation. In short, the situation is one of back-scratching — both trying to make each other look highly informed and effective. The reporter is guaranteed good stories and the senators are assured a good press.

The same kind of situation goes on much more intensely on the presidential level. The president is very interested in getting favorable treatment by the newspapers and television commentators. To insure that the news gets at least an administration overview, the White House staff handles the news releases, conducts background sessions for reporters, and arranges seminars for media people to inform them of new developments and to put the administration in the best possible light. The administration will also leak secret documents and information when that information tends to support its position. Leaking secret information is such a time-honored practice that the government's case in the Pentagon papers episode is almost ludicrous.[5] The government says in effect that it is patriotic for it to leak favorable secrets but treasonous for anyone else even when the information is years old.

The view that the media reporters desperately need the administration spokesmen is reflected by Walter Cronkite: "Television news requires more cooperation from its subjects than any other reporting medium, and this creates a demand for a new kind of talent among news personnel. In other types of journalism it is possible to compile a rather sound report without the cooperation of the central individual."[6] Most Washington reporters tend to view their official access as irreplaceable. They also tend, under fairly intense deadline pressure, to be unable and unwilling to develop the network of sources similar to Jack Anderson's. Therefore, they tend to parrot the administration line and to be relatively uncritical especially during those periods when investigative reporting is most needed to present the alternative view to the American people. This is most true in foreign affairs where the White House has almost total control of policy with little effective interference from Congress, the courts, or public opinion. In no way can the Washington press be blamed for the Vietnam War or any other tragedy; the central point is simply that the press is woefully inadequate in telling or getting the whole truth on critical foreign and domestic issues. Its failure may be a completely understandable one; but nonetheless it is a failure and others, like Anderson, seem to regularly scoop the entire Washington press corps with investigatory reporting. Most regrettably, though, it is a failure that could be corrected if the Washington press really desired to do so.

Weapons of the President

In spite of the weakness of the press in general, one should keep in mind the vast array of communication weapons the president has at his disposal to use exactly as he sees fit. First, the president can make news whenever he wishes. He is a national hero figure whose every action commands the attention of both national and local press. The president can demand and get national television and radio time to make announcements or speeches. He also has an extensive staff and the entire national bureaucracy to provide him with the latest and most complete information, which he can give to the press selectively or not at all. No president offers complete information to anyone not on his staff; no president should since some secrecy in government is necessary and justified for effective administration.

The most effective weapons employed in the president's attempt to manage and manipulate the news via the reporters are the personal interviews, the backgrounder conference, the special seminar, the selective leak to a friendly journalist, or the trial balloon. The personal interview with key advisers or the president himself may be used to explain policies or to announce new additions to old ones. Reporters chosen to interview value the selection highly and would be expected to give a relatively friendly account of the discussion. Of course, the reporter selected would be chosen for his previous fair treatment of the administration. The backgrounder is the most frequently used conference for reporters. Reporters are called in by the White House press staff and are given a talk-discussion by key advisers. Most of the talk is "off the record" and not directly quotable but it is in effect a direct handout to the press. In the backgrounder a rumor or trial balloon may be launched to test the public's reaction to an administration plan that is not official. A few years ago one such trial balloon suggested that the United States and Russia were going to send troops to the Middle East to keep peace there. This raised such a negative reaction that it was quickly disavowed by official Washington. The special seminar is something like the backgrounder only somewhat more elaborate, more specialized, and somewhat more a joint effort of the

White House staff, the Defense Department, and the State Department. The selective leak is simply the unofficial but approved leaking of previously secret information to a friendly journalist for the specific purpose of making the administration look good on some issue. It is done regularly by the White House, the Defense Department, and the State Department and is, according to the government's Pentagon papers case, a treasonable act. In any case, the president and the White House staff have a vast array of news devices to offer reporters. Management of the news and manipulation of seasoned reporters may be a harsh description of what goes on; nevertheless, the White House makes an intensive effort to ensure that its view of events is the one most likely to be reported.

A Brief History of President-Press Relations

For purposes of perspective and case analysis, we will examine the historical development of president -press relations in this century with special emphasis from FDR and the New Deal to President Nixon.[7] One of the first effective communicators with the press was Theodore Roosevelt. He had a flair for the journalistic phrase ("trustbuster," "speak softly and carry a big stick") and was highly regarded by the press corps both as an effective president and as a source of excellent news stories. Woodrow Wilson was the first to schedule a regular news conference, although Wilson attempted to control what reporters said in an overt manner, one similar to that used by Lyndon Johnson.

The administration of Franklin D. Roosevelt proved a watershed in presidential relationships with the press. According to many[8] Washington correspondents, FDR knew the value and influence of a news paragraph written as he wanted it written. Roosevelt's words seemed to have a decisive effect on public opinion. He carefully dramatized movement for social reform and the new laws which sanctioned these reforms. Of course, his direct efforts to mobilize public opinion were less successful. His court-packing scheme failed as did his attempt to defeat Conservative Democrats who opposed his social legislation. His "fireside chats" institutionalized radio as an effective device to communicate with the American people. One should point out that it was none other than quiet and correct Calvin Coolidge who first used the radio to talk to all Americans who owned radios (then a rather limited number). FDR used newsmen in the same manner he used his staff and cabinet.

He tried to find out what was going on throughout his bureaucracy and to find out what the people were thinking. Publicity, public debates between his staff members, reporters' investigations — all became part of the elaborate and seemingly dysfunctional presidential attempt to control the government in a period of social crisis.

The White House staff continued to expand during the Truman administration. Truman, like all presidents, felt the press was hostile to him. Nonetheless, Truman's penchant for direct talk and unwavering loyalty to his staff made a great number of headlines, most of which were favorable. The image of Truman as the aggressive, combative, average man just trying to do the best job he possibly could was the one most Americans received through the media. Press conferences were staged to the extent that all questions had to be submitted in advance.

The Eisenhower years were generally barren for the press. Ike did not understand how to manipulate the press, did not really try, and was unable to realize that the press, which had treated him as a genuine war hero during World War II, could criticize his every action as president. His former very favorable W. W. II treatment was to become almost totally negative because of his simple lack of political finesse. Since he was also an ineffective president, the negative treatment was compounded. When Ike delivered his attack on the nation's press during the 1964 Republican Convention, it was a result of his eight years of total frustration with both the print and electronic media.

Whatever favorable treatment that he received was usually the result of his excellent press secretary, James Hagerty. Hagerty talked about his "woodworking" for Eisenhower, in which the press secretary would attempt to make news (good news) for him. His handling of Eisenhower's illnesses was superb press work. He also attempted to control the entire administration news apparatus by placing his personally selected men at the State Department and the Defense Department. Eisenhower was the first president to talk to reporters at live, televised press conferences. Hagerty edited the television tapes to insure that only the best, grammatically correct answers would be broadcast. Hagerty's efforts were generally regarded as effective press communication even though the president himself was ineffective.

While John Kennedy was generally liked by the press, he worked hardest at manipulating the reporters. Kennedy tried to become personal friends with influential columnists, inviting some to his home, giving personal backgrounders, and favoring those writers who reported favorable stories. His attempt at news management and moral suasion was overt yet most of the press corps did not seem to resent it. The spectacle of an American president actively courting the working press surely flattered them, as it was intended to. Just before his assassination, Kennedy's "honeymoon" with the press seemed to be diminishing. However, much of the Kennedy image — dynamic, brilliant, energetic, handsome, charismatic — was due to his almost uniformly favorable press coverage. One might suggest that JFK was the first consummate McLuhan president, emphasizing how things were said and done as much as what was said.

In addition to his energetic attempts to win the press, Kennedy was the first to hold live, unedited press conferences on television. He held fewer conferences than FDR, Truman, and Eisenhower because he worried about the danger of overposure. The meticulous preparation necessary for each press conference may have been another reason for the relative infrequency. Pierre Salinger says that before each conference — and conferences were always scheduled beforehand — the press secretaries of the various executive departments met with Salinger as JFK's press secretary and compiled a list of questions they expected the reporters would ask.[9] President Kennedy was provided with a list of these questions together with suggestions for answers. Often he requested additional information. The whole process was topped off by a session with his White House advisers at which the possible answers were weighed and analyzed. Such preparations were necessary since one slip could put the foreign and domestic relations of the United States in great disrepair.

Lyndon Johnson was conscious of his image, especially in comparison to JFK, but he followed the Kennedy technique. He was often criticized for his overly longwindedness and his tendency to use a large part of his conference time for announcements. In addition, in his desire to appear well-briefed, LBJ "planted" many questions. He held meetings with reporters off camera and was considered most relaxed and candid during these encounters.

Johnson displayed restraint in his use of television early in his administration, but in 1965 he wanted to use the medium so much that the industry was surprised. He constantly attempted to improve the physical mechanics of his "performances." Such an enormous amount of exposure proved to be self-defeating.

LBJ's press relations differed from those of the previous administration. LBJ was more folksy and informal. He tended to hold more frequent conferences, many of which were impulsively called on short notice or held at unusual places, such as from a bale of hay at the LBJ ranch. Johnson engulfed newsmen with the news stories he wanted them to print. When newsmen would not be flattered, LBJ would threaten and sometimes actually speak to the reporters' publishers. Also, Johnson would direct investigations of the correspondents with whose work he disagreed. The credibility gap was Johnson's own fault because he attempted to browbeat journalists into writing favorable stories. LBJ preferred to confuse anyone attempting to guess his next appointment or announcement.

President Nixon in his first years in office held relatively few regularly scheduled press conferences. When questioned about this lack at a December 10, 1970, televised press conference, Nixon responded by saying that he felt he had a responsibility to do "my job to the people," through press conferences, reports to the nation, and interviews with individual reporters. Earlier Nixon had been criticized for dominating television and, when the opposition demanded equal time, the networks complained; the president decided to limit the press conferences.

Nixon realized that his television image reoriented his public policy and the public opinion of his policies and activities. He employed several public relations men to handle his appearances and smooth his relationship with the public. To Nixon, his effectiveness as an official and his personal political success depended greatly on strategic, tactical press relations.

Nixon always distrusted the press and was frustrated with his inability to get favorable coverage. His strategy was to ignore the reporters, use highly skilled public relations men to handle most of his communications with them, and to talk directly to the American people on free television prime time. When this strategy only seemed to increase unfavorable treatment, he tried a more direct approach and authorized Vice-President Agnew to attack both the print and electronic media. Polls showed that Agnew's attacks had wide support among the American public. The direct attack seemed to mute much of the criticism of reporters on television and in the national press.

By most reasonable standards, the coverage of President Nixon must be judged fair. Perhaps it is because most reporters expected Nixon to be a reactionary in domestic and foreign affairs and were pleased that he could be innovative in both areas. Another possible reason is that Nixon as president concentrated on his press relations and his personal image. The White House staff seemed engulfed with former advertising and public relations executives. The man who attributed his earlier defeats to the press and to his television performances in the Kennedy-Nixon debates rose to be among the most skilled television-public relations performers.

While most presidents have been resentful of criticism by the press, all presidents have had a vast array of information sources and specialists to talk directly to the public and to manipulate and use the press. Previously, we discussed some weapons of the White House — a felt obligation to lie for the public interest, selective leaks to favorite reporters, background sessions given by top advisers, information sheets on news stories the president wants published, and classification systems that can coverup any information the executive wants suppressed.

How the President Manipulates

In the previous section we discussed the extensive White House staff and its attempt to manage the news. Also, we looked briefly at some of the techniques employed by various presidents to win over the correspondents. No president is completely successful in getting good coverage for the simple reason that he has enemies, usually party but sometimes personal, who work hard to ensure some criticism. In addition, all or most of the opposition leadership in both the House of Representatives and the Senate are certain to disagree with almost anything the president does or proposes.

That the White House dominates the news is undisputed. Its control over information makes it indispensable to reporters. They must have access in order to do their jobs. Some suggest there exists a Department of Defense-contractor system between newsmen and public officials. The newsmen live off their access to public officials, and since public officials like to receive favorable publicity, there is a constant stream of news items given or leaked to the press. Some of the information leaked can be adverse, as Jack Anderson has shown, but most of it supports whatever the administration wants. Because the source of information is vital to the reporter and can be cut off immediately, most reporters think very hard before they criticize openly or challenge their handouts. In addition, many reporters without national reputations must be cognizant of their editor's feelings. To be sure, there are many fine reporters who continually challenge and investigate, yet the evidence indicates that too many are quite happy to accept whatever the White House wants to hand out.

There are many more examples besides the obvious ones of the Pentagon papers and the White House releases during the India-Pakistan War. The U-2 affair in which Eisenhower lied about American spy planes, the State Department's effort to suppress an NBC documentary from airing, a filming of an escape through the Berlin Wall, the Stanton (president of CBS) admonition to his news executives to stop the dove-hawk talk so as not to "unsteady the hand of the President" are just a few of the White House's direct attempts to manage the news.

The question of how the president manipulates the news can best be answered by looking at the vast informational organization at his disposal. One major part of it is the Armed Forces Information Services and the public relations sections of the army, navy, and air force. Senator J. William Fulbright has documented this component of the president's public relations effort very well.[10] Besides the Defense Department, the president has the State Department, the Central Intelligence Agency, and all the public relations bureaus of the federal bureaucracies as well as his personal White House staff.

The Pentagon
Propaganda Machine

In his book, Senator Fulbright says he often wondered how his speeches that were critical of the Defense Department would be so quickly rebutted throughout the country. Only after some investigation did the senator find out what a vast informational network was arrayed against his ideas. All the cabinet-level bureaucracies have extensive public relations and information divisions. Indeed, it is part of the mission of each agency to tell the American public what it is doing and to offer its services to any American that needs them. The fine line between information and the active attempt to persuade tax-paying citizens to support a given program is in some dispute. One should realize that it is vitally important to any major agency to cultivate and encourage client groups. Thus, the Department of Interior, through some of its bureaus, makes certain conservation groups are kept well informed of its programs and its requests to Congress for new programs. Congress responds favorably to agencies with well-organized client-interest groups.

Thus, one of the most powerful departments in the executive branch has been and is the Department of Agriculture. Its subsidy is passed with large majorities because of effective farm lobbies. Therefore, it would be unfair to suggest that the Defense Department is doing something unAmerican when it attempts to develop and encourage client groups of its own. However, with questions of peace and war in the balance and expenditures that range up to eighty billion dollars, in addition to thousands of lives, the efforts of the Defense Department should come under careful scrutiny.

In 1967, the Associated Press estimated that the executive branch was spending $400 million for information and public relations activities.[11] While not all this money was for propaganda purposes, the cost is approximately twice the combined cost on newsgathering by the two major wire services, the three major television networks, and the ten largest American newspapers. The number of persons engaged in informational activities in the Defense Department alone is 4,430. In one year, the Armed Forces Information Service sends to military units 8.5 million copies of 70 publications, 104,000 clip sheets for service newspapers, and 1.5 million posters.[12] Another large number of clip sheets (sheets with selected newspaper clippings) and newsletters goes to editors throughout the country. The Armed Forces Radio and Television is the world's largest television and radio network under single control. It consists of 204 radio stations and 80 television stations throughout the world. In addition, there are 56 radio stations and 6 television stations on ships in the navy. Since all the stations are under direct military control, the news presented on the stations is subject to some censorship. In recent years there have been several cases where military superiors refused to allow the broadcast of information deemed detrimental to the service. However, one should expect some type of scrutiny in all military news operations.

The scope of activities involving the Office of the Assistant Secretary for Public Affairs is quite large.[13] This office is the official information office of the Defense Department and is usually headed by a political appointee who is loyal to the president. The activities of the office include five television crews in South East Asia doing features for distribution to commercial TV stations;[14] a speaker's bureau that provided 492 high-ranking military officers and civilian officials to organized groups throughout the United States; a magazine and book branch that acts as a literary agent, seeking out commercial markets for material written by members of the armed services; an organizations' division that maintains liaison with 500 defense-oriented private groups, including veterans organizations, and that mails material to 287 groups on a regular basis; and a projects division that schedules everything from parachute jumpers and aerobatic teams to marching bands and color guards for fairs, celebrations, and other public events. Since this is only one of the informational outlets of the president, one can get some idea of the vast extent of the operation.

Some insight into the effectiveness and largeness of the Defense Department's information effort is given in the following letter to Senator Fulbright from a former army soldier who worked in an Information Office at an air force base. Admittedly, the man is somewhat disaffected from his army work. Nevertheless, the letter portrays one small segment of the air forces' informational efforts very completely.

> Most Americans are unaware that they are the target of a ceaseless propaganda campaign waged by the largest advertising agency in the world. . . . The U.S. military maintains an active, professional advertising department (information office) on every one of its thousands of installations around the world.
>
> For two and one-half years . . . , I was assigned to one such "information" office. Our mission . . . [was] to "push" our product [the Air Force] as hard as we could — to capitalize on its successes and to conceal its blunders, creating a favorable public image of the Air Force.
>
> The information office had a lavish budget (25 persons including well-paid civilian employees, NCO's, and officers through the rank of colonel). . . . The local news media were receptive to our efforts, which consisted largely of glorifying the Air Force's role in Vietnam."[15]

Fulbright provides us with some specific examples of how the army and the entire Defense Department attempts to influence public opinion.[16] In 1967, for example, the army provided 1,000 speakers per month to speak to groups around the country on Vietnam. General William C. Westmoreland scheduled fifty-nine appearances between August 1968 and May 1969, a truly enormous and taxing speaking tour. The army, like the other services, encourages personal contact. Another specific case is the Anti-Ballistic Missile-Sentinel Affair.[17] To encourage favorable opinion in Congress and in the general public, army officials with the cooperation of the Defense Department embarked on a widespread publicity campaign that embellished the danger to the United States and the missiles' deterrent effect. The *Washington Post* carried a story on February 16, 1968, by Paul Geyeline that said army officials were conducting an "extraordinarily intricate and comprehensive campaign" to persuade the American people and their representatives of the need for ABM. The *Post* followed this story with an editorial captioned "the Big ABM Brainwash."

"Operation Understanding"[18] is another Defense Department propaganda method designed to convince important business and public leaders that the department is virtually always right and needs all the money it gets and much more to protect America from its enemies. This operation is an ingenious attempt to create an effective, widespread client group that insures congressional and White House support for programs. Seventy local officials are selected at a time for transportation to the Joint Civilian Orientation Conference, which is an eight-day, sumptuous tour that is almost free to bases around the country. Presentations are geared to convince these officials of the necessity for all the programs that the department has. It includes briefings by high-ranking officers, fire and action displays arranged especially for the visitors, and the very highest VIP treatment. The "graduates" of this conference are then invited to form alumni groups called the Defense Orientation Conference Association which attempts to further spread the favorable messages to other civic groups and help convince Congress that the Defense Department should get whatever it wants.

Perhaps the most invidious operation of the information office is the staged films it produced on the Vietnam War. To show how effective the South Vietnamese army had become, the office staged combat assaults for television tapes. These tapes were then released to television stations throughout the country. In addition, the "Big Picture" television tapes were produced especially for local television stations. These tapes attempted to show how alert and effective the armed forces were. The Defense Department authorized substantial help to movie producers whose productions tended to glorify one of the services. When John Wayne wanted to film his picture from Vietnam, he was accorded everything he desired from tanks to hundreds of extras for battle scenes. Since the film was blatantly hawkish on the war, the Department received large benefits for its efforts.

The Defense Intelligence Agency (DIA), the Central Intelligence Agency (CIA), and the Federal Bureau of Investigation (FBI) are among the agencies primarily responsible for gathering intelligence about enemies of America. Under the Nixon administration it was disclosed that some army intelligence units were keeping detailed dossiers on many activists in this country, and among these activists were several congressmen. Secretary of Defense Melvin Laird and the White House reportedly stopped the practice; nonetheless, it was a potential means of direct manipulation of both public opinion and opinion leadership.

The CBS documentary, "The Selling of the Pentagon,"[19] told how the Pentagon went about using public funds to propagandize the Vietnam War to the public. The Pentagon denied the charge, insisting it was only informing the public on how tax dollars were being spent. However, the documentary showed an active, planned indoctrination campaign to sell the Vietnam War to the American people. The military often suggested that anyone critical of the Vietnam War was an enemy of the United States. Of course, the Pentagon papers indicated how completely the American public was deliberately misled by the White House and the Defense Department. While often the government was not lying, it was not telling the whole truth and was allowing a misinterpretation of known facts.

Nixon-Agnew Attacks
on the Mass Media

Agnew's direct attacks on bias in both the print and electronic media were unusual only because he voiced what every other president has felt. The polls taken after the attacks indicated widespread support from the American people for the Agnew speeches. President Nixon authorized and directed the Agnew speeches and, of course, followed the reaction by both the public and the working press very closely. Nixon's management of the media reached the ultimate in his years in office. He hired more former advertising and public relations executives than any other president. He was the president most concerned with how things appear and how things are said. His "New Nixon" image was carefully constructed to avoid his previous image of a scheming opportunist.

Perhaps McLuhan puts the debate of the media's bias and the presidential management of the news in perspective. He says that the content of the media, regardless of how important, is really trivial and transitory; the power is the media itself.[20] Upon reflection, one can see that the power of reporters and television commentators accrues to them not necessarily because of their gifted reflections but because they use the media daily to communicate with millions of people. The media themselves are the instrument of power that frightens presidents, cabinet secretaries, high-level bureaucrats, and university presidents. McLuhan is simply suggesting that the media are transforming society, changing the parameters under which we live, so that what anyone says on or in the media is unimportant by comparison.

Reporters have been criticized severely for printing misinformation and relying on government handouts instead of independent sources. Yet some observers have pointed out that the news-gathering system mitigates against such intensive investigatory writing. In the print media, a certain number of columns a week is normally expected if not required by reporters at all levels. In the electronic media, the newsman is paid directly by how often his material is used on television or radio. Robert MacNeil says, "A man may spend three or four days quietly digging for facts to support a story, only to find himself receiving a fee of $50 if his story is used — or nothing if the story does not pan out. His colleagues, meanwhile, may use the same amount of time rushing to snatch an interview here and put together a few superficial facts there and may place ten pieces on the air for $500."[21] To pursue stories for a long time is to lose money.

Jack Anderson has a staff of several reporters to check stories and leads for him. He also has a syndicated column that is highly remunerative. So, to some extent, Anderson is doing what most other reporters would like to do if they had the money and time. Many American newspapers, such as the *New York Times*, the *Washington Post*, and other national newspapers, could do much more and choose not to. One cannot expect all newspapers to sacrifice financial gain, yet the responsibility of the press is of such importance to a democracy that we have a right to demand some sacrifice on the part of the major national, regional, and large city newspapers. If the press is the "fourth branch of government" which helps set the agenda for the nation, then it should do no less.

The Agnew attacks on the media were carefully planned by Nixon's staff and written by Pat Buchanan, one of Nixon's chief writers. Because the president has some indirect control of the press through information power, the Federal Communications Commissions, and his friendships with newspaper publishers and television network executives, the attacks were seen to be powerful thrusts at the media's existence as an independent, uncensored informational source to the American public.

In his speeches, Agnew examined the power of the press.

At least forty million Americans each night. . . . watch
the network news. . . . In Will Rogers' observation, what
you knew was what you read in the newspaper. Today,
for growing millions of Americans, it is what they see
and hear on their television sets. How is this network
news determined? A small group of men, numbering
perhaps no more than a dozen "anchormen," commentators, and executive producers, settle upon the 20
minutes or so of film and commentary that is to reach
the public. This selection is made from the 90 to 180
minutes that may be available. Their powers of choice
are broad. They decide what forty to fifty million
Americans will learn of the day's events in the Nation
and the world. . . .

Through news, documentaries and specials, they have
often used their power constructively and creatively to
awaken the public conscience to critical problems. The
networks made "hunger" and "black lung disease"
national issues overnight. The TV networks have done
what no other medium could have done in terms of
dramatizing the horrors of war. . . . But it was also the
networks that elevated Stokely Carmichael and George
Lincoln Rockwell from obscurity to national prom-
inence. . . ."[22]

To Agnew, the mass media, especially the electronic media, are
quite powerful. The power comes not from what the commentators
say but from the power to talk to approximately forty million people
every day.

Walter Lippmann commented on the dominance of the network
news over public opinion, although his opinions are somewhat
biased since he believes that the print media and reporters like
himself ought to have that dominance. He said, "There is an essential and radical difference between television and printing . . . . The
three or four competing television stations control virtually all that
can be received over the air by ordinary television sets. But, besides
the mass circulation dailies, there are the weeklies, the monthlies,
the out-of-town newspapers, and books."[23] Of course Lippmann ignores the hour-long local news that is broadcast in all areas throughout the major cities. In large cities, the news staff is large and often
does investigatory reporting that supplements and sometimes con-

tradicts national network news. In the Washington area, four stations spend one hour each evening doing local news and special reports. The work is surprisingly good since many reporters have aspirations to report for the national networks. "Networks," Lippmann stated, "which are few in number, have a virtual monopoly of a whole medium of communication."[24] Lippmann is probably overstating his case and is simply substantiating the lessening of the power of the print media and the increasing power of television and radio in communicating with both the elites and masses of America. Only the elites would take the time to read the interpretive columns and the editorials even when television and radio news was in its early stages. The print media never really informed the masses of Americans while the electronic media are doing just that. Perhaps some of the increased awareness and political activity among the masses is the result of such information. There has been a noticeable increase in protest activity that goes from civil rights activities to women's and gay liberation. The new information available to the masses of citizens may have contributed to this new activism.

Agnew makes a point that Daniel Moynihan and columnists Rowland Evans and Robert Novak reiterate. Agnew talks about the geographical and intellectual biases of newsmen. "We do know that, to a man, these commentators and producers live and work in the geographical and intellectual confines of Washington, D. C. or New York City — the latter of which James Reston terms the 'most unrepresentative community in the entire United States.' Both communities bask in their own provincialism, their own parochialism. We can deduce that these men thus read the same newspapers, and draw their political and social views from the same sources. Worse, they talk constantly to one another, thereby providing artificial reinforcement of their shared views."[25] Do they allow their biases to influence the selection and presentation of the news? David Brinkley states, "objectivity is impossible to normal human behavior. Rather," he says, "we should strive for 'fairness'."[26]

Walter Cronkite suggests that the American people do not understand journalism. He stated that "they do not know how we work, they do not believe we can hold strong private thoughts and still be objective journalists."[27] What Cronkite is defining is the scope of a possibly widening credibility gap that exists between the national news media and the American public. There is some evidence that suggests this credibility gap is not as large as Agnew suggested. Most Americans believe that television news is the most trustworthy of all news sources available.

Agnew also examined some documentaries presented on national network television. The attempt in most documentaries is to present the story in its most graphic terms. The overall message is stressed rather than every exact detail. The detail, of course, is what bothers Agnew and other establishment figures in America. There is some embellishment in such productions if only to get the biggest name for an interview regardless of substantive qualifications. The writers sometimes give the script to a well-known television commentator who regurgitates what is written with only the slightest double-checking. Misquotes, misinformation, and fabricated answers sometimes result from the production deadlines and the attempt to make the documentary exciting and newsworthy.

One of the documentaries Agnew talked about specifically was CBS's "Hunger in America." This was released during the Johnson administration and suggested that large numbers of Americans may be starving to death while the Department of Agriculture keeps storing more and more surplus farm products. Secretary of Agriculture Orville Freeman demanded equal time, but CBS refused, repeated the program, and added to the presentation a review of the substantial efforts made by the administration and Congress to remedy the situation. Agnew pointed out that an investigation of the documentary showed

that the infant who was filmed by CBS in the nursery, and who was shown in the relevant segment of the program . . . was born prematurely . . . apparently as the result of a fall taken by the mother on the previous day. . . . The infant died on October 29, 1967; the death certificate shows the cause of death as . . . prematurity. There is no evidence to show that either the mother or father was suffering from malnutrition. . . . The baby shown dying of starvation in fact died of other causes.[28]

Nor was this, Agnew related, the only distortion in this production.

Evidence was submitted that CBS personnel had, in the words of the report, "paid participants on the program to appear before its cameras and perform as per their instructions." The segment of the program featuring a more balanced view of the problem on malnutrition in the areas was edited out for being "too technical."[29]

One should note that Agnew does not quarrel with the overall message of injustice presented by the documentary. In fact, he praises the results of the production, one of which was congressional legislation to remedy the situation. However, some of the details appear to have been staged for dramatic effect, embellishing the problem and enraging bureaucrats who were at fault.

Another more startling example of network embellishment involves the Columbia Broadcasting System again. "Project Nassau" involved the participation of CBS personnel in an aborted effort to film a 1966 invasion of Haiti that was to be partially funded by CBS. The network's role in the effort was investigated by the Special Subcommittee on Investigations of the House Commerce Committee. The report found that "the activities preparatory to 'Project Nassau' involved more than the filming of sham events, manipulation of sound tracks, and the like. Underlying the whole activity was the earnest endeavor by a group of dangerous individuals to subvert the laws of the United States. Had it been successful, the conspiracy would have produced a crisis for American foreign policy in the sensitive Caribbean area. Six men have now been convicted for their part in this conspiracy."[30]

CBS funds were provided for the leasing of a 67-foot schooner which was to be utilized by the invasion force; expenses were reimbursed for the transportation of weapons which were to be subsequently used by the conspirators; various payments were made to . . . the leader of the invasion conspiracy, with full knowledge of his identity and his criminal intentions. If these acts did not actually involve the network in the conspiracy to violate the U.S. Neutrality Act, they came dangerously close to doing so.[31]

If these charges are true, and it appears that they are, then CBS was violating moral values and the constitutional privileges of free speech. The network's action reflects the danger of the concentrated power which appears to be in the hands of the national news networks. It is both easy and tempting to subvert this power and as far as "Project Nassau" goes, one would have to agree completely with the former vice-president.

Another documentary, again produced by CBS, conforms more to the "Hunger in America" case. Agnew mentioned the "Selling of the Pentagon" only briefly in his media addresses. But the Department of Defense and its vast informational apparatus spent considerable time attempting to discredit both the details of the story and the overall message. The department did an effective job with the details since there were many inaccuracies in the broadcast, but the overall message was that the Pentagon was using tax money to sell its policies — especially in the Vietnam War — to the American public. We have documented the extensive effort employed by the Defense Department for "informational purposes." Most of the effort is blatant propaganda done by the slickest, most expensive public relations people available. However, there were serious inaccuracies, tape splicings, and misquotes evidenced in the film. These were deliberate mistakes done to embellish and highlight the documentary's message. It is unfortunate that CBS and other networks feel obliged to include misinformation and inaccuracies for it clearly dilutes the themes presented and encourages the public to disbelieve everything in the documentary. The story in its most balanced form is poignant enough; the embellishment through deliberate mistakes is unnecessary.

Claude Witze elaborates on the inaccuracies in "The Selling of the Pentagon"[32] in a publication of the Air Force Association, which consists of military men and friends of the military. Witze examines the television script and points out the inaccuracies. For example, Rodger Mudd narrated a scene showing the colonels, a group of officers who travel around the country talking to civic groups. The selection shown suggests that the colonels were trying to justify the Vietnam War and prove it was consistent with national goals and ethical values. The overall point was that the colonels were propagandizing the war and speaking directly of the foreign policy implications of the U.S. involvement in Vietnam. Witze answers this by indicating that the Industrial College of the Armed Forces (ICAF) consists of five military officers and a State Department officer and does not speak on such implications, a clear violation of military regulations. The regulations governing ICAF say the material used must be cleared for accuracy, propriety, and consistency with official policy. Both the State Department and the Defense Department have a hand in the clearance of all such presentations. Of course, this explanation does not answer the charge since the entire presentation of the colonels was strongly pro-Vietnam War and quite hawkish. It is true that Mudd took part of the speeches out of context to dramatize the propaganda effect, but one could see easily that the presentation was very unbalanced and extremely hostile to critics of the war.

Another inaccuracy was an answer given by former Assistant Secretary of Defense for Public Affairs Donald Z. Henkin concerning the public's right to know. The answer broadcast was not the one given by Henkin to the question posed. Again, the real answer supported the overall point of the film but was not as effective as the one used. Also, a press conference was broadcast showing Jerry Friedheim, President Nixon's spokesman for the Defense Department Office of Public Affairs. At the conference, Friedheim was asked a number of questions, to three of which he replied "No comment." The documentary showed him responding to a few questions and included each time Friedheim said "No comment," leaving the impression that most of the questions were answered this way. The effect of the episode was to show that the Defense Department releases just what information it wants and attempts to manage the news, but the filmed version was simply an unfair presentation of the news conference.

Daniel Moynihan, former presidential adviser on domestic affairs, wrote an article concerned with the entire question of newspaper reporter bias and presidential newsmaking. Moynihan describes the advantages the president has to manage and make news.

It is to be acknowledged that in most essential encounters between the President and the press, the advantage is with the former. The President has a near limitless capacity to "make" news which must be reported, if only by reason of competition between one journal, or one medium, or another. (If anything, radio and television news is more readily subject to such dominance. Their format permits many fewer "stories." The President-in-action almost always takes precedence.) The President also has considerable capacity to reward friends and punish enemies in the press corps. . . . And for quite a long while, finally, a President who wishes, can carry off formidable deceptions. (One need only recall the barefaced lying that went with the formal opinion of Roosevelt's Attorney General that the destroyer-naval-base deal of 1940 was legal.) [33]

Moynihan then explains why and how the press distorts the news about the White House to the extent that nothing the president does can be regarded as successful even though it may be of great significance. He argues that a fierce journalistic tradition of independence and an increasing cultural pattern of deep suspicion of anything government does makes it hard for any government to succeed. In addition, there seems to be a messianic image of the presidency pervading the country. The feeling is that the president can solve all the country's social and economic problems in a very short time if he only wants to. Anything the White House does, then, is compared with this ideal panacea image of what he can do. The former presidential adviser also points out that the press is power without responsibility. Increasingly, the reporters from the national newspapers are graduates of the elite schools of the country. The national press is not value-free; the liberal biases of the newspapers must show somewhere in the stories printed. The press has become a too-willing outlet for the Joe McCarthys and the New Left activists, creating an imbalance that cannot be corrected unless some restrictions on the independence of the press is introduced. Moynihan does not argue for censorship but does indicate that the complete independence of the press may be too much power for a group to exercise without some provisions to insure responsibility.

He then relates two examples of blatant irresponsibility both involving the *New York Times*. The first concerned the reporting of numbers of blacks holding federal jobs, where only one segment of the black labor force was examined. The story resulted in a misleading impression in an area where the facts are easily accessible to investigative reporters. The second involved the Nixon administration's attempt to help black colleges. The story indicated a strong lack of interest or desire to do anything. The actual story was one of considerable effort led by Robert J. Brown, special assistant to the president. Brown was especially eager to insure that black colleges and universities received needed financial assistance and was able to increase funds available from $80 to $100 million. The story was almost completely at odds with the facts. The *Times* reporter was not deliberately reporting untruths; he was simply slanting the facts so that they constituted a strong indictment of the Nixon administration.

Two other examples Moynihan relates concern the reporting of Joe McCarthy's allegations and paranoias in addition to news accounts of the Students for a Democratic Society and other New Left groups. "The American style of objective journalism made McCarthy. He would not have gotten anywhere in Great Britain, since most knew he was lying."[34] The headlines printed after some wild charge were equally as guilty as McCarthy himself. Reporters and publishers were simply afraid to assert themselves as the "fourth branch of government" when the crisis situation developed. Moynihan asks, "If McCarthy was lying, why print what he said; or why print it on the front page? If SDS stages a confrontation over a trumped up issue, why oblige them by taking it as face value?" Editorials do help correct false impressions, but why make them in the first place?

Finally, he calls for the establishment of a department of internal criticism within each major paper, especially the national ones. The *Washington Post* already has an individual assigned to evaluate the work of its reporters. However, it is one of the few papers with such an institutional arrangement. In the end, the issue is one of culture, not politics, for the culture of disparagement seems to color all the stories of reporters regardless of how objective and impartial they attempt to be.

Conclusion

We have discussed the interaction of the press with the president and indicated that the relationship is a symbiotic one with the president holding the advantage. The characterization of the press as the "fourth branch of government" is erroneous since the press refuses to do the kind of investigatory reporting necessary to be an important check on and agenda maker for the country. It is true that the newspaper and television system of rewarding those who are the most productive mitigates against intensive researching of stories. However, the vital function of the newspapers is being left to a self-selected few who adamantly refuse to mouth the handouts from the White House and who establish an intricate set of overlapping resources to report what is happening in the national government.

Also discussed were the weapons of the president. Moynihan indicates that the president has never-ending opportunities to make news and has all the control and access to information he needs. Reporters harried by deadlines need these resources, thereby giving the White House considerable opportunity to manage the news. Specific emphasis was placed on the "Pentagon Propaganda Machine," the elaborate and massive informational office of the Defense Department. The well-organized, well-financed public information apparatus of the Defense Department is just one part of the informational resources of the president.

NOTES

1. Jack Anderson and Carl Kalvelage, *American Government — Like It Is* (Morristown, N.J.: General Learning Corp., 1972).

2. Ibid., pp. 93-94.

3. William Rivers, *The Adversaries* (Boston, Mass.: Beacon Press, 1970), p. 81.

4. Donald R. Matthews, *U.S. Senators and Their World* (Chapel Hill: University of North Carolina Press, 1960).

5. The selective leak to friendly reporters is an extremely useful bureaucratic weapon. Before Robert McNamara organized weapons procurement for the Department of Defense, each service would battle for its special plane, gun, missile, or ship. To influence the public and Congress, various high-ranking military officers would leak classified military secrets damaging to the other services' weapons system. The Nixon administration's outrage against Jack Anderson for publishing secret administration conversations during the India-Pakistan War and against Daniel Ellsberg for release of the Pentagon papers must appear a bit hypocritical. All presidents have used leaks of classified information to their advantage. To call others traitors for doing what the executive branch does every day is hypocrisy. Of course, excessive concern for secrecy by Nixon and Kissinger led to wholesale wiretapping of White House staff and the Washington press. In addition, the "plumbers" unit of Howard Hunt and Gordon Liddy was organized to stop these unauthorized leaks without regard to law or constitutional protections. The most comprehensive treatment of government leaks is David Wise's *The Politics of Lying* (New York: Random House, 1973). In the next chapter, the White House transcripts reveal how Nixon felt about the leaks problem.

6. Quoted from an address by former Vice-President Spiro T. Agnew, Boston, Massachusetts, 18 March 1971.

7. Much of the following historical discussion is taken from Patrick Anderson's excellent book *The Presidents' Men* (Garden City, N. Y.: Anchor Books, 1969), especially pp. 158-232. For an earlier elaboration of presidential press relations see James E. Pollard, *The Presidents and the Press* (New York: Macmillan, 1947). Pollard's book goes from George Washington to Harry Truman while Anderson's book goes from Franklin Roosevelt to Lyndon Johnson.

8. Pollard, ibid., pp. 773-845.

9. Anderson, *The President's Men*. See especially pp. 276-90. See also Bernard Rubin, *Political Television* (Belmont, Calif.: Wadsworth, 1968), p. 82.

10. J. William Fulbright, *The Pentagon Propaganda Machine* (New York: Random House, 1970).

11. Ibid., p. 17.

12. Ibid., p. 46.

13. Ibid., pp. 33-34.

14. Ibid.

15. Ibid., p. 88.

16. Ibid., p. 80.

17. Ibid., pp. 2-3.

18. Ibid., pp. 34-35.

19. For an elaborate investigation into the effects of "The Selling of the Pentagon" on public attitudes see Michael Jay Robinson, "Public Affairs Television and the Growth of Political Malaise: The Case of the Selling of the Pentagon" (Ph.D. diss., University of Michigan, 1972).

20. Marshall H. McLuhan, *Understanding Media: The Extensions of Man* (New York: McGraw-Hill, 1964).

21. Robert MacNeil, *The People Machine* (New York: Harper and Row, 1968), p. 31.

22. U.S., Congress, Senate, *Congressional Record,* 91st Cong., 1st sess., 1969, 115: 187.

23. U.S., Congress, Senate, Address by the Vice-President, Midwest Regional Republican Committee Meeting, *Congressional Record*, 91st Cong., 1st sess., 13 November 1969, 115: 187.

24. Ibid.

25. Ibid.

26. Ibid.

27. Ibid.

28. Address by Vice-President Agnew, Middlesex Club, Boston, Massachusetts, 18 March 1971. The whole controversy involving bias of the national television news was investigated by Edith Efron in *The News Twisters* (Los Angeles, Calif.: Nash, 1971). Efron taped all three national television news programs (ABC, NBC, CBS) for the "critical" seven weeks prior to the presidential election (September 16 through November 4). She limited her analysis to ten selected issues and the three presidential candidates. Her coding categories, units of analysis, and interpretations have elicited an enormous controversy. The book charges mass and pervasive bias by the networks against "conservative" opinion. Several researchers who reevaluated her data came to different conclusions. For an elaboration of the controversy and a re-interpretation of the data, see Robinson, "Public Affairs Television and the Growth of Political Malaise," pp. 169-80. Several other books have investigated the problem of television news bias and the general problem of bias in the mass media: Robert S. Frank, *Message Dimensions of Television News* (Lexington, Mass.: D.C. Heath, 1973); William Small, *To Kill a Messenger: Television News and the Real World* (New York: Hastings House, 1970); Edward Jay Epstein, *News from Nowhere* (New York: Random House, 1973); and Marvin Barrett, ed., *The Politics of Broadcasting* (New York: Crowell, 1973). For an inside look into one investigative reporter's mind see Tyler Abell, *Drew Pearson Diaries, 1949-1959* (New York: Holt, Rinehart, and Winston, 1974).

29. Agnew, ibid.

30. Ibid.

31. Ibid.

32. Claude Witze, "Airpower in the News," *Air Force Magazine,* April 1971.

33. Daniel P. Moynihan, "The Presidency and the Press," *Commentary* (March 1971), pp. 41-53.

34. Ibid.

5 The Watergate Scandal: The Opinion-Policy Process Exposed

Watergate is perhaps the worst government scandal in American history. It is also the most perfect example of the impact of the mass media on public opinion and the adversary role of the media toward the president. It shows clearly that investigative reporters will eventually find out the truth regardless of obstacles; indicates the general mediocrity of the White House press corps, which relies chiefly on executive branch press handouts; and gives a fantastic amount of insight into the media effect on opinion and the effects of public opinion on congressional decision making. The public outcry after President Nixon fired Special Prosecutor Archibald Cox forced the House of Representatives to consider seriously the first impeachment of a president in over 100 years. The public's reaction to the Watergate evidence showed how important the scandal was. Congressional by-elections and the 1974 election have shown that the voters were angry because of the Watergate corruption and voted against a candidate supporting the administration.[1]

This case study will be divided into three general topics: (1) the story of the outstanding investigative reporting of the Pulitzer-prize winning *Washington Post* reporters, Bob Woodward and Carl Bernstein; (2) an examination into President Nixon's desperate attempt to control, manipulate and muzzle the investigation. The White House transcripts will provide much of the basic information for this analysis; and (3) a presentation of Gallup public opinion polls showing the effects of Watergate on Nixon's popularity, the public's view of Watergate, and the public's ideas on impeachment. All the tables will reflect the trends in public attitudes over time. An attempt will be made to link directly the public attitudes on congressional and presidential decision making.

A Chronology of the
Watergate Story

The seemingly innocuous burglary that was to lead to the mass resignations and jail sentence of almost the entire White House staff occurred on June 17, 1972. Two young reporters of the *Washington Post* were assigned to cover the story.[2] Bob Woodward (then twenty-nine) had been at the *Post* for less than one year. Carl Bernstein (then twenty-eight) regularly handled Virginia politics but, through chance, was asked to investigate.

The two reporters knew that five men had been arrested at 2:30 a.m. dressed in business suits and all with rubber surgical gloves. Police confiscated a walkie-talkie, forty rolls of unexposed film, two 35-millimeter cameras, lock picks, pen-size tear-gas guns, and bugging devices that were capable of picking up both telephone and room conversations. Some of the arrested men had substantial amounts of money, mostly in $100 bills in sequence.

Ron Ziegler, Nixon's press secretary, and John Mitchell, then in charge of the Committee to Re-elect the President (CRP), called the burglary a "third-rate job." Both disclaimed any knowledge of the incident and suggested it was simply a bizarre enterprise of some misguided Nixon loyalists. Former Vice-President Agnew was to claim later that he thought the Democrats instigated the whole incident to cause the Nixon administration and presidential campaign embarrassment.

The *Post's* first big break came two days later when the name of E. Howard Hunt was discovered in two address books of those arrested. Woodward called the White House directly and found out that Hunt had an office there and worked for Charles Colson, the man who said he would "walk over his grandmother" for Richard Nixon. With strong support from *Post* editors, both Woodward and Bernstein started spending long hours checking information and talking to any Republican official available.

The first breakthrough came when Bernstein, sifting through the records of a Florida prosecutor investigating the Cuban-Americans arrested in the break-in, found that a $25,000 cashier's check apparently earmarked for President Nixon's campaign had been deposited in the Florida bank account of Bernard L. Barker, one of the five men arrested at the Watergate.

The reporters then began to go at night to the homes of staff members of the Republican reelection campaign committee. Most refused to say anything but some, thoroughly disgusted, offered tips or became cooperative after several inconsequential visits.

Woodward remembers one source who was extremely helpful, but who first "had to purge his soul of all his anti-*Washington Post* feeling."[3] After twenty minutes of condemning the *Post*, his anger shifted to his bosses and the official became a valuable source.

Perhaps the most intriguing source was a member of the executive branch who had access to information at the Committee to Re-elect the President as well as the White House. He could be contacted only in emergencies and through an elaborate procedure. If he wanted to contact Woodward he would somehow get Woodward's morning *New York Times* and indicate the time on page 20. They would meet at some underground garage at 2 a.m. If Woodward wanted to contact him, he would move a flower pot with a red flag in it to the rear of his balcony.

On September 17, the two reported that funds for the Watergate espionage operation were made available by several principal assistants of John N. Mitchell, former manager of CRP and former attorney general, and were kept in a special account. Later they were to name Mitchell as one of those controlling the direct disbursements from the fund.

In late September, Woodward and Bernstein received a clue into the overall dimensions of Watergate. They found that Donald Segretti had been hired to carry out a series of "dirty tricks" on Democrats. They also learned that Segretti was just part of a massive espionage and disruption effort by CRP.

On October 10, they reported that FBI agents had established that the Watergate bugging incident stemmed from a massive campaign of political spying and sabotage conducted for President Nixon's campaign. Federal agents discovered that between $350,000 and $700,000 of campaign contributions had been set aside to pay for an extensive undercover campaign aimed at discrediting other presidential candidates and disrupting their campaigns. These activities represented a basic strategy of the Nixon reelection effort.

On October 15, they reported that Nixon's appointments secretary, Dwight L. Chapin, had served as liaison man in the White House for Segretti. The next day, they reported that Nixon's personal attorney, Herbert W. Kalmbach, was one of five persons authorized to approve payments from the Nixon campaign's secret intelligence-gathering and espionage fund. Their biggest story concerned H. R. Haldeman, the former chief of staff of the Nixon White House.

On October 25, they reported that Haldeman was one of the five high-ranking presidential associates authorized to approve payments from the secret Nixon campaign cash fund. Although Woodward and Bernstein had four sources confirming the Haldeman connection, the story was to cause them severe anguish. One of their chief sources, Hugh Sloan, denied he had told the grand jury the above information. He did not deny the story but simply denied that he had told it to the grand jury as alleged in the *Post* article. The denial by Sloan and the vehement denials by the White House cast considerable doubt on the entire effort by the two reporters. As the White House transcripts later showed, Nixon and his staff attempted to attack both the reporters and the *Post* by using license challenges to the *Post* television subsidiaries and by personal attacks on both Woodward and Bernstein. In the confusion following the story and the landslide reelection of Nixon, Haldeman received a great deal of sympathy from both press and public. *Post* editor Ben Bradlee simply stated, "We stand by our story," and refused any retraction.

Subsequent events proved that story and the rest to be true. When James McCord told Judge Sirica the truth about the burglary and the cover-up, the affair dominated the national news. After Jeb Magruder, deputy campaign director of CRP and John Dean, counsel to the president, told the grand jury and the Senate Watergate Committee the truth, mass resignations of the White House staff, including Erlichman and Haldeman, followed. The inescapable conclusion was that the president himself was deeply involved in the cover-up and therefore was obstructing justice, an impeachable felony offense.

One should note that Woodward was a major factor in the discovery of the White House taping systems.[4] After learning that Alexander Butterfield was in charge of White House "internal security," Woodward pressed the Senate Watergate Committee staff to interview him. Sam Dash, the committee's chief counsel, overlooked the matter, but finally he interviewed Butterfield and found out that Nixon had "bugged" himself. While Nixon probably felt he would never have to release any of his personal conversations, the tapes and his handling of them became the most damaging evidence that implicated the president in at least the cover-up. Without the tapes, only John Dean's unsubstantiated evidence would have directly implicated Nixon. Nixon's release of the transcripts confirmed much of Dean's testimony and showed an amoral, petty, and sometimes vicious president attempting to try almost anything to rid himself of the Watergate scandal. Many observers were unable to understand why Nixon did not destroy those tapes and claim "national security" forced him to do so. Perhaps, as Eric Sevareid commented, the whole episode was a Greek tragedy with Nixon having a fatal character flaw that would lead to his destruction as a president and he simply was unable to prevent it.

The White House Transcripts

One of the reasons the Watergate scandal is an almost perfect case study of the media-opinion-policy process is that we have direct evidence from the decision makers at the White House. In addition, the formal testimony of various White House aides at the Senate Watergate hearings is available.

After the initial White House characterization of the Watergate burglary as a "third-rate" attempt not worthy of comment, Ron Ziegler issued a broad statement that no one presently employed at the White House was involved in any way. To the story about Donald Segretti and the overall espionage and sabotage effort of Nixon's campaign strategists, a principal spokesman for CRP said, "The *Post* story is not only fiction but a collection of lies."[5]

After the story appeared linking Herbert Kalmbach, the president's personal attorney, with the "GOP Spy Fund," Erlichman dismissed it as part of "mud month"[6] (the period just before the election when political charges would be thrown about). Ziegler was more direct: "I'm not going to dignify these types of stories with a comment .... It goes without saying that this administration does not condone sabotage or espionage or surveillance of individuals, but it also does not condone innuendo or source stories that make broad sweeping charges about the character of individuals."[7]

Clark MacGregor, who replaced John Mitchell as director of CRP, charged that "the *Post* has maliciously sought to give the appearance of a direct connection between the White House and the Watergate — a charge which the *Post* knows and half a dozen investigations have found to be false."[8] Attacks by Senator Robert Dole and former Vice-President Agnew followed. All charged the *Post* with deliberate and malicious fabrication and Agnew suggested that the whole story was some monumental hoax perpetrated by the Democrats.

Woodward and Bernstein found out that the blanket denials were being handled by H. R. Haldeman, Nixon's chief of staff. The handling of a "third-rate" burglary by someone as important as Haldeman meant that the stories were extremely important. When

Ron Ziegler stated that all previous White House denials were "inoperative," the following April, the *Post* reporters were vindicated.

All presidents are concerned with their image. Richard Neustadt shows how vital it is to convey a proper image to the various publics with which the president deals.[9] However, the Nixon White House seemed obsessed with public relations and image, partly because it viewed the mass media as anti-Nixon and partly because many of the important staff people were former professional public relations people. Haldeman and Ziegler were both from the J. Walter Thompson Agency, one of the largest public relations firms in the country. Some critics quipped that the White House staff was a subsidiary of the J. Walter Thompson firm. The strong denials and pointed attacks by the White House on the *Post* provide a useful look at the public attempts to halt the Watergate inquiry.

The White House transcripts of selected presidential conversations provide a fascinating look at the former president's attitude toward the mass media. An incisive perspective on how Nixon viewed the world in general and the media in particular is reflected in the September 15, 1972, conversation with John Dean. (P is the president; D is John Dean, counsel to the president).

P — We are all in it together. This is a war. We take a few shots and it will be over. We will give them a few shots and it will be over. Don't worry. I wouldn't want to be on the other side right now. Would you?

D — Along that line, one of the things I've tried to do, I have begun to keep notes on a lot of people who are emerging as less than our friends because this will be over some day and we shouldn't forget the way some of them have treated us.

P — I want the most comprehensive notes on all those who tried to do us in. They didn't have to do it. If we had had a very close election and they were playing the other side I would understand this. No — they were doing this quite deliberately and they are asking for it and they are going to get it. We have not used the power in this first four years as you know. We have never used it. We have not used the Bureau and we have not used the Justice Department but things are going to change now. And they are either going to do it right or go.

D — What an exciting prospect.

P — Thanks. It has to be done. We have been (adjective deleted) fools for us to come into this election campaign and not do anything with regard to the Democratic Senators who are running, et cetera. And who the hell are they after? They are after us. It is absolutely ridiculous. It is not going to be that way anymore.[10]

To examine the transcripts in some logical order, the president's media characterizations are divided into four groups: (1) presidential control and suppression of the mass media; (2) concerns about "the public relations" aspects of the situation; (3) the leak problem or leaks that the president did not like; and (4) general remarks about the media consumption habits of the president.

Presidential Control and Suppression of the Media

Nixon's views on the suppression of the press came out in a general conversation with John Dean concerning the lawsuit against the Republican Committee to Re-elect the President by the Democrats for the Watergate burglary. In the following exerpt we find that Nixon believed that few people cared about the suppression of the press and also obtain some insight into Nixon's assessment of media support. One should point out that Robinson's study of media bias showed an overwhelming press support for Nixon in both 1968 and 1972 — approximately eight of every ten newspapers endorsed him in 1968, and nine out of ten in 1972.[11]

P — Well, one hell of a lot of people don't give one damn about this issue of the suppression of the press, etc. We know that we aren't trying to do it. They all squeal about it. It is amusing to me when they say I watched the networks and I thought they were restrained. What (expletive omitted) do they want them to do — go through the 1968 syndrome when they were 8 to 1 against us. They are only three to one this time. It is really sickening though to see these guys. These guys have always figured we have the press on our side. You know we receive a modest amount of support — no more. Colson's sure making them move around, saying we don't like this or that and (inaudible).
D — Well, you know Colson's threat of a law suit which was printed in Evans and Novak had a very sobering effect on several of the national magazines. They are now checking before printing a lot of this Watergate

junk they print. They check the press office trying to
get a confirmation or denial, or call the individuals
involved. And they have said they are doing it because
they are afraid of a libel suit on them. So it did have
a sobering effect. We will keep them honest if we can
remind them that they can't print anything and get
away with it.[12]

In a further conversation on the lawsuit and campaign finances,
Nixon showed that one way to control stories was to leak information. Nixon and Dean indicated that Charles Colson, former special
counsel to the president, would be a useful conduit for favorable
leaked information.

D — They have now, but it gets about that much coverage in the paper. They can't even figure out what
McGovern's done, the books are such a mess, but you
haven't seen them say anything yet. And that is one
of the things that hopefully we will bring out in hearings, as to what a mess this was et cetera.
P — How are you going to bring it out? You can't bring
it out in these hearings.
D — Well I think I would rather do it independently,
so that the media types will bring it out. Chuck is going
to be of aid when he is out there not connected with
the White House, coming through with bits of tidbits.
Chuck will still have his channels to flip things out.
P — Sure! Sure! In my view — of course it is hard to
believe since he loves the action and the rest — but
apart from the financial — for the country's aid, etc. —
I don't care what you think: Colson can be more valuable out than in, because, basically in, he has reached
the point that he was too visible.[13]

In another conversation concerning the Senate's Watergate hearings to be chaired by Senator Sam Ervin, Dean tells the president
that he (Dean) is planning a number of brain sessions with some of
the media people. The president tells him this is a terrible waste
of his time but "all this business is a battle" and must be done
vigorously.

D — This is a heck of an idea, Mr. President. Some of
these early articles said — will Sam Ervin, Constitutional man, be a judge? Will he admit hearsay? We can
try to get some think pieces out to try to get a little

pressure on him to perform that way, to make it look like partisan when he doesn't.

P — The point that Kleindienst gets out: no hearsay, no innuendo. There will be no hearsay, no innuendo. This will disappoint the (adjective deleted) press. No hearsay! No innuendo! No leaks!

D — Well, there are a lot of precedents. I have been involved in two Congressional investigations. One was the Adam Clayton Powell investigation when I was working over there as the Minority Counsel of the House Judiciary. We didn't take hearsay. We stuck to the facts on that. We did an investigation of the Oklahoma judges. Again, the same sort of thing. We went into executive session when necessary. I bet if we look around, respectable investigations that have been held up there that could be held up, and some of it should be coming forth to set the stage for these hearings. I am planning a number of brain sessions with some of the media people to —

P — I know. It is very important, but it seems like a terrible waste of your time. But it is important in the sense that all this business is a battle and they are going to wage the battle. A lot of them have enormous frustrations about those elections, state of their party, etc. And their party has its problems. We think we have had problems, look at some of theirs. Strauss has had people and all the actors, and they haven't done that well you know.

D — Well I was — we have come a long road on this thing now. I had thought it was an impossible task to hold together until after the election until things started falling out, but we have made it this far and I am convinced we are going to make it the whole road and put this thing in the funny pages of the history books rather than anything serious because actually —

P — It will be somewhat serious but the main thing, of course, is also the isolation of the President.[14]

Discussing the L. Patrick Gray hearings for Senate confirmation of him as director of the Federal Bureau of Investigation, Nixon and Dean contemplated using Clark Molenhoff, a Pulitzer-prize winning journalist who briefly worked at the White House as an ombudsman and stopper of potential scandals. Molenhoff was to become one of the administration's most vitriolic critics, referring to much of the White House staff as "those bunch of Nazis."

P — Rather than going to a hearing, do "Meet the Press," and that will force the hearing to call him. That is quite the way to do it. Have him give an interview to *US News*, "Wires in the Sky" or something. A respected reporter — why not give it to Molenhoff?

D — Well that is interesting. Molenhoff is close, but our guy gets near Molenhoff. Molenhoff may not do anything.

P — No, and we are in a position with Molenhoff that he has been fighting us some. Maybe Molenhoff would be a pretty good prospect for this thing. It is the kind of a story he loves, but he digs on something. You couldn't call him, however, (inaudible) — The (characterization deleted) loves to talk too much, although he is a hell of a guy.

D — OK. Can I call Clark and say "listen Clark, a guy has brought me a piece of dynamite that I don't even want in the White House?"

P — He will write that, won't he?

D — Yeah. Because that doesn't look like a set up deal. Well Clark Molenhoff is the first guy to uncover a shield of anything, and he will say no way —

P — But he would do it. That is a very important piece (unintelligible). Getting back, don't you feel that is the need here to broaden the scope?[15]

The cloak of national security was used throughout the scandal to justify the lawlessness of the White House. A conversation with Dean, Haldeman, and the president concerning the break-in in Dr. Ellsberg's psychiatrist's office indicates some of their thinking about the blanket use of the national security excuse. Dean's comment, "I think we could get by on that," shows the White House's use of this excuse to manipulate the opinions of both the mass media and public opinion in general.

P — The point is this, that it is now time, though that Mitchell has got to sit down, and know where the hell all this thing stands, too. You see, John is concerned, as you know, about the Ehrlichman situation. It worries him a great deal because, and this is why the Hunt problem is so serious, because, it has nothing to do with the campaign. It has to do with the Ellsberg case. I don't know what the hell the — (unintelligible)

H — But what I was going to say —

P — What is the answer on this? How you keep it out,

I don't know. You can't keep it out if Hunt talks. You
see the point is irrelevant. It has gotten to this point —
D — You might put it on a national security grounds
basis.
H — It absolutely was.
D — And say that this was —
H — (unintelligible) — CIA —
D — Ah —
H — Seriously,
P — National Security. We had to get information for
national security grounds.
D — Then the question is, why didn't the CIA do it or
why didn't the FBI do it?
P — Because we had to do it on a confidential basis.
H — Because we were checking them.
P — Neither could be trusted.
H — It has basically never been proven. There was
reason to question their position.
P — With the bombing thing coming out and everything
coming out, the whole thing was national security.
D — I think we could get by on that.
P — On that one I think we should simply say this
was a national security investigation that was conducted. And on that basis, I think the same in the
drug field with Krogh. Krogh could say he feels he did
not perjure himself. He could say it was a national
security matter. That is why —[16]

In a conversation with Henry Peterson, assistant attorney general, and Ron Ziegler concerning the resignations of Haldeman,
Erlichman, and Dean from the White House staff, the president
told Ziegler to give the story to the wire services. This was decided
upon presumably because the wire services would spread the story
almost verbatim with a minimum of interpretive or investigating
reporting.

Z — Give it to a wire service story — the wire services
can confirm it later instead of calling (inaudible).
P — No, no, no, no — I wouldn't call — I'd just give
it to the wires.
HP — That's right — yeah.
P — Just give it to the wires. Say gentlemen you wonder what the President has been doing? — where is he
today? — he's in the EOB. But I want them to know
that since the 21st I've been working my tail off, which

I have, — I — I'm so sick of this thing — I want to get it done with and over, and I don't want to hear about it again. Well I'll hear about it a lot, but I've got to run the country too. (Ziegler leaves).[17]

Concern for PR

The transcripts show clearly that the White House had a pervasive concern for public relations. A number of times the president or his associates discuss the PR of the situation. Erlichman's celebrated comments about "It'll play in Peoria" revealed the public relations obsession of the Nixon administration. In true McLuhan fashion, it was always concerned with image or how people would receive the information rather than the substance itself. Harry Trelevan's comments with regard to Nixon's 1968 campaign continued to dominate the thinking of the White House. "It's not what's there that counts, it's what he projects — and carrying it one step further, it's not what he projects but rather what the voter receives."[18]

In the March 22 meeting, the president, Haldeman, Ehrlichman, Dean, and Mitchell discuss the upcoming Watergate hearings and the membership of the Senate committee. They appear obsessed with the possibility of television and are worried about the activities of Senator Kennedy during the hearings. The LBJ fear of the Kennedys seems to have been adopted by Nixon and his advisers.

H — Is there an executive session of a Senate Committee where other Senators can come in, where any Senator has the privilege of submitting questions? Senator Kennedy would want to sit there I am sure.
P — He can't ask questions.
H — He can't?
D — Not unless (inaudible)
P — All the members (inaudible) but we shall see. But it is normal practice that no one can ask questions but members of the Committee.
H — But Teddy could still sit there in the audience and then go out to the TV camera and say (inaudible) look this is what is being said, et cetera.
P — Oh, well we are going to have that.
D — I think if he did that he would be terribly criticized.

H—I was just thinking in the membership of the Committee. We are in reasonably good shape and that the people we have on the Committee are not as bad as some Senators who would turn the use of TV afterwards for their own purposes.

P — Not as spectacular.

M — (inaudible) Could I point out (inaudible)

D — (Inaudible)

H — When do they start hearings now?

D — (Inaudible)

P — The topic — here — we have plenty of time for those hearings, but what Bob is concerned about is the PR. We don't have much time.

D — PR is going to start being better right away with the termination of the Gray hearings for 10 weeks that will let some steam out of that —

P — The PR. What I meant is, and anyway that the main thing is to do the right thing. Don't rush too fast with the PR but it takes time to write, et cetera. John has to have time to write this report. Do we broach this whether we have a report or not? (Inaudible voice and answer.) [19]

In the March 27 discussion, the president rejected the idea of a "super-panel" to determine White House involvement saying, "I think the damn thing is going to come out anyway, and I think you better cut the losses now . . . ." Concerning the testimony of John Dean to the Grand Jury, the president said:

E — I can't imagine (unintelligible)

P — Well, if called, he will be cooperative, consistent with his responsibilities as Counsel. How do we say that?

E — He will cooperate.

P — He will fully cooperate.

E — Better check that with Dean. I know he's got certain misgivings on this.

Z — He did this morning.

P — Yeah. Well then, don't say that.

E — Well, I think you can pose the dilemma without saying flatly what you are going to do.

P — Yeah. We — but maybe you just don't want to. You better not try to break into it, Ron.

Z — You get into posing the dilemma —

P — Then they are going to break into questions. I

would simply stall them off today. Say that is not before us at this time, but let me emphasize, as the President has indicated, there will be complete cooperation consistent with the responsibilities that everybody has on the separation of powers. Fair enough? And, of course, consistent with Mr. Dean's other responsibilities as a Counsel. See? How about just saying it that way? Well, John, do you have doubts?

E — No. But if Ziegler opens, Ziegler has to answer something. About the only thing that occurred to me when I read this thing yesterday was somehow or another, he should be introducing the fact that Dean is going to get a chance to clear his name.

P — Yeah.

E — Eventually there is going to be an opportunity for that in some forum, at some time, in some way. But maybe you get into —

P — I don't think this is the day to do it.

Z — I think that is right. Give them more than a day to see how we approach the whole matter (unintelligible —RZ exit).[20]

In the April 16 meeting, Dean and the president discussed the resignations of Dean, Haldeman, and Ehrlichman. Their entire emphasis was on the public relations aspects of them and how to avoid presidential involvement.

P — You see we got that problem today that the thing may break. You know with Magruder, et cetera and I. You know that is what I wanted to run over with you briefly. You know to get your feeling again as to how we handle it. You were saying the President should stay one step ahead of this thing. Well, we've got — the only problem is what the hell can I say publicly? Here is what we have done. I called in Kleindienst, I have been working on it all week. As soon as I got the Magruder thing I got in Kleindienst and then at 4:00 P.M. we got in Petersen. Kleindienst withdrew and assigned Petersen. I said, "Alright, Henry, I don't want to talk with Kleindienst anymore about this case. I am just going to talk to you. You are in charge. You follow through and get to the bottom of this thing and I am going to let the chips fall where they may." We have covered that all the way down the line. Now I had to follow him to a certain extent on the prosecution side.

On the other hand on the PR side I am sure as hell
am not going to let the Justice Department step out
and say look we dragged the White House in here. I've
got to step out and do it, John. Don't you agree?
D — That right.
P — Again, I don't want to walk out and say look
John Dean's resignation has been accepted. (Expletive
omitted) That isn't fair.[21]

When discussing possible clemency for Howard Hunt (a leader
of the Watergate break-in group), the president again focused on
public relations.

P — Clemency is one thing. He is a friend of Hunt's.
I am just trying to put the best face on it, but if it is
the wrong thing to do I have to know.
D — Well, one of the things, I think you have to be
very careful. And this is why the issue should be very
good is, if you take a set of facts and let the prosecutors
who have no PR judgment but they will give you the
raw facts as they relate to the law, and it's later you
have to decide what public face will be put on it.
P — Oh, I understand. You can help on that, John.[22]

Leaks

President Nixon made constant reference to national security
leaks. While these unauthorized leaks are identical to the authorized
national security leaks in general substance (leaking secret information — a felony offense), the White House was intent on stopping
the unauthorized ones at all costs and, as we later found out, without regard to law or individual civil liberties. Obviously it is crucial
for any government to control its national secrets. However, many
have observed that the essence of democracy is government by leaks.
In a general discussion of the implications of the proposed Senate
Watergate hearings, the president and John Dean discussed leaks.

D — I have got to say one thing. There has never been
a leak out of my office. There never will be a leak out
of my office. I wouldn't begin to know how to leak and
I don't want to learn how you leak.
P — Well, it was a shocking thing. I was reading a
book last night. A fascinating book, although fun book,

by Malcolm Smith Jr. on Kennedy's Thirteen Mistakes,
the great mistakes. And one of them was on the Bay of
Pigs. And what had happened, there was Chester
Bowles had learned about it, and he deliberately leaked
it. Deliberately because he wanted the operation to fail!
And he admitted it! Admitted it![23]

In a discussion of the wire-tapping of White House personnel
and some reporters, Ehrlichman and the president recalled its necessity because of national security. They attempted to suggest that
such wire-tapping went on in previous administrations and, in any
case, it was in the national interest.

E — The, the line of response would be this as I see it.
Starting back in the days when I was Counsel to the
President, we were very concerned with our national
security leaks and we undertook at that time a whole
series of steps to try and determine the source of the
leaks. Some of this involved national security taps duly
and properly authorized and conducted. We had three
very serious breaches. After I left the office of Counsel.
I continued to follow this.
P — Yeah. At your request.
E — We had three very serious breaches. One was the
whole Szulc group; one was the Pentagon Papers and
the other was the Pakistan-India situation; but there
were leaks all through there and so we had an active
and on-going White House job using the resources of
the Bureau, the Agency and the various departmental
security arms with White House supervision. In this
particular instance, Hunt became involved because at
the time of the Pentagon Papers break we had dual
concerns. We had concern about the relationship of
this particular leak to other security leaks that we had
across the government — Rand etc. — and so we moved
very vigorously on the whole cast of characters in the
Pentagon Papers thing. Some of our findings have
never come out. It was an effort to relate that incident
to the other national security breaches we had, and to
find out as much as we could about this. We put a
number of people into this that we had at work on
other things. One was Hunt and he in turn used Liddy.
I didn't know — and this is fact — I checked this two
or three ways. I didn't know what they were doing
about this operation in Los Angeles until after it oc-

curred and they came to me and told me that it had
been done and that it was unsuccessful and that they
were intending to make a re-entry to secure papers that
they were after. I said no and stopped it at that time.
Young and Krogh operated that, the whole operation.
From the beginning as a matter of fact with the Szulc
leaks and so on and they laid it out perfectly. And
Krogh is very frank in saying, "I authorized this operation in Los Angeles, no two ways about it." He says,
"If I am asked, that's what I will say and I will resign
and leave the Department of Transportation and get
out of town." He said, "I thought at the time we were
doing the right thing and —"
P — Should he?
E — I don't think he will have to. Number one, I don't
think Hunt will strike him. If he did, I would put the
national security tent over this whole operation.
P — I sure would.
E — And say there are a lot of things that went on in
the national interest where they involved taps, they
involved entry, they involved interrogation, they involved a lot of things and I don't propose to open that
up to (unintelligible) just hard line it.[24]

Media Consumption by the President

Finally, the transcripts show that Nixon was very aware of what
was written in major newspapers and what television commentators
had stated. Previously, Nixon's staff indicated that the president
received detailed summaries of all significant news and did not have
time to read the actual newspapers.

In an early discussion of Watergate implications, Nixon revealed a
close perusal of both the *Washington Post* and the *New York Times*.

P — Well, as I said, the *New York Times,* the *Washington Post* and all the rest. They put it in terms of
executive privilege because they were against the investigation. So the real question now is say that I having
been through that — we have talked it over and I have
always felt very miffed about that because I thought
that was very wrong and now this is another matter. But
I think we ought to cooperate in finding an area of
cooperation. Here it is. You see, the Baker theory is

that he wants to have a big slam-bang thing for a whole week and then he thinks interest in the whole thing will fall off. And he is right about that. But his interest in having a big slam-bang for a week is that we bring all the shots up right away. The big shots you could bring up. They could bring up Stans. They have to put him on, and they've got to put Mitchell on. They would like, of course, to get Haldeman, Ehrlichman and Colson.

D — I understand that you and Bob have talked about running Stans out as sort of a stalking horse on it, on another post.

P — It is not my idea. I guess Moore or somebody mentioned it.

D — I think it was my idea. I think it could be one defusing factor in the hearings. Stans would like to get his story out. He is not in any serious problem ulti-mately. It could be rough and tumble, but Maury is ready to take it and it would be a mini-hearing there is no doubt about it. But this further detracts from the other committee.

P — It would be a mini-hearing, it is true. Except knowing the Press and knowing — like they have taken — they sold several copies of these stories about Colson and Haldeman about four times.

D — Well, I know that.

P — Well, I just wonder if that doesn't do that?

D — At present I hesitate to send Stans. They would give him a hot seat.

P — Somebody is after him about Vesco. I first read the story briefly in the Post. I read, naturally, the first page and I turned to the Times to read it. The Times had in the second paragraph that the money had been re-turned, but the Post didn't have it.

D — That is correct.

P — The Post didn't have it until after you continued to the back section. It is the (adjective omitted) thing I ever saw.

D — Typical.[25]

The president denounced an NBC story on Howard Hunt in a March 13, 1973, discussion with Dean.

D — The focus is right on us. That the problem.

P — Nothing on the Democrats. — Nothing on what the previous three Administrations did?

D — Nothing. If Hunt is still a walking story we'll pull out of this thing. You can't find anybody who even knows what is happening. Although it has increased in the network coverage. That NBC thing last night, which is just a travesty as far and we're talking about shabby journalism, they took the worst edited clips out of context, with Strachan saying he was leaving. And then had a little clip of Ron saying, "I deny that." And he was denying something other than what they were talking about in their charge. It was incredible. Someone is going through and putting that altogether right now and Ron ought to be able to (unintelligible) to that one on NBC. It was a very, very dishonest television reporting of sequence of events, but out of sequence.[26]

Both PR and the press are discussed in the following transcript. Dean stated, "they would never buy that" with regard to a PR story intimating little White House involvement. Their worry was clearly on what would sell to the public, not the truth.

P — I mean put the story out PR people, here is the story, the true story about Watergate.
D — They would never believe it. The two things they are working on are Watergate —
P — Who is "they?"
D — The press, (inaudible), the intellectuals —
P — The Packwoods?
D — Right — They would never buy it as far as one White House involvement in Watergate which I think there is just none for that incident which occurred at the Democratic National Headquarters. People here we just did not know that was going to be done. I think there are some people who saw the fruits of it, but that is another story. I am talking about the criminal conspiracy to go in there. The other thing is that the Segretti thing. You hang that out, and they wouldn't believe that. They wouldn't believe that Chapin acted on his own to put his old friend Segretti to be a Dick Tuck on somebody else's campaign. They would have to paint it into something more sinister, more involved, part of a general plan.
P — Shows you what a master Dick Tuck is, Segretti's hasn't been a bit similar.[27]

Ehrlichman and the president discussed the testimony of Jeb Magruder, the deputy director of CRP. They were afraid of what

Magruder would say and how it would "play in Peoria." Peoria, Illinois, had become famous because it represented "middle America" to the public relations-conscious White House. Haldeman was also part of the meeting.

H — If Magruder goes public on this, then you know —
P — Incidentally, if Magruder does that, let's see what it does to Magruder.
E — It depends on how he does it. If he does it under immunity, it doesn't do anything to him.
P — All right — except ruin him.
H — Well, yeah. It ruins him in a way he becomes a folk hero to the guys.
P — He becomes an immediate hero with the media. You know, in terms of — I know how these things work.
E — Mike Wallace will get him and he will go on "Sixty Minutes" (a CBS news program) and he will come across as the All American Boy who was doing, who was just doing — who was serving his President, his Attorney General, and they misled him.[28]

Both Haldeman and the president expressed great fear of television if it carried the Senate Watergate hearings. They seemed to be hoping that the networks would not carry it because of the expense; however, as the summer of 1973 showed, the televised hearings became the television hit of the year.

H — The way it will be played is not that the Committee is being unreasonable by insisting on television, but that we are being unreasonable by insisting against it.
P — Well, that would be true unless you go out and hammer that the whole record could be made public.
H — Yeah.
P — And that we think it is reasonable.
H — The question then is that you lose something obviously by doing that, and do we really gain enough to make it worth it? How bad is it if we go on television? I am not at all sure it is all that bad. In the first place, it is going to be in the daytime. In the second place, as of now it is not going to be carried live by the networks.
P— Yeah.
H — Now it might be, but I would guess it won't be after this other stuff breaks, it isn't going to be that important anymore. The networks don't want to carry it. It would cost them money. What will probably end up happening is, it will be carried on the public broad-

casting which has virtually no audience in the daytime.
P — Uh huh. I suppose what happens there is that every new break is carried for five or ten minutes in the evening news.
H — That's right.
P — That's the point.
H — It is going to be carried anyway. It is a question of whether it is carried for five minutes with one of us on camera for a couple of those minutes, or whether it is carried for three minutes with —
P — Weicher —
H — Weicher and John Chancellor and Dan Rather saying: "Trembling with fear and obviously trying to hide the truth, ah . . ."[29]

Watergate and the
Opinion-Policy Process

While the transcripts and books about Watergate are fascinating insights into the decision making of the Nixon White House, public opinion pressures seemed to play a direct role in getting the Senate hearings started, in addition to the appointment of the special prosecutor and the beginning of the formal House of Representatives hearings into the possible impeachment of President Nixon. We will attempt to link the opinion polls with the decisions of both the president and the Congress.

While the linkage must be indirect since one cannot really know exactly why the president and Congress made certain decisions, it is clear that the mass media acted as a catalyst, almost exactly as posited in the linkage chapter. The mass media energized various interest groups to pressure Congress to investigate and prosecute those responsible. Without the hard investigative reporting of Woodward and Bernstein, it is unlikely the full scandal would have been exposed. The transcripts show that the Justice Department was quite willing to ignore evidence pointing to high White House staff personnel. The revelations by the *Washington Post* reporters kept public attention and pressure on the Congress, the White House, and Judge John Sirica's court.

Three broad aspects of public opinion pressure which can be examined are: (1) President Nixon's popularity or the public's view of how capable a president he was at the time; (2) the public's view of Watergate; and (3) the public's view of impeachment or resignation of the president.

Table 5-1

Nixon's Popularity Ratings (average for each year)

	Approve	Disapprove	No Opinion
1969	62%	16%	22%
1970	57	29	14
1971	50	37	13
1972	51	30	19
1973	42	47	11
1974 (to May)	26	63	11

SOURCE: Gallup Poll Index, 1969 to May, 1974.

As table 5-1 shows, the Nixon popularity dropped to an all-time low and approached the record disapproval rate of 23 percent for President Truman, right after he fired General Douglas MacArthur. In order to link the approval rate to issues, figure 13 will graph Nixon's approval rate and indicate major policy decisions made during that time.

The figure indicates that Nixon's popularity was closely tied to revelations concerning Watergate and national issues. The televised Senate hearings and the various revelations had a disastrous effect on Nixon's public approval. While it is impossible to find out how the Attentive public felt about Nixon, Gallup did ask the Republican county chairmen how they felt about the effects of Watergate on Republican congressional chances (table 5-2).

Table 5-2

Effects of Watergate on Republican Congressional Chances[a]

	National	East	Midwest	South	West
A great deal	11%	17%	11%	8%	15%
Somewhat	40	43	42	36	46
Hardly at all	31	26	33	34	23
Not at all	17	13	14	22	15
No opinion	1	1	*	*	1

[a]To what extent, if at all, do you think Watergate will hurt the chances of congressional candidates in your area?"
SOURCE: Gallup Opinion Index, April 1974, p. 5.

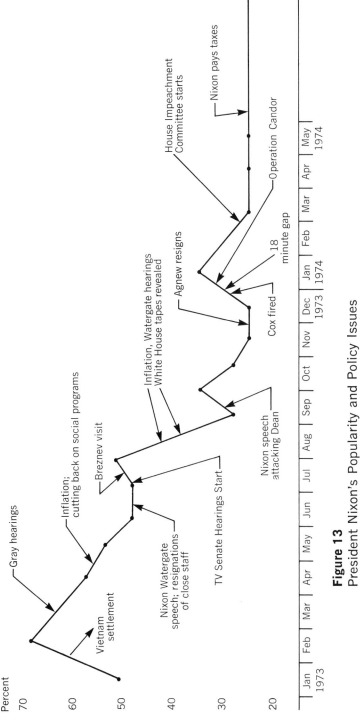

Figure 13
President Nixon's Popularity and Policy Issues
(in percent approval)

Over 50 percent of the Republican chairmen in every area except the South stated that Watergate will hurt from "somewhat" to "a great deal." Recent elections in supposedly Republican safe districts (including President Ford's old district) show that voters are affected by Watergate and may change their vote to Democrats in significant numbers. The 1974 congressional elections did result in large gains for the Democrats but not as bad as some predicted. In fact, some argue that, had President Ford waited until Christmas to give Nixon the pardon, the Republicans' loss would have been minimal. One should remember that the Nixon landslide of 1972 was a personal victory; his "coattails" carried in very few Republican congressmen and senators. Nixon was severely criticized by Republicans for ignoring the congressional candidates in 1972.

As table 5-3 shows, the majority of the American public was convinced that the president was guilty enough to be impeached by the House of Representatives. While impeachment in the House would simply transfer the case to the Senate for trial, a majority of Americans believed the president should be convicted and removed from office.

The incredible public awareness of this issue is shown by table 5-4. Even before the televised Senate Watergate hearings started, over 90 percent of the American public had heard or read about Watergate.

Table 5-3
The Public's Attitudes toward Nixon's Impeachment,[a] 1973-74

	Yes	No	No opinion
June 22-25	19	69	12
July 6-9	24	62	14
Aug 3-6	26	61	13
Oct 19-22	33	52	15
Nov 2-5	37	54	9
Nov 30-Dec 3	35	54	11
Jan 4-7	37	53	10
Apr 12-15[b]	46	42	12
Apr 12-15[c]	52	33	15

[a]"Do you think President Nixon should be impeached and compelled to leave the presidency or not?"

[b]"Just from the way you feel now, do you think his actions are serious enough to warrant his being removed from the presidency, or not?"

[c]"Now, let me ask you first of all, if you think there is enough evidence of possible wrongdoing in the case of President Nixon to bring him to trial before the Senate, or not?"

SOURCE: Gallup Opinion Index, 1973 to May, 1974.

Table 5-4

Trend in Public Awareness about Watergate[a]

	Aware	Not Aware
Sept. 22-25, 1972	52%	48%
April 6-9, 1973	83	17
April 27-30, 1973	91	9
May 11-14, 1973	96	4
June 1-4, 1973	97	3

[a]"Have you heard or read about Watergate?"
SOURCE: Gallup Opinion Index, June 1973, p. 2.

By the beginning of the televised hearings, 97 percent of the American public was aware of Watergate. Such public awareness shows that the mass public is informed on major issues and has definite opinions on them.

The televised hearings seemed to have a major impact on President Nixon's popularity. In September, 1973, Gallup reported that 100 percent of his interviewees had either seen the hearings live or seen a rebroadcast during one seven-day period in August.[30] Perhaps Nixon's fears of television and the mass media were justified.

To examine how much the public felt Nixon was involved in various aspects of Watergate, Gallup asked the public a series of questions over a three-month period. Table 5-5 indicates that the majority felt that Nixon participated in at least the cover-up with 8 percent believing he planned the Watergate bugging from the beginning. In the August 17 survey, 73 percent felt Nixon knew about the cover-up at the least. Even on June 1, at the beginning of the surveys, 67 percent of the American public felt Nixon was involved with the cover-up at least.

Table 5-5 shows a pervasive awareness of Watergate and a constant pressure on Congress to investigate and impeach the president. Overall, these tables indicate a strong public knowledge and interest in Watergate and clearly indicate the pressure of public opinion on American government.

Conclusions

This examination of the Watergate scandal showed the direct effects of the mass media on the opinion-policy process. The media,

Table 5-5

Nixon's Involvement in Watergate[a]

	June 1	June 22	July 6	Aug 3	Aug 17
Nixon planned the Watergate from the beginning	8%	8%	9%	8%	9%
Nixon did not plan the bugging but knew about it before it took place	28	27	30	29	24
Nixon found out about the bugging after it occurred but tried to cover it up	31	36	34	37	40
Nixon had no knowledge of the bugging and spoke up as soon as he learned about it.	19	17	15	15	23
No opinion	14	12	12	11	4

SOURCE: Gallup Opinion Index, 1973, especially September 1973, p. 2.

especially the *Washington Post*, kept the public aware of the scandal and eventually helped force the White House staff to admit their guilt or resign. The presidential transcripts provided a fascinating inside view into the former president's views toward the media, the public relations mentality of the White House, and his pervasive fear of leaks. The Gallup polls provided us with clear evidence of the casual pressures of public opinion on policy makers.

Perhaps the most fascinating evidence was the almost 100 percent awareness of the issue by the American people. Clearly, on issues of importance the citizens are not only aware but also able to make intelligent decisions. The overwhelming pressure on congressmen led directly to the resignation of one of the strongest presidents in American history.

NOTES

1. The elections showed the most direct effects of public opinion on congressional action. Of the four elections, only one Republican won. All the districts were considered safe Republican districts and at least one district

had not had a Democrat represent it in Congress for over fifty years. In one Michigan district, former President Nixon himself campaigned (the Republican lost). These losses prompted several senior Republicans in both the House and Senate to call for the president to resign for the good of the country and the Republican party. While no Republican incumbents were involved, the trend of voting indicates a shift to the Democrats of 5 to 10 percent. The 1974 elections resulted in a major shift of congressional and gubernatorial seats to the Democrats. Watergate, the Nixon pardon, and the recession economy were the primary factors in the Democratic victory. President Ford's campaign efforts and his honest nice-guy image seemed to help somewhat. However, the overwhelming Democratic victory possibilities diminished considerably as soon as Nixon resigned.

2. Much of this section is based upon various press accounts and the book, *All the President's Men,* by Carl Bernstein and Bob Woodward (New York: Simon and Schuster, 1974). Also extensively referred to is James McCartney's "Here's the Scoop," *Philadelphia Inquirer,* 15 July 1973, sec. H, p. 1, 5.

3. McCartney, ibid., p. 5.

4. Woodward and Bernstein, *All the President's Men,* pp. 330-32.

5. Ibid., p. 143.

6. Ibid., p. 161.

7. Ibid., p. 162.

8. Ibid., p. 164.

9. Richard E. Neustadt, *Presidential Power* (New York: Wiley, 1960).

10. *The White House Transcripts* (New York: New York Times, 1974), p. 63.

11. John P. Robinson, "Perceived Media Bias and the 1968 Election," *Journalism Quarterly* 49 (Summer 1972): 239-46.

12. *White House Transcripts,* p. 75.

13. Ibid., p. 79.

14. Ibid., pp. 90-91.

15. Ibid., p. 109.

16. Ibid., p. 573.

17. Ibid.

18. Joe McGinniss, *The Selling of the President* (New York: Trident Press, 1969), p. 23.

19. *White House Transcripts,* pp. 211-12.

20. Ibid., pp. 225-26.

21. Ibid., p. 506.

22. Ibid., p. 520.

23. Ibid., p. 86.

24. Ibid., pp. 237-38.

25. Ibid., pp. 71-72.

26. Ibid., pp. 109-10.

27. Ibid., p. 120.

28. Ibid., p. 243.

29. Ibid., p. 415.

30. Gallup Opinion Index, September 1973, p. 31.

6

Blacks
and the Mass Media

The Media Habits of the
Ghetto Residents

There are a number of studies that have explored this area in some detail. Most of the studies are based on limited samples; however, the findings seem to agree. Roper Research Associates reported in 1969 that television is the main source of news for most Americans and is considered the most credible.[1] Also, they found that there is an inverse relationship between median income and the time spent watching television. Adults in low-income homes watch television for more than four hours each day with the trend going higher. For low-income blacks the time increased to six hours per day. Bradley S. Greenberg reports that 95 percent of the public own at least one operating television and that the same percentage holds for persons qualifying for Office of Economic Opportunity assistance.[2] While televisions seem to be available to most ghetto residents, newspapers are not. A *Washington Post* survey showed that newspaper circulation in black neighborhoods is 60 percent less than in white areas. The large metropolitan newspapers, even those with great sympathy for black interests, seem to be largely ignored by the ghetto resident.

In an intensive study of the media habits of blacks in Pittsburgh, Thomas Allen interviewed one hundred households.[3] In his study, the median education was 8.2 years, the average income was $2,800, and male unemployment was 19 percent. Each household had at least one television and one radio. Only 14 percent received a daily newspaper. Of those that did, very few read anything other than sporting news, entertainment, and so on. The ghetto resident depended almost entirely on television for news—with 86 percent watching television news sometime between five and seven o'clock at night. There was widespread ignorance about contemporary events, indicating that blacks in Pittsburgh seemed to hear the news without really listening. At least, it appeared that they felt the information did not concern their daily lives.

In 1966, Walter Gerson conducted a survey to investigate the effect of mass media on the socialization of behavior of whites and blacks.[4] In San Francisco 351 blacks and 272 whites were questioned. The average age was 15.2 years. He found that more blacks than whites used the media as an agency of socialization. Many suggested that they used the media to learn how to behave like whites. In a sense, the media were providing the social access for the black to the larger white world—one that he does not understand and that normally ignores him.

Other studies have found that while 40 percent of the general public say they get most of their news via television, over 70 percent of the low-income citizens say they get most of their news via the electronic media. A study by Greenberg and Brenda Dervin confirms this finding.[5] They found that an approximately equal percentage of low-income types own TV sets as did a general population sample (see table 6-1). However, when it came to newspapers, one-quarter of the low-income sample said they did not have any delivered, while only 14 percent of the general population said no.[6]

Table 6-1

Television Sets and Ownership

Number of Working TV Sets	Low Income			General Population
	Total	White	Black	
0	3%	3%	2%	3%
1	63	66	60	58
2 or more	34	31	38	39

Source: Bradley Greenberg and Brenda Dervin, "Mass Communications Among the Urban Poor," *Public Opinion Quarterly* 34 (Summer 1970): 228. Used with permission of the publisher and the authors.

This study would seem to point out that there are distinct class biases in the uses of news media. The lower economic classes and the submerged ethnic minorities received most of their news from television, and newspapers are less widely read in these groups than in others.[7]

Another significant fact brought out by the Greenberg and Dervin study concerned world news sources. They showed that over two-thirds of their low-income sample relied on TV for *world* news as compared to only one-third of the general population (table 6-2).

Table 6-2

TV and News Information

Attitude	Low Income			General Population
Medium Preferred for World News	Total	White	Black	
Television	69%	68%	68%	38%
Radio	16	13	21	28
Newspapers	15	19	11	34
Attitude	Low Income			General Population
Medium Preferred for Local News	Total	White	Black	
Television	30%	33%	27%	21%
Radio	34	34	32	31
Newspapers	22	26	19	41
People	14	7	22	7

SOURCE: Bradley Greenberg and Brenda Dervin, "Mass Communication Among the Urban Poor," *Public Opinion Quarterly* 34 (Summer 1970): 234. Used with permission of the publisher and the authors.

Note the *decreased* use of television and increased use of people for local news. Indications are that this pattern is magnified during a stress period such as a riot.

The picture of the ghetto resident's viewing habits and information sources is quite clear. He does not use the metropolitan newspaper for information about either local or national news; he uses primarily the TV news. The next step is to find out how blacks regard the news they are consuming. It is important to note that the ghetto blacks are being given a picture of the real world primarily through the television and, to some extent, the radio. Television interprets the outside world and socializes blacks to what is acceptable there. Since we know that low-income people travel very little, television is their only effective link with the outside world, except for some opinion leaders in the neighborhood. Since control of communications is thought to be political and social power (direct influence), the television becomes a powerful force in the lives of the black residents.

Donald R. Matthews and James W. Prothro compared the media consumption of blacks and whites in the eleven states of the former Confederacy. Their sample constitutes one of the largest black samples ever collected and their work remains an extremely important contribution to the study of public opinion. They report that while media consumption habits of blacks and whites are quite similar, 22 percent of black adults expose themselves only to the electronic media.[8]

Figure 14 compares mass media consumption with black and white political participation. It shows clearly that as media use increases, the percent participating beyond talking increases. The white rate levels off after three kinds of media (TV and radio, newspapers, magazines) while the black rate continues to increase. The white rate increase is significantly lower than the black rate in-

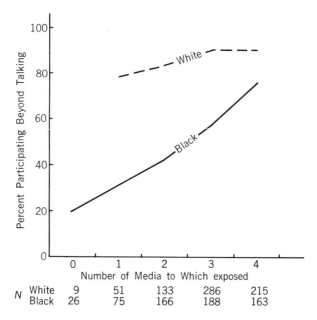

Source: From *Negroes and the New Southern Politics* by Donald R. Matthews and James W. Prothro, p. 253, © 1966 by Harcourt Brace Jovanovich, Inc. and reprinted with their permission.

Figure 14

Political Participation in the South, by
Exposure to Mass Media and Race

crease with whites going from 75 to 80 percent while blacks go from 20 to almost 70 percent. The media exposure appears to affect black political participation greatly.

Table 6-3 compares the exposure of southern blacks with selected political attitudes. It shows that as blacks are exposed to more media, their political interest increases, their level of political information increases, and their sense of civic competence increases. Most of the increases are large ones and suggest a definite impact of media exposure.

Table 6-3

Exposure of Southern Negroes to Mass Media and Selected Political Attitudes and Cognitions

	Number of Media to Which Exposed		
	0–1 (N = 90)	2–3 (N = 278)	4 (N = 248)
EXTENT OF POLITICAL INTEREST			
Great Deal	17%	25%	37%
Somewhat	7	21	29
Not much	76	54	34
Total	100%	100%	100%
LEVEL OF POLITICAL INFORMATION			
6–7 (high)	1%	5%	15%
4–5	13	34	36
2–3	50	43	35
0–1 (low)	36	18	14
Total	100%	100%	100%
SENSE OF CIVIC COMPETENCE			
3 (high)	15%	24%	35%
2	21	35	34
1	34	33	22
0 (low)	30	8	9
Total	100%	100%	100%

SOURCE: From *Negroes and the New Southern Politics* by Donald R. Matthews and James W. Prothro, p. 257, © 1966 by Harcourt Brace Jovanovich, Inc. and reprinted with their permission.

All three attitudes are indexes compiled from a series of questions concerning political interest, political information, and civic competence. In other tables that control for income and education the same pattern continues to hold.[9] While such findings do not conclusively prove the impact of the media, they definitely show strong tendencies and support conclusions that suggest the media influences such political attitudes.

How Blacks View the
Mass Media

If one accepts the argument that the media are a powerful force in the ghetto, then the critical question of impact is raised. What do blacks think about television, radio, and the newspapers (both local and metropolitan)? Do they view them all as tools of the white establishment, emanating lies always? Or do they view them as legitimate sources of fairly accurate information about happenings in the local and world community?

Louis Harris reflects on the questions just posed. His work is important for several reasons. First, it is one of the very few samples to examine the degree of disenchantment with American society by blacks generally. Second, it gives a comparative view of how blacks view American institutions, both public and private. Finally, it presents an idea of how blacks compare the Kennedy, Johnson, and Nixon administrations with regard to their sensitivity to black problems. The majority of the article is presented below.[10]

Disenchantment among black citizens with some of the principal institutions of American society has grown when compared to a year ago. Surprisingly, television leads the list when blacks are asked whether they feel these institutions "really care about blacks achieving equality," running eight points higher than the U.S. Supreme Court. But most of the organizations of a dominantly white society fail to attract the confidence of a majority of blacks today.

In the critical area of law enforcement, the nation's highest court stands alone as a symbol among blacks of fairness rather than discrimination, although its rating has slipped sharply among blacks compared to a year ago. Both this summer and last, a cross section of 1,200 black households was asked this question nationwide:

"Let me ask you about some government enforcement agencies. For each, tell me if you feel they would apply the law equally to both blacks and whites, or if they would be more likely to discriminate against blacks in favor of whites."

	1971	1970
U.S. Supreme Court	%	%
Apply equality for blacks and whites	52	62
Against blacks	26	21

	1971	1970
	%	%
Not sure	22	17
FBI		
Apply equally	39	50
Against blacks	39	27
Not sure	22	23
Justice Department Under Nixon		
Apply equally	20	22
Against blacks	56	50
Not sure	32	28
Local Police		
Apply equally	21	20
Against blacks	60	62
Not sure	19	18
Local Courts		
Apply equally	19	23
Against blacks	56	55
Not sure	25	22

Basically, blacks in this country have by and large ceased to look to the federal government as a force which can be depended upon to help blacks. Today's attitudes represent a drastic change in black orientation toward government since the Kennedy and Johnson years.

The national cross section of blacks was asked this year and also last year:

"Thinking back over the past 10 years, do you feel that when Presidents Kennedy and Johnson were in the White House, the federal government could be depended on to help blacks a great deal, some but not a lot, or not much?" and "How about today under the Nixon Administration — do you think the federal government can be depended on to help blacks a great deal, some but not a lot, or not much?" and "And how about the next five years — do you think the federal government can be depended on to help blacks a great deal, some but not a lot, or not much?"

	1971	1970
Under JFK and LBJ	%	%
A great deal	72	63
Some not a lot	23	30
Not much	3	4

	1971 %	1970 %
Not sure	1	3
Under Nixon		
A great deal	3	3
Some not a lot	26	21
Not much	65	66
Not sure	6	10
In Next 5 Years		
A great deal	14	17
Some not a lot	22	26
Not much	22	24
Not sure	42	33

Asked about U.S. institutions generally, only television and the U.S. Supreme Court emerged among pluralities of blacks as clearly committed to black equality, with Congress regarded in an ambivalent light. Newspapers, corporations and white churches were judged to be relatively indifferent or hostile to black aspirations.

"How much interest do you feel the following have in seeing blacks achieve full equality — do you feel they really care, are indifferent or have tried to prevent blacks from achieving racial equality?"

	Really Care %	Indifferent %	Tried to Prevent %	Not Sure %
Television	47	26	13	14
U.S. Supreme Court	39	23	12	26
U.S. Congress	30	28	14	28
Newspapers	27	33	17	23
Local Government	23	30	27	20
Large Corporations	22	32	18	28
Local Police	21	28	35	16
State government	20	35	22	23
Nixon administration	20	31	29	20
Small local companies	17	31	26	26
White churches	16	30	29	24
Local real estate	14	28	31	27

The principle finding with regard to the media is that television is rated first in really caring about minority citizens. Harris seems surprised by this finding; however, other studies have clearly shown that blacks simply do not read the newspapers, so their knowledge about the newspapers' fairness would be quite limited.

Jack Lyle made a study of newspapers in Los Angeles and devoted a special portion of it to the minority press and the attitudes of minorities towards newspapers in general.[11] He took a limited telephone survey of black residents and found that: (1) only 25 percent of the respondents said black stories had an equal chance of being used as a white story in the white press; (2) only 33 percent thought black political candidates could get equal treatment as a white political candidate; and (3) only 13 percent thought the white press "always" prints both sides of a story on issues involving blacks and whites. Lyle's findings indicate a fairly widespread distrust of the white newspapers in Los Angeles. Others have found similar results in less systematic approaches.

Joseph Shoquist reports the following conversation with a young ghetto resident. "He argued that the majority of Milwaukee's 100,000 Negroes — the poorest and the blackest of the blacks — don't read the *Journal* and couldn't care less about what it says or thinks. 'You simply are not relevant to the ghetto black man,' he told me. 'You are economically and socially oriented away from him, and what you write does nothing to extend his existence. The black man has lost his trust and faith in the established press and doesn't believe you want to serve him. You might as well forget him'."[12] While these words are both eloquent and succinct, they describe how blacks feel about the metropolitan newspapers, which most blacks think are for whites only.

There are, of course, a great number of hard, rational reasons for this pervasive distrust of the newspapers by blacks. Benjamin Bagdikian reports that it is still possible to see a sensationalized story of a black rape in Oregon on the front page of Jackson, Mississippi, newspapers.[13] All southern blacks knew of the biases of the white-controlled press throughout the South and expect the same from the northern press — they are seldom disappointed since prejudice toward blacks in the North is a bit more covert but sometimes even more degrading than in the South. Bagdikian comments that, for the average white, the black never leads an average, uneventful middle-class life joining the PTA, the Masons, and the like. He is always portrayed as a low-class, lazy, crime-oriented person.

A very moving story is told by Budd Schulberg, founder of the Watts Writers Workshop, that indicates how ghetto blacks view the white middle-class world portrayed on television. He talks of an experience in a Watts pool hall where he was the only white among a number of young black men. "I went into a pool room. There were about eight or ten young people in the pool room. They just looked up and down the wall. But I stayed there. They had a beat-up television set there. I sat in the back and I watched it as the pool game went on . . . and I got my first little flicker of education. The television show, especially the commercial made me very uncomfortable. They were showing all the things — the houses and other things — that these people, ragged and pretty beat, would obviously never have. It finally got to a commercial about how you could have your own home, only so much down, right on the golf course, every house opening out on the golf course with a swimming pool, etc., and they started to laugh. One of them said, 'I'm going to have two.' They were funny, but I do not think I have ever looked at commercials in the same way again after coming from that pool hall."[14]

The Community Press

While many studies have found that ghetto residents do not read the metropolitan newspapers, they do read their black newspapers in significantly greater numbers. Few have studied the impact of these black newspapers; however, from a brief perusal of some of them, it seems that the papers deal primarily in stories of sensationalized violence, overwhelming black success in the white world against great odds, and community stories about black middle-class activities. Of course, the 1960s saw many black newspapers develop a strong civil rights posture and a much better social consciousness. However, for the most part, the papers serve the establishment black, with some emphasis on the problems of poor blacks. For the ghetto resident, then, the black press is a little less guilty of bias and misrepresentation, but only a little less. To some extent, the successful black publisher, to be successful, has to act and appear like the white press. His stories cannot be too militantly black or he will lose advertising and various other benefits.

The importance of the community press in local issues is quite large. The local press can be a vigorous interest group for a locality and can transform an unorganized community into an effective lobbying group. In an intensive study of the community press in the Chicago area, Morris Janowitz finds some indication of widespread bias representing the overall biases of the particular communities.[15] He notes that while the community press in and around Chicago neighborhoods circulate in working-class areas, the mention of local labor union activities is noticeably absent. It appears that some publishers have a known anti-union bias so trade union publicists seem to neglect community newspapers as a potential source of publicity.

Janowitz found that, in terms of the news penetration on the citizenry, mentions of municipal services seem to vary directly with socioeconomic status. Those that had the best service wanted to keep it maintained and constantly improving. Also, he indicated that the citizens seemed to remember the news printed in the local newspaper much longer and with much greater intensity than news from the metropolitan press.

Janowitz also studied the kind of image the community press has with the citizenry. First, the local press is seen as an addition to the regular press and the other news media. Also, the press is thought to be relatively uncommercialized. Significantly, it is viewed as being politically neutral and a strong agent for community good. Finally, the community press is considered an extension of the reader's personal and social contacts, a kind of good, helpful neighbor.

Thus, the community press could play a great role in the everyday lives of blacks. The fact it has not condemns the present black publishing establishment. There is some evidence that the black community press does play a major informative function for minority citizens.

Blacks and the Media from a Historical Perspective

Anyone at all familiar with the history of black-white relations in the United States should not be surprised with the negative feelings of blacks toward the white press. The electronic medium gets better reception probably because of the positive role it played during the civil rights struggle and because the entire industry is only in its third decade (excluding radio).

The cries of racism within this country are well founded. Slaves in this country were treated much more inhumanly than anywhere else in both American continents. Cultural genocide was practiced openly; blacks were treated like cattle and no social avenues of great consequence were open to them. Even the northern areas that espoused great sympathy for the slaves offered little opportunity in terms of education or business activities. Blacks when freed were to keep their place at the bottom of the economic ladder.

The local white press condoned racial hatred and even instigated it as a kind of promotional sales activity. The record of southern newspapers (where the overwhelming majority of blacks lived until World War II) is incredibly bad. Righteous journalists were frightened or were otherwise willing to substantially alter facts in news stories involving whites and blacks. The injustice, which continues today in many small towns and some large ones especially in Alabama and Mississippi, was so obvious and widespread that it needs no documentation. For anyone to argue otherwise is a clear statement of his parochialism. The hypocrisy of the northern press with its denunciations of practices in the South that were going on a bit more covertly in the North is also unchallenged history. It is ironic that the greatest strides toward rectifying the situation come not from the liberal North but from the South, which is steeped in racial hatred.

The Kerner Commission's report documents this lamentable state with regard to all the media and race relations: "... the news media have failed to analyze and report adequately on racial problems in the United States and, as a related matter, to meet the Negro's legitimate expectation in journalism. By and large, news organizations have failed to communicate to both their black and white audiences a sense of the problems America faces and the sources of potential solutions. The media report and write from the standpoint of a white man's world. The ills of the ghetto, the difficulties of life there, the Negro's burning sense of grievance, are seldom conveyed. Slights and indignities are part of the Negro's daily life, and many of them come from what he now calls 'the white press'—a press that repeatedly, if unconsciously, reflects the biases, the paternalism, and indifference of white America. . . ."[16]

The Commission then makes a number of recommendations that, surprisingly, have been accepted by at least the major newspaper and television stations in the country. National newspapers now recruit young black reporters vigorously. Black reporters have formed associations to make sure that more than tokenism is practised by industries. The overall effect is greatly improved; however, the old wounds of the past remain imprinted in the minds of most reflective blacks from all socioeconomic classes. They assume bias; they expect bias; and their expectations are still frequently realized.

The Media in the
Civil Rights Movement

Looking back on the civil rights movement of the 1960s, one has to be awed with the gains of the movement over incredible obstacles. Southern laws, judges, newspapers, television, elected officials, police, and white southerners generally with all the powers that go to the establishment were arrayed against an organized group of blacks with few legal rights and with a history of violent persecution that should have frightened off any rational person. Yet these few blacks accomplished in a few short years what some have called a social revolution, most significant in the South but also with great economic, social, and political significance in the North.

The role the media played in this battle, especially television, was very important. Dr. Martin Luther King and other black leaders realized the power of the media and knew that their cause was morally and constitutionally right. Their strategy was to show the rest of the country and the world clear evidence of their plight via the media, primarily the national newspapers and the national television news companies. The specter of Police Chief "Bull" Connor and his men using cattle prods on defenseless women, children, and young adults rightfully shocked the national conscience.

When pictures of state and local police clubbing women and men were shown from Selma, all the legal power in the world could not oversome the injustice being presented. The Congress of Racial Equality sponsored a series of "freedom rides" to and through the South. Several of the buses, which, under federal law, were supposed to be integrated and whose passengers were supposed to use integrated facilities, were burned by local racists with some police help. After a few years of ineptitude, the southern police and politicians finally realized that their intimidation was counterproductive and attempted to insure that future disturbances would be well protected from local Ku Klux Klan organizations and other racists groups. In fact, for some time before Dr. King was assassinated, many blacks and some white sympathizers noted that he was becoming less and less effective. The simple reason was that peaceful demonstrations well guarded by local police were poor news, certainly not worthy of national news telecasts. The black militants, with their intemperate allegations and boasts of guerrilla warfare, received the national media attention.

The strategy of using the national media was a brilliant one. It enabled the world to see the horrible conditions under which blacks lived in the South and, to some extent, in the North. The words and films emanating from the confrontations presented such a *prima facie* case of injustice that Congress and the entire nation mobilized to change things. Besides the changes engendered by the civil rights movement, one of the more intriguing results of well-organized minority protest was to give other minorities hope and a successful model to follow. The organized protests of Chicanos, enthic groups such as Italians, Indians, college students, and the women's liberation movement were inspired to some degree by the success of the powerless blacks demanding their rights guaranateed by the Constitution with few weapons other than prayer, dedication, and the mass media. This role was of great significance as former Attorney General Nicholas Katzenbach noted:

> Newsmen have been the occasion of violence in the South in large measure because the segregationists realize an unquestionable truth: that press coverage is an essential part of the civil rights movement. Exposure, after all, is a central means of making a private moral conviction public, of impelling people all over to see and confront ideas they otherwise would turn away from.
> . . . Yet news coverage has been a powerful deterrent to racial violence in the South. For every assault on newsmen, many more incidents have been diffused by their presence. Reporters and cameras, particularly the network television cameras, which symbolize the national focus on Southern violence, have had a tempering effect. . . . Only because of the extensive reporting and film evidence on the University of Mississippi rioting in September, 1962, was it possible to show how absurd were the persistent claims that the United States marshals had started it all.[17]

Unfortunately, the coverage became crisis oriented. Little Rock, Selma, and Meridian were given all of the publicity. White America saw only news of violence, civil disobedience, and arrests. Many people became sick of hearing about civil rights. Sadly, only one side of the story was being shown, and the underlying causes for the discontent were never brought out. Furthermore, little attempt was made to understand what these causes might be. The Kerner Commission concurs:

> Ultimately, most important, we believe that the media have thus far failed to report adequately on the

causes and consequences of civil disorders and the underlying problems of race relations.[18]

MacNeill comments on the effect of this role of television:

When "Bull" Connor was hosing and dog-biting the Birmingham Demonstrators shown on National Television, the Negro Revolution became widely known to white America.

Television was a primary agent in conveying to fair-minded white Americans for the first time the depths of Negro humiliation and frustration. From the days of the Freedom Riders, through the March on Washington in 1963, to the march from Selma, Alabama in 1965, television moved with the fresh tide of goodwill that swept the country.

Sympathy was dictated by the defensive posture of non-violent, moderate Negroes.

After Selma, militants took over and the tide of goodwill stopped.

Television was presenting Negroes as attacking, looting, burning, and shooting as they rioted in the big cities.

The important role of the mass media was clearly evident during the civil rights demonstrations.[19]

The Black Media and
Blacks in the White Media

One of the blacks interviewed by Thomas Allen said: "The average black person couldn't give less of a damn about what the media says. The intelligent black person is resentful at what he considers to be a totally false portrayal of what goes on in the ghetto. Most black people see the newspapers as mouthpieces of the 'power structure'."[20] Earlier we suggested that many black people also regard the black media with the same contempt, suggesting that black journalists and broadcasters had to "sell out" to the whites to "make it."

The reasons for the distrust have been suggested previously. Another practical reason is that most reporters writing and talking about blacks are white, usually living in some comfortable suburb with no idea of what it is like to exist in the ghetto. In addition, many media people are either lazy or frightened. They tend to rely chiefly on police reports and statistics, a combination of circumstances usually resulting in a totally false portrayal of what goes on in the ghetto. The police and press are viewed as working together in presenting a slanted and distorted version of ghetto life and problems.

One of the most interesting developments in the black media is the black owned and operated radio stations. There is a strong movement among blacks to organize and pool their resources to buy as many of these stations as possible. Of course, the next logical step would be to purchase a television station in a large city. With the coming of cable television and a wired nation, this may not be necessary since cable television will give the television receiver the opportunity to originate and send his own broadcasts. However, widespread cable TV seems to be a long way off, especially since the national networks have mobilized all their resources to fight it.

In the series of articles on "Black Radio," Hollie West discusses the needs that black radio fulfills for black media professionals and the black community.[21] Black news is frequently overlooked or given little attention on most white stations. Because of the increasing number of black stations and the need for in-depth black news coverage, the Mutual Broadcasting System has begun a mutual black network service which offers daily five-minute newscasts featuring black news events to seventy stations around the world.

One additional advantage of black-owned stations is that they develop black media managers. As one manager, Ron Pickney, stated, "If there weren't black stations blacks wouldn't be working in radio. I don't think I could rise to be news director at a white station."[22] While white television and radio stations are adding more and more black managers, black stations offer the best management opportunities for black professionals.

The picture, then, is an improving one for blacks, but only a slowly improving one. There just are insufficient numbers of qualified blacks to fill the demands of metropolitian newspapers. The situation is getting better as more and more blacks see opportunities in the media. As far as black ownership is concerned, the trend toward community economic development suggests that more and more radio and television stations will be owned and operated by blacks. But this also will take some time and a great deal of effort by blacks themselves. Reliance on white goodwill is over for most blacks; they want and will assert themselves as independent operators of economic and political power.[23]

Urban Riots

Many have suggested that the mass media really caused the urban riots of the 1960s. Some, especially police chiefs and politicians, charge that newspapers and television stations sensationalized, rationalized, and even abetted the disturbances. It is true that many national newspapers expressed a great deal of sympathy for the plight of the black minority. Also, it is true that the television and radio reports tended to sensationalize the actual disturbance, even attracting crowds by their mere presence.

Edward C. Banfield suggests that the media have been telling blacks it is all right to rob and steal because of society's transgressions against minorities, especially blacks.[24] The overall effect of this rationalization on blacks has been to increase their belligerence, their feeling that all law is racist, and their feeling that some kind of reparations payment is due them. What is happening, Banfield suggests, is that the media are encouraging and helping blacks to riot, rob, and plunder — thereby undermining the slow but constantly increasing assimilation of blacks into middle-class society.

With regard to the riots, Banfield stated that television and newspapers sensationalized the coverage of the disturbances. The media reported that the police were not stopping the rioters or would not enter certain parts of the city. Each riot became a prototype for blacks in other cities, showing how and what to do. The coverage often emphasized the helplessness of the authorities. He suggested that other major race riots in America — 1943 in Detroit, Harlem in 1935 and 1936 — did not spread to other areas of the United States because of the absence of television coverage. Banfield's overall point is that the media acted as a catalyst and justifier for the disturbances.

There is some evidence to substantiate Banfield's comments. There were cases of a lack of cooperation between police and reporters. Newark Police Director Dominick Spina complained that "television seems to have the knack of picking people off the street and leading them into making the most violent kinds of statements."[25] Some feel that the pressure of constant deadlines forces the reporters to take a quick look. Accuracy is often sacrificed for speed. In their rush to be first with the best story, reporters' initial reports in major newspapers and television networks are distorted. In many cities the way the press interpreted the role of black leadership was seriously distorted. Often, they were accused of doing nothing, when in actuality they were doing all that was humanly possible.

The Kerner Commission's Report

In discussing the Watts riot, Anthony Obershall observed:

> The success of the store breakers, arsonists and loot-
> ers in eluding the police can in part be put down to the
> role of the mass media during the riot week. The Los
> Angeles riot was the first one in which rioters were
> able to watch their actions on television. The concen-
> tration and movements of the police in the area were
> well reported on the air, better than that of the rioters
> themselves.[26]

However, the Kerner Commission agreed that, on the whole, the media did attempt to give a balanced, accurate account of the disorders.[27] The press did try to calm emotions and behavior. Of 837 television sequences of riot and race news, 494 were calm, 262 were emotional, and 81 were normal. Only 4.8 percent of the television footage showed looting and sniping. Many of the events were portrayed as national rather than local events. After Martin Luther King, Jr., was assassinated, the broadcasters tried to present calm images. Walter Cronkite and Chet Huntley were stable, reassuring figures. Rather than show Stokely Carmichael delivering an inflammatory speech, CBS had Cronkite summarize the speech.

There are numerous examples of the mass media's responsible record in the coverage of the 1967 riots. The media often set up their own guidelines. Bill Sheehan, vice-president of television news for ABC, set up four important conditions:

1. The story had to be kept in perspective.

2. The nature of the problem was to be described with precision.

3. The reporter was to find out the reasons for the trouble and follow up on them.

4. There was to be no staging of events.[28]

On August 9, 1967, in a letter to Senator Hugh Scott, CBS President Frank Stanton outlined the steps he had taken.

1. We use unmarked cars. . . .

2. We do not use lights. . . .

3. Reporters and technicians have standing orders to obey the police. . . .

4. Extreme caution is to be exercised in estimating the size of crowds.

5. Eyewitness reports are checked for accuracy.

6. Statements by riot participants or apologists are balanced by reports by responsible officials.

7. Rumors are run down. . . .

Reuben Frank, executive vice-president of NBC news, in a staff memo dated August 21, 1967, wrote similarly:

We cover events. We report them, we do not arrange them, modify them, stage them or schedule them. We do not re-enact them. . . . If a rally is to take place and the sponsors ask us when is the best time for us, we are to have no opinion.[29]

While the Kerner Commission did find that the media coverage was balanced overall, it also suggested a significant imbalance between what happened in the cities and what newspapers, radio, and television coverage told the public, especially at the beginning of the disorders. It found the disorders less destructive, less widespread, and less a black-white confrontation than most people believed. In addition, it found that the cumulative effect of concentrated national news coverage on the riots was that the entire nation seemed to be engulfed by pitched battles between blacks and the police.

The specific findings of an intensive study done for the Kerner Commission were as follows:

The results of this analysis do not support our early belief. Of 955 television sequences of riot and racial news examined . . . only a small proportion of all scenes analyzed showed actual mob action, people looting, sniping, setting fires, or being injured or killed.

Of 3,779 newspaper articles analyzed more focused on legislation which should be sought and planning which should be done to control . . . and prevent future riots than any other topic.[30]

By its own admission, the Commission's results do not support the charge that the media sensationalized the riots. Yet further in the report, in apparent contradiction, the Commission states, "We suggest that the main failure of the media last summer was that the totality of its coverage was not as representative as it should have been to be accurate."

Some critics have blamed the news managers and editors for the media's negative influence on riots and disorders. The Kerner report suggested that while there is not much beyond the exercise of sound judgment that news managers can do to stem the spread of disorders from city to city, there are significant opportunities to improve the underlying causes. Many agree that the root causes stem from a myriad of socioeconomic ailments that plague the central cities. One possible reason is the lack of understanding by the general white society, plain indifference by most whites, which is indicated by public opinion polls showing gross misconceptions.

Studies on the Riots

A number of studies have focused on the effects of the media on the riots. Researchers found that in seven cities, 79 percent of 567 ghetto residents heard about the disorders in their cities by word of mouth. They reportedly distrust the media as an instrument of the white power structure.

Fred Pawledge stated:

We know that riots occur, by and large after sudden relatively minor confrontations with persons of authority — the cops. We know that word of these confrontations is often magnified and carried by rumor at high speed through the Negro community. There is probably a better system of internal communications in the ghetto than in the National Guard. During the early hours of a riot, it functions like lightning.[31]

In a study done by Benjamin D. Singer, 499 black males were surveyed who had been arrested during the Detroit riot.[32] He found the mass media to be a prime source of initially informing a portion of the ghetto, but after that, interpersonal channels take over with great effect (table 6-4). It might be interesting to see whether there is a hidden relationship between the fact that those who found out through interpersonal means were incited or encouraged to participate in a disorder more than the ones who heard it through a news media.

Table 6-4

Channel Through Which Those Arrested
Found Out About Detroit Riot

Channel	Percentages of Responses
Direct Experience	26.9
Interpersonal: Phone*	8.8 ⎱ = 48%
Interpersonal: Person*	39.0 ⎰
Radio	16.5 ⎱ = 26%
Television	9.0 ⎰

*It should be emphasized here that these persons who phoned or told somebody else
about the riot were inclined to have heard it themselves through the media.
SOURCE: Benjamin D. Singer, "Mass Media and the Communications Process in the
Detroit Riot of 1967," *Public Opinion Quarterly* 34 (Summer 1970): 243. Used by
permission of the publisher.

One final word regarding perceptions. In line with the Kerner
Commission's content analysis of riot sequences, that they constituted only a small proportion of all scenes analyzed, Singer has
some interesting findings (table 6-5).

Table 6-5

Perceptions of What People Were
Doing in Television Riot Sequences

Perception	% of Responses
Violent Acts Against Persons	49.8
Looting	21.1
Property Destruction	6.5
People Running, Standing, Milling	10.2
Arrests, Crowd Control	5.2
Peaceful Demonstrations, Other Responses	7.2
Total (Some Respondents Gave More Than One Answer)	100.0% (N = 650)

SOURCE: Benjamin D. Singer, "Mass Media and the Communications Process in the
Detroit Riot of 1967," *Public Opinion Quarterly* 34 (Summer 1970): 238. Used by
permission of the publisher.

Singer's findings show that most people in the riot area received
their information through interpersonal contact. However, the
primary source of the information came through the electronic
media, television or radio. Table 6-5 indicates what ghetto residents
thought the rioters were doing. Most thought they were committing
violent acts against persons. This misconception was probably based

on wild rumors and the sensationalized stories reported by the press based on police misinformation.

Charles Daly reports the following findings of the mass media effect on the riots:

1. Despite some sensationalizing, distortion, etc., newspapers, radio, and television made a strong and somewhat successful effort to give a balanced, factual account of the 1967 disorders.

2. Despite attempts to be fair, the media accounts failed to reflect accurately the riots' scale and character. The media presented an exaggerated atmosphere in mood and event.

3. The media failed to report accurately the causes and consequences of civil disorders and the problems of race in the United States.[33]

He further suggests that in the long-range struggle to produce an egalitarian society, the mass media can be extremely important. Their role in riots is marginal, however. When the level of anger in the black ghetto gets so close to the flash point, any event could be the spark that sets off the chain of violence and destruction. The real causes are the conditions that establish the tensions in the first place and not in the media.

Benjamin Badgikian investigated the indirect effects of the media on riots.[34] He found that the riots are influenced by police-ghetto relations, schooling and job opportunities, and general black-white relations — all of which can be influenced directly through presentations in the mass media. He suggests that journalism can be most influential in the reporting and discussion of causes for riots or rational theories of cause. This discussion should be channeled to the inner city communications network through television or the use of black radio and newspapers. The media, Bagdikian suggests, should be the forum for the regular collection, publication, and dissemination of suggested solutions to urgent problems affecting blacks. Newspapers and broadcasters should seek out the most creative thinkers and attempt to spread their ideas.

Students, Chicago, and
Protest Politics

We have discussed the central role the media played during the civil rights movement, giving the movement a world audience and exposing the horrible conditions that existed for blacks in the South. Many have suggested that the media have played a similar role in student disorders, the 1968 Chicago convention disorders, and other protest movements.

As long as we accept the premise that communications are power, we must give the media an important role in almost anything that happens. Their role in recent protest movements has been intensified because of the lack of power of most of the dissident groups. The power of the media was these groups' only source of influence. They used it effectively on a frightened bureaucracy, abetted by a willing TV news crew. That the media were their only effective weapon opened the way to charges that the media caused the violence and protests that ensued. To some extent, the charge is true since a media blackout would have made the protest action inconsequential. However, the causes for the protest were there long before the reporters and TV cameramen arrived. So while the charge of media causation is somewhat plausible, it is basically untrue since adverse conditions were the real motivating factor.

Marshall McLuhan suggested that the medium used to convey a message had a separate message of its own independent of the content of the original message. When there was a civil rights protest, viewers saw oppression occurring and by looking became a part of the entire action. They became participants, with their felt participation being almost as intense as those persons actually in the demonstration. To some extent, the electronic media encouraged a new and independent reaction from the viewers, one that led to considerable pressure on Congress and other institutions for redress, and that added a significant new dimension to protest politics. The student disorders and the Chicago convention also used the media for maximum impact. Students, without any power, demonstrated to get a policy input in the university community.

The power of the media was used to frighten usually timid administrators and to communicate student demands to the university and the public at large. The Chicago demonstration at the 1968 Democratic National Convention sought to do the same thing — to force so much attention on the policy makers that they would have to accede to the demands of the protesters.

Few would question the power of the media, especially the electronic media. Communist governments control all the media; most democratic governments have a large measure of control, especially over television and radio. In fact, until the British introduced a commercial television station in their country, the United States was one of the few nontotalitarian governments that allowed its television stations a large measure of independence.

Black Political
Attitudes

Although we discussed briefly the effects of the mass media on
black political attitudes, we will review some of the more important
literature in this area. Much of the literature focuses on the development and change patterns of these attitudes with only peripheral
discussion of mass media influence. The Kerner Commission report did focus some attention on the mass media influence on the
urban riots.

Few would dispute that the focus of media attention on all
aspects of the social and political lives of black Americans had
some impact on attitudes of both whites and blacks. The question
to resolve is how and to what extent the mass media changed
attitudes.

In a study examining the effects of mass media on attitudes toward desegregation, Melvin Tumin found that the media act as an
instrument through which people of different regions of the country
keep in contact with the mass culture.[35] He hypothesized that the
greater one's exposure to the mass media, the greater one's readiness for desegregation. He found that increases in exposure were
associated with consistent and persistent increases in readiness for
desegregation. Also, the data showed that small differences reach
statistical significance when extremes of low and high exposure are
compared to readiness for desegregation.

Louis Harris devotes a large study to black attitudes in the
1970s.[36] He finds black hostility toward whites to be deeply felt and
increasing. To the statement "whites feel that blacks are inferior,"
81 percent of blacks agree for both 1970 and 1971. To the statement, "whites give blacks a break only when forced to," 77 percent
agreed in 1970 and 79 percent in 1971.[37] By a majority of 58 percent
to 19 percent blacks felt that "most whites are less honest than
blacks."

Harris suggests that the Nixon policy of "benign neglect" seemed
to be working by 1973.[38] He states that the number who felt dis-
criminated against in "getting hotel and motel" accommodations
had dropped 24 points from 68 percent in 1969 to 44 percent in
1973. Also perceived discrimination in "providing a quality education for black children" fell 19 points from 72 percent in 1969 to
53 percent in 1973. Blacks also felt less discrimination in obtaining
skilled labor jobs, getting white-collar jobs, getting in labor unions,
and getting decent housing.[39]

Kenneth P. Langton and M. Kent Jennings looked at political interest, discussion, and media usage by black students.[40] They found that black students used television more often than whites.[41] They also found that the more civics courses blacks took in high school, the less likely they were to seek political information in newspapers, magazines, and television.[42] They suggest that a civics course may increase a student's political interest while acting as a substitute for political information gathering in the media. The mass media, however, remain a primary source of political information for black students.

Joel Aberbach and Jack Walker examined political trust and racial ideology.[43] They found that blacks are less trusting than whites. They suggest that the data represent a change in the usual pattern since the federal government has been the black man's friend with regard to freedom rights and national legislation. Aberbach and Walker state that "the government in Washington has been the symbol of the American Negro's intense identification with and 'faith in the American Dream.' Now, at least in cities like Detroit, this sense of trust is being undermined as many black people are beginning to reject their traditional ties with paternalistic friends and allies and are striking out at the more subtle forms of discrimination and deprivation in the North."[44] While there is no direct mention of media influence, it seems arguable that the massive television coverage of the riots of the 1960s encouraged this decline of political trust.

While the study of black political attitudes constitutes a massive literature,[45] we can only speculate on the effects of the mass media in changing black attitudes. It is clear that the electronic media, especially television, are the major source of political information for blacks. It is also clear that the mass media played a central role in the civil rights movement and in the urban riots of the 1960s. Many observers, especially policemen and public officials, suggested that without the media neither the civil rights movement nor the urban riots would have taken place. No one suggests the media caused these incidents but the media made them national and even international news immediately. The spotlight of national attention was focused on them for long periods of time.

The linkage model suggested in chapter 2 appears useful again in that the mass media seem to energize both blacks and sympathetic whites to put pressure on policy makers for action. Those pressures produced a number of major civil rights bills from the Congress and a series of presidential Executive Orders to end discrimination. They also forced the federal government to reflect on the causes of the urban riots and to take a number of formal and informal actions to alleviate poor housing, poor education, and lack of employment opportunity. The media were a catalyst for action, building a small civil rights movement into a nationally coordinated operation and forcing the government to eliminate the causes of urban disorders.

Conclusions

We discovered that most blacks get almost all of their news via the television and the radio. We found a white press that was, at the least, unresponsive to black hopes and aspirations and, at the worst, printing absolute lies and distortions concerning any black-white incidents. To some extent, this situation is improving, especially since the electronic media's record is much better than that of the printed media. The central question raised was whether the media caused the riots. The answer is clearly negative since a whole set of socioeconomic factors could have caused the disturbances. However, the media gave the riots new significance because they gave the protesters a world audience and worldwide airing of their grievances. The media will continue to be an important weapon in protest politics; they are an effective, available, and powerful tool when skillfully employed by protesters, whatever the cause.

While the influence of the media on black political attitudes was indirect, it was important in spotlighting attention on injustices. We found that the media influence model could be successfully applied here also.

NOTES

1. Burns W. Roper, *A Ten-Year View of Public Attitudes Toward Television and Other Mass Media* (New York: Television Information Office, 1969).

2. Bradley S. Greenberg, "Mass Communication Behaviors of the Urban Poor," in *Why Aren't We Getting Through: The Urban Communication Crisis,* ed. Edmund M. Midura (Washington, D.C.: Acropolis Books, 1971), p. 25.

3. M. Thomas Allen, "Mass Media Use Patterns and Functions in the Negro Ghetto in Pittsburgh" (Ph.D. diss., West Virginia University, 1967).

4. Walter Gerson, cited in ibid.

5. Bradley S. Greenberg and Brenda Dervin, "Mass Communications Among the Urban Poor," *Public Opinion Quarterly* 34 (Summer 1970): 224-35.

6. Ibid., p. 228.

7. Ibid., p. 234.

8. Donald R. Matthews and James W. Prothro, *Negroes and the New Southern Politics* (New York: Harcourt Brace Jovanovich, 1966), p. 249.

9. Ibid., p. 259.

10. Louis Harris, "TV is Rated First in Care About Blacks," *The Washington Post,* 31 August 1971. Reprinted by permission of the Chicago Tribune-New York News Syndicate, Inc. Copyright 1971.

11. Jack Lyle, *The News in Megalopolis* (San Francisco, Calif.: Chandler, 1967), p. 155.

12. Joseph W. Shoquist, "The Role of the Press in a Continuing Urban Crisis," in *Why Aren't We Getting Through,* ed. Midura, pp. 43-60.

13. Benjamin Bagdikian, "Editorial Responsibility in Times of Urban Disorder," in *The Media and the Cities,* ed. Charles W. Daly (Chicago, Ill.: University of Chicago Press, 1968), p. 15.

14. Budd Schulberg, "Can the Disadvantaged in the Inner City Learn to Communicate?" in *Why Aren't We Getting Through,* ed. Midura, pp. 113-32.

15. Morris Janowitz, *The Community Press in an Urban Setting* (Chicago, Ill.: University of Chicago Press, 1967), p. 142.

16. U.S. Riot Commission, *Report of the National Advisory Commission on Civic Disorders* (The Kerner Commission) (New York: Bantam, 1968), pp. 362-89.

17. Paul L. Fisher and Ralph L. Lowenstein, *Race and the News Media* (New York: Anti-Defamation League, 1967), p. 38. Used by permission of the authors.

18. *National Advisory Commission Report,* p. 363.

19. Robert MacNeil, *The People Machine: The Influence of Television on American Politics* (New York: Harper and Row, 1968), pp. 70-71.

20. Allen, "Mass Media Use Patterns," p. 374.

21. Hollie West, "Black Radio," *Washington Post,* 28 January 1973, sec. L-3. This was in a series of in-depth articles on black radio.

22. *Washington Post,* 29 January 1973, sec. B-1.

23. For an excellent overview of the development of the black press in America see Roland E. Wolseley, *The Black Press, U.S.A.* (Ames: Iowa State University Press, 1971). See chapter 15 for the impact of the black press on black Americans. An excellent round-table discussion on blacks and the press can be found in Jack Lyle, ed., *The Black American and the Press* (Los Angeles, Calif.: Ward Ritchie Press, 1968). Some other historical treatments of the black press can be found in Frederick G. Detweiler, *The Negro Press in the United States* (Chicago, Ill.: University of Chicago Press, 1922) and Carter Royston Bryan, *Negro Journalism in America Before Emancipation* (Lexington, Ky.: Association for Education in Journalism, 1969). See also Wolseley, pp. 333-41, for a complete bibliography.

24. Edward C. Banfield, *The Unheavenly City* (Boston, Mass.: Little, Brown, 1968), p. 198.

25. *Time*, vol. 90, 25 August 1967, p. 63.

26. In Hugh Davis Graham and Ted Robert Gurr, *Violence in America* (New York: New American Library, 1969), p. 418.

27. "TV Networks Rule of Riots," *Vital Speeches* 34-53, 1 November 1967.

28. Ibid.

29. Ibid.

30. *National Advisory Commission Report,* pp. 364-65.

31. Fred Pawledge, "What We Failed to Learn," *New Leader,* 14 August 1967, p. 5.

32. Benjamin D. Singer, "Mass Media and the Communications Process in the Detroit Riot of 1967," *Public Opinion Quarterly* 34 (Summer 1970): 243.

33. Daly, *Media and the Cities,* p. 5.

34. Badgikian, "Editorial Responsibility," p. 14.

35. Melvin M. Tumin, "Exposure to Mass Media and Readings for Desegregation," *Public Opinion Quarterly* 21 (Summer 1971): 237-51.

36. Louis Harris, *The Anguish of Change* (New York: Norton, 1973).

37. Ibid., p. 233.

38. Ibid., p. 253.

39. Ibid. For a general discussion of the impact of black voting in the North and South, see Frederick G. Dutton, *Changing Sources of Power* (New York: McGraw-Hill, 1971).

40. Kenneth P. Langton and M. Kent Jennings, "Political Socialization and the High School Civics Curriculum in the United States," in *Black Political Attitudes: Implications for Political Support,* ed. Charles S. Bullock III and Harrell R. Rodgers, Jr. (Chicago, Ill.: Markham, 1972).

41. Ibid., p. 66.

42. Ibid., p. 67.

43. Joel D. Aberbach and Jack L. Walker, "Political Trust and Racial Ideology," in ibid., pp. 133-62.

44. Ibid., p. 141.

45. One of the most thorough treatments of black attitudes and political participation is James Walton, Jr., *Black Politics* (New York: Lippincott, 1972). See also Angus Campbell and Howard Schuman, *Racial Attitudes in Fifteen American Cities* (Ann Arbor, Mich.: Institute for Social Research, 1969); Howard Schuman and Barry Gruenberg, *The Impact of City on Racial Attitudes* (Ann Arbor, Mich.: Institute for Social Research, 1970); Robert L. Crain and Carol Sachs Weisman, *Discrimination, Personality, and Achievement: A Survey of Northern Blacks* (New York: Seminar Press, 1972); Richard M. Burkey, *Racial Discrimination and Public Policy in the United States* (New York: Heath Lexington Books, 1971); and Allen D. Grimshaw, ed., *Racial Violence in the United States* (Chicago, Ill.: Aldine, 1969).

7

The Media and Society: Theories of Media Effect

In this chapter, we will examine the theoretical impact of the mass media from three different perspectives. There has been much scholarly inquiry concerning the total impact of the mass media on society in general. Among those who have pioneered in this effort has been Marshall McLuhan, who has attempted to show how technology molds society and determines a significant portion of its culture.[1] Therefore, our initial thrust will concern McLuhan's writings.

Second, we will examine communications theory as it has been applied to politics specifically. Karl Deutsch,[2] Lucien Pye,[3] and Daniel Lerner[4] have attempted to show how the media affects politics and change, with special emphasis on national development. They have sought answers to the following questions: What part do the media play in transitional or changing nations? What does the nature of the communications system developed in a society tell us about that society? Finally, can communications theory help us predict the future of a given nation-state?

Third, we will explore the various theories of media effect regarding attitude and behavior change. The questions we will investigate are: (1) To what extent does the media induce attitude change? (2) What are the mediating circumstances? and (3) What are some of the formal theories of media effect on attitude change? More specifically, we will examine the possible effects of the media on voters. The question of changing voters has been dealt with in chapter 1.

Media and Society:
Culture and Technology

McLuhan sees the electronic age of the media inducing profound effects on politics as Americans are traditionally accustomed to viewing it.

The day of political democracy as we know it is finished. . . . Individual freedom itself will not be submerged in the new tribal society, but it will certainly assume different and more complex dimensions. The ballot box, for example, is the product of a literate Western culture—a hot box in a cool world. . . . Voting in the traditional sense is through as we leave the age of political parties, political issues and political goals and enter an age where the collective tribal image and the iconic image of the tribal chieftain is the overriding political reality.[5]

While he goes on to talk about the end of bloc voting in politics and the supremacy of the icon, the inclusive image, it seems a great deal of time will pass before these predictions are consummated.

The ultimate importance of McLuhan's insights is that society and its politics are being changed because of electronic technology. Of course, the observation that major technological changes transforms a society is not a new one nor a particularly insightful one; it is quite obvious. The telephone, the printing press, the computer, the airplane, various machine inventions, the production line — all have contributed to change that sometimes approaches large-scale transformations within a given society. The electronic age, especially television, and perhaps even more important, cable television, is bringing about radical change within our American society and, in McLuhan's view, in the world at large. Immediate communication, the power of information and knowledge, and the ability of societies and individuals to communicate immediately over vast distances will push the world community into a new age. It will be most effective in democratic societies where there is a free flow of information and new ideas, but eventually it will spread throughout the world. Although it will take some time for the full effects of the electronic age to engulf us, let us look at some of the more immediate predicted influences on American society.

The Media and
Education

Today children know about riots, wars, politics, and vast array of subjects previously known only to the educated. McLuhan and Quentin Fiore suggest a larger share of changes for the educational system entirely.[6] Instead of the educational patterns developed by print and book-oriented educators with their fragmented courses and curricula, we will have schedules and subjects replaced by a system where the student is totally involved immediately. The trends toward unstructured education now apparent at all levels of the educational process seem to substantiate this transformation. Even though the technical specialist is still revered, it is the generalist who makes the overall policy choices. Increasingly, specialized areas have a large overlap into many areas such as school decision making and governmental policy making. McLuhan suggests that all these changes are a direct result of our electronic age.

The Media and
Government

We have already related some of the changes that the electronic age is forcing on government. However, McLuhan suggests that the public is no longer a mass of distinct viewpoints but a mass audience that strives to be creative and participatory. The new politics sees the living room as a voting booth and changes passive television viewers into direct participators in freedom marches, wars, revolution, and pollution, with the felt involvement becoming stronger and stronger every day. Minority groups cannot be ignored any longer because "we are a part of each other."[7] The politician must be right for television, giving off the proper amounts of integrity, education and charisma to his vast audience. It is not what he says but how he says it, and what the public thinks he said, that is important. Television provides the electorate with a new set of criteria that enables viewers to shape expectations of what an American president, senator, or governor should be and to help them to decide who is the most qualified — all according to television performance.

Jack Newfield, assistant editor of the *Village Voice*, in reviewing Scammon and Wattenberg's *The Real Majority*, said:

The most conspicuous weakness, perhaps, of Scammon and Wattenberg is their inability to understand the transcendent importance of television. One doesn't have to agree with all of Marshall McLuhan's puns and probes to understand that he is on to something big. Television *is* a surrogate reality for millions of people, and the result is that television is absorbing and centralizing the authority that was once dispersed among the shop steward, the district leader, the minister and the print publisher. Television is making irrelevant the political middle-man or interpreter. Every voter can now see the candidates in his own living room and make a judgment, perhaps frivolous or irrational, about how he will vote. The historic effect of this has been to break down the political party structure, and to project personality above party—a Lindsay or a Kennedy.

The most telling variable in the campaigns this year has not been the law and order issue but the use of television.[8]

The Media and the Cities

McLuhan predicts the demise of the cities.[9] If policy makers were to listen to his advice, they would stop worrying about the decay of American cities and start planning how to make them all Williamsburg-like museums for the future children of the world. Just as the railroads and highways gave us new patterns of living and provided the catalyst for the growth of large metropolitan areas growing outward from the central city, the electronic age and new modes of transportation have made these vast concentrations of people, materials, and industry much less useful. So today we see a trend to build new cities, a trend for industry to locate away from the central city, and negative growth rates for most central cities in America. Whether these trends are due directly to the new conditions created by the electronic age is open to some question; however, many have documented these transformations.

Hot and Cool Media: Linear and Mosaic Man

The simulated sense of participation apparent in television defines it as a cool medium. Hot media exclude the receiver's participation; they furnish all the information one needs and define the situation or event completely. The cool media demand that the receiver bring to the communication his experiences and his information, that he participate in the process. They are low definition. Thus, the viewer watching a political advertisement "reads" into the slogans and stories what he wants to. In effect, the viewer creates an ideal candidate according to his own specifications. Hot media are the radio and the movies; cool media are the telephone and the television. The basic difference lies in the amount of participation allowed the receivers. In a hot medium, there is low participation, but in the cool media, there is high participation or completion by the audience.

McLuhan asserts that the radio tends to provoke violence on non-literate or semiliterate peoples.[10] For those tribal peoples with their entire social existence centered around and an extension of family life, the radio is a violent experience. It is violent because it threatens this very secure and stable living pattern. The power of radio is to retribalize mankind, with its almost instant reversal of individualism into collectivism — both Fascist and Marxist. The Orson Welles broadcast on the "invasion from Mars," the power of radio propaganda in Nazi Germany, the revival of native tongues in Ireland, Scotland, Wales, and Israel since the coming of the radio — all are powerful commentaries on the impact of this hot medium on societies.

McLuhan relates the world situation to radio as follows: "Hot medium like the radio used in cool or non-literate culture has a violent effect; quite unlike as in England and America, radio is considered entertainment. As for the cold war and the hot bomb, the cultural strategy needed is humor and play. It is play that cools off hot situations by merging them. However, competitive sports between Russia and the West is not the answer — it is actually inflammatory."[11]

With the television image, we have the supremacy of the general outline. Instead of bloc voting, we have the inclusive image. Instead of the political viewpoint, we have the inclusive political posture or stance. Television as a low intensity, cool medium forces the audience to fill in the details of the images presented. The process entails a high degree of audience involvement with television's simultaneously occurring "mosaic mesh." One must appear cool on television and not assert one's singular status and role position. One must look as if he could be a teacher, a doctor, a lawyer, or a businessman offering simply blurred outlines that the viewer colors in according to his selective perceptions.

Linear and Mosaic Man

The linear culture that stems from the print-oriented man denotes perceptions that are sequential, fragmented, compartmentalized, alienated. Linear man thinks in sequence and in a step-by-step process. Government for this linear culture is a machine that runs on "balance of powers" and checks and balances. Government is a morass of hierarchical bureaucracies based on a step level of authority and pay.

For the electronic age, government is a nervous system with the federal government as the brain center. The government is seen as centralized, from which all monies, information, and policies emanate. The nervous system government is the cybernetic approach, the swift processing and reacting toward information. Man in this age is mosaic man, seeing things in totality. He perceives himself as what he does. He is attached to pop culture and an inclination "to do his own thing."[12] He is basically antiscience and inclined toward mysticism. Government is viewed without checks or balances. The Supreme Court legislates, the executive legislates and interprets the Constitution, and the Congress does what it is told to do.

Obviously, our government and citizenry are somewhere between the two models. With the increasing importance of the federal government in all phases of domestic and foreign policy, with the increasing power of the presidency, one can see the trends for the electronic age. When cable television is developed with its capacity to put nerve endings in every household in the country, the trend will be stimulated. One often gets the feeling that McLuhan and his followers perceive social change as being caused only by the new communications systems such as radio, television, and now cable television. Certainly they are an important factor — theoretically the most important — however, many other factors are equally significant, such as economic and political development in a given society.

As A. D. Whitehead said, "Electronic technology is reshaping our entire culture and forcing us to reconsider every thought, finding and action. And that includes the individual, the family, the neighborhood, education, jobs, governments — your entire relationship to others."[13] Thus media alter the environment in which we live and develop a unique ratio of sense perception. The extension of these senses alters the way we perceive the world. When these ratios change, men and society change.

What McLuhan sought to show was that people are being affected by the mass media in a powerful, indirect way. The mass media do not change the individuals directly; they change the environment of the individual. The individual then reacts and adapts to the changed environment. What we have is a Gestalt (worldly, complete, or overall) approach to the study of mass media. We must recognize that technology changes the environment and indirectly society, politics, and culture.

Cybernetics and the
Nerves of Government

Norbert Wiener, one of the founders of cybernetics, has said: "It is my thesis that the operation of the living individual and the operation of some of the newer communication machines are precisely parallel. . . . Society can only be understood through a study of the messages and communication facilities that belong to it."[14] Cybernetics is concerned with the study of steering and communication, especially control and the feedback process. Integration, disintegration, and responsiveness are key communications topics.

Information is a patterned relationship between events. All messages must be received, stored, and sent. Any channel of communication, whether face-to-face or through the media, has a given capacity that can be exceeded and can result in overload. Feedback is a producing action which tends to modify the original message or behavior. The feedback process has load, or the amount of information involved; lag, or the delay in time for the message to be received; and gain, or the amount of speed of reaction to information. But how does all this relate to political systems? Karl Deutsch sees the process of communication in a society as an indicator of societal cohesion.[15] Thus, one measure of social cohesion is the speed and accuracy with which information is received and transmitted. Deutsch suggests that since it has become quite possible to estimate in advance the problem-solving capacities of an electronic calculator, it should be possible to estimate, although far more roughly, the problem-solving capacity of a government or society as well as to estimate its ability for innovation — that is, its capacity to put a new solution actually into operation. Deutsch is suggesting that communications theory may result in predictive political theory. When one views nations as communications systems, one can generate verifiable evidence on the capabilities of that system and ultimately, how that system is likely to react under stress. Since communications theory is multidisciplinary, it has a wealth of useful models and operational definitions that can be applied to political analysis. For example, in studying the communications system in Nigeria, we note that there has been a mail flow increase by a multiple of eight from 1929 to 1948. This suggests great internal development within the country.

Deutsch says that "the interchange model of the political subsystem, and of its relations to the other main subsystems of society, has quantitative implications."[16] Not only can the volume of effective demands made on a government be estimated but also the range of matters for which a polity assumes responsibility as well as the amount of relevant resources and capabilities at its disposal.

The rates of many of the transaction flows between government and interest groups can be measured or estimated. Savings rates and investment rates are familiar to economists. In a similar fashion, it should be possible to estimate roughly the rise in the volume of political demands made upon the government from the rate of social mobilization. Social mobilization is the rate at which people leave the seclusion of subsistence agriculture and village life and their control on tradition and general isolation from the central society in metropolitan areas. Deutsch shows that the rates at which people enter the money economy, urban life, literacy exposure to mass media, and partial acculturation to modernity can be measured in part.[17] In addition, the rate at which the responsibilities of the government are expanding might be estimated from the expansion of the portion of the gross national product expended by government at the local, state, and federal levels.

The rates of political integration and alienation can be measured also. Deutsch states:

> More directly, from voting data and perhaps from sample surveys, estimates could be derived for the political integration ratio, that is the proportion of persons extending generalized political support to the government or to the political parties pledged to such support including "loyal opposition" parties. Similarly, a political ratio could be estimated as the proportion of people denying generalized support to the country and its type of government, or supporting opposition parties repudiating any such generalized allegiance to the state and its regime.

The rates of political integration and alienation are, then, the ones at which the respective ratios change over time; and a rate and ratio of political neutralization for the indifferent, the apathetic, and perhaps for those paralyzed by cross-pressures, might also be estimated in order to complete this part of the picture.[18]

Deutsch shows that all governments depend upon the processing of information. The important focus should be on the pattern of information sending and receiving. Thus, he states, *"information can be defined as a patterned distribution, or a patterned relationship between events."*[19] With regard to information and change, he suggests that at least some parts of the receiving system must be in unstable equilibrium, so that the very small amount of energy carrying the signal will be sufficient to start off a much larger process of change.

For example, when a given society has numerous strikes, protests, or other political disturbances, an inevitable debate arises concerning whether and to what extent domestic or foreign agitators are involved. On a higher level, the problem reappears as the question of the role of new ideas in inducing or prompting social change, and it is directly applicable to studies of the conditions favoring political reform.[20]

Deutsch notes that power itself is intrinsically related to information. Information always precedes both compulsion and compliance.[21] He then makes an important distinction between impersonal communication (radio, newspaper) and personal, face-to-face communication. For example, during World War II many governments-in-exile were considered legitimate by their Nazi-dominated citizens; however, the underground organizations, especially the highly organized Communist ones, had less legitimacy but much more power because of good face-to-face contact with the people. When the countries were liberated, the organizations with good personal communications were far more effective than those broadcasting in exile from London. Thus, legitimacy beliefs and social communications are the mainspring of political power. Deutsch goes on to note that the manipulation of political symbols must be distinguished by the means of manipulation — impersonally as in a speech or book or personally as in human and institutional chains of communication.

He suggests that the communications network should enable one to measure a country's information-carrying capacity, that is, its stability. This suggests that a communications overload or decision overload may be a major factor in the breakdown of states or government.[22] Deutsch states, ". . . we may be able to identify political decision systems that are equipped with adequate facilities for the collection of external and internal information as well as for its transmission to the point of decision-making. . . ."[23] The concept of communications overload then becomes a key to understanding and predicting the rise and fall of both totalitarian and democratic regimes.

Political Development and Political Theory

Another important theoretical problem with which communications systems have great significance is political and economic developmental theory. Many scholars have stated that mass communication has a mysterious positive impact upon the modernization of traditional societies. Daniel Lerner comes closest to assessing the importance of mass communication and its relation to societal modernization. He states:

> The media teach new desires and new satisfactions. They depict situations in which the "good things" of life — of which most Middle Easterners never dreamed before — are taken for granted. They portray roles in which these richer lives are lived, and provide clues as to how these roles can be enacted by others.[24]

In similar assessment, Matthews and Prothro comment on the modernization effect of the mass media on southern Negroes. They state:

> Exposure to the mass media increases both political motivation and and political unmotivated activity in politics. These two empirical findings suggest that mass communications are contributing to the modernization of the South. . . .[25]

While the comparison of the South with traditional Middle Eastern society is rather farfetched, the basic point is sound and meaningful — mass communications tend to modernize communities and individuals simply by familiarizing them with the world in which they live.

Other scholars see the pattern of communications within the society as a basic means to differentiate society. Daniel Lerner explores this line of reasoning and argues that in a traditional society there is little information outflow or feedback; the masses depend upon the village wisemen for all their information about the outside world.[26] In a transitional society there are usually one or two means of mass communication available to the general public with the distribution tending to be somewhat limited. However, in the modern society, there is a differentiated mass communications structure with wide distribution to the masses.

Deutsch sees the process of communication in a society as an indicator of societal cohesion. Thus, one measure of social cohesion is the speed and accuracy with which information is received and transmitted on wide ranges of different topics. To be more specific, Deutsch believes that communications and control theory may lead to new insights about change in all societies, whether underdeveloped or well-developed.[27] Thus the ratio between the internal and external communications is an indicator of the degree of the nation's self-preoccupation, the way it views itself as a member of the world community. Viewing this ratio over time will reveal some data about changes within a given country.

James V. Toscano applied a Deutsch-derived model to examine the Wilmington, Delaware, region and the cohesiveness of the counties surrounding Wilmington.[28] He used transaction flows as measures of political integration. His findings indicated that most of the counties were well integrated with Wilmington but that one was essentially divorced from the other communities. Of course, one would have to follow up this finding to find out why this situation occurred. However, communications systems do offer an incisive look into the workings of political systems, whether at the county level or at the national level.

Lucian Pye suggests that the development of the mass media can be linked with the interests and demands of the citizenry, with the challenge of new ideas and values, and with all the problems that underlie the general problems of building political consensus. The need for political agreement on the goals and values of a society is especially pressing in a developing country, where tribal loyalties and family loyalties take precedence over nation identification. It is in nation building that Pye sees an impact for communications. "The two most fundamental problems in political modernization are those of changing attitudes and reducing the gap between the ruling elite and less modernized masses."[29]

For David McClelland the achievement motivation is crucial to both political and economic development.[30] He suggests that certain types of media content help to raise achievement motivation and help to develop a consensus supporting it. He studied children in different countries that represented all levels of economic development and he noted that one of the largest gaps related to the attitudes toward achievement and receptivity to change. Obviously, those children with the best attitudes came from countries that were well developed. Part of the nation building then is inculcating correct attitudes toward change in the children. Gabriel Almond and Sidney Verba in their five-nation study of culture examined peoples in societies of differing economic and political development.[31] They found that attitudes toward government, trust in government, and ability of government to meaningfully change a citizen's world were quite different for the five countries. They suggested that the building of a strong participatory, democratic government depended upon socializing citizens to participate in government and to view government as a major means of change. They found that Americans were most interested, participated more, and viewed government with more positive feeling than any of the other countries (Britain, Germany, Mexico, and Italy were the other nations). We can conclude that communications systems have a vital role to play in both economic and political development.

Wilbur Schramm sees all social change accompanied by tension and indicates that the flow of information helps to relieve tension.[32] It acts as a temperature control agent, raising the temperature by raising expectation and reducing the temperature by providing explanations. He sees three major roles of the media: (1) the watchman role to scan the world and report back; (2) the police role to set the policy agenda to be discussed by the government or sometimes to decide policy; and finally (3) the teacher role to socialize the new member of the country and to show all citizens new skills, values, and new ways to do and think about things.

Deane E. Neubauer notes the strong relationship between literacy and other measures of development and media usage. The strong relationship indicates that well-distributed and well-organized media systems increased the likelihood of economic growth, but he points out that it does not necessarily bring about democratic development.[33] Some have suggested that fast economic growth brings about so much dislocation and instability within a given country as to prevent any possibility of developing strong democratic and participatory institutions and processes. In fact, the experiences of many developing countries suggest that economic growth takes place most rapidly under authoritarian regimes. Certainly, these regimes can easily deny citizens consumer goods so that they can invest heavily in industrialization.

Communication and
Attitude Change

There are two major schools of thought concerning the effects of mass media on people.[34] One is the classical behaviorist theory that suggests man is primarily a responder to stimuli. When stimuli (political messages) are channeled to appropriate response-dispositions within planned reward contexts, the behavior of individuals can be manipulated, modified, induced, eliminated, or changed directly and immediately almost at the will of those projecting the messages. Consequently, the greater the number of rewarding messages a voter receives on behalf of one candidate, the more likely he is to vote for that candidate — even in the event that he was originally committed to another candidate.

The second school is the phenomenological or functional school which suggests that there are many important influences other than exposure to the mass communication message, which influences the voter to choose one candidate rather than another. These influences stem more from the totality of conditions of life that surround the voter both before and during a political campaign than from the individual messages he is exposed to during the campaign. Thus, the functional school investigates the effect of media on the total environment and, specifically, the more remote factors affecting the candidate selection.

Effects on the
Political Environment

According to Harold Mendelsohn and Irving Crespi, the media have altered the processes of nominating candidates at party conventions.[35] This is especially true for presidential races, but it is also true for gubernatorial, senatorial, and local political nominations. The media give the potential candidate (especially one with a considerable amount of money) an opportunity to bypass the political organizations and appeal directly to the voters. The recruitment process is separated from the smoke-filled rooms of the political bosses but still is limited to those who either have strong party backing or those who have lots of money. Milton Shapp in Pennsylvania is just one example of a rich man interested in politics who was able to win his party's nomination with very little party backing. In the presidential nomination process, we see the media (especially the newspaper and television commentators) deciding who is the front-runner and who is to be disregarded as a serious candidate. They determine which candidate will get most of the attention and which candidate will be ignored. Television and newspaper coverage is an important part of a candidate's media campaign.

Second, the media have altered the campaigning process. The emphasis today is on media experts, image makers, television slogan producers, poll-takers — the total communications effort. The overall goal is to indicate that the candidate would make a good governor, senator, or president, that he knows what is bothering the voters, and that the messages presented over the electronic media have maximum effect on the electorate.

Also, the electronic media have altered the traditional party structures and party functions. Very few candidates will abandon the party organization, the poll watchers, the last minute "get out the vote" campaign, but the media-oriented candidate wants to talk directly to the 95 percent of the electorate that is unaffiliated with a formal party organization. The candidates still attend the rallies and kiss the babies; however, the traditional reliance on party bosses and party organization is usually abandoned. Most of the effort is directed at talking to the voters via the electronic media.

Finally, the media have helped to encourage the questioning of the traditional ways of choosing and electing candidates, helping to usher in the new politics and the acceptance of reform and social change. The reform and new politics is often less effective and less able to implement change than some of the old party machines. However, the media-politics opened up the recruitment, nomination, and election process in such a complete way as to force significant changes in the way Americans go about the business of politics.

A Catalogue of Media Effects
on Attitude Change

Below are some of the effects, extracted from both laboratory and field experiments, which scholars have found the media have on individual attitudes. They are:

1. Actual conversion is small, but there is considerable modifying, crystallization, and reinforcement effect.

2. When the media contribute to attitude change, the mediating factors will be found ineffective and the effect of the media will be direct, or the mediating factors, which normally reinforce, will themselves contribute to change.

3. Sources regarded highly tend to be more effective since they are deemed very credible by the citizens.

4. The mass media themselves are regarded with awe by the public and tend to confer status on people using them.

5. The sleeper effect — if a message is repeated often enough over time, people will tend to forget the sources and remember the message. Carried to its extreme, this is the "Big Lie" technique popularized by the Nazis.

6. The main effects of the media involve reinforcement, neutralization, crystallization, or activation of attitudes. The purpose of persuasion is not to change the attitudes of the committed but to shift the perception of voters with low involvement. Important mediating factors in the conversion process are the intelligence of the listeners, their ego-involvement, and the cross-pressures and the opinion leadership to which they are subjected.

7. Formal personal appeal is more effective than radio. The television and movie films fall somewhere in the middle.

8. Two-sided presentation is always more effective than one-sided. Messages with an explicit conclusion are better than those in which the audience is allowed to form its own conclusion.

9. Repetition over time, with innovative variations, increases the effectiveness of the communication.

10. Persuasive communications that appear to encompass the majority view are always more effective unless the minority is very small and very dedicated.

Theories of
Attitude Change

There are at least five different perspectives from which one can view attitude change. The message has to gain the attention of the listener; the listener has to understand the communication; he must yield to the suggestion for change contained in the message; he should retain the attitude change; and, finally, his behavior must reflect the attitude change. The behavior dimension is, of course, the crucial one. There are a few classic examples concerning the relationship of the attitude and the behavior. One famous experiment was attempted after World War II in which the researcher wrote to motels across the country asking whether the owners would accept a Chinese couple for one-night stays during a trip across the country. A large percentage of the motel owners said they would refuse the couple and indicated they would not serve nonwhite persons. However, when the researcher accompanied the Chinese couple on the actual trip, they were never refused by any of the motel owners.

Leon Festinger investigated attitude change and behavior and found conflicting studies.[36] He concluded that even when opinions are changed because of strong messages, they are quite unstable and will disappear unless some environmental change can support it. Thus, behavior modification starts with attitude change but is a much longer process involving groups and families and emphasizing the total attitudinal environment.

Individual Difference Theory

This theory suggests that humans vary greatly in psychological makeup and that they come from different learning environments. Thus, the personality variables were the basis for viewing messages or events. The audience selectively perceives communications on the basis of its different personality makeups. Therefore, the effect of the media is not uniform but varies greatly from person to person.

The individual difference theory[37] is related closely to the psychodynamic model of persuasion. This model suggests that the key to persuasion lies in modifying the internal psychological structure of the individual so that the psychodynamic relationship can operate according to the wishes of the persuader. Thus, many appeals are directed to small groups of people; for example, ethnic, racial, or social groups, which may consist of individuals with similar psychological traits.

The importance of groups or information leaders has been noted continuously by researchers. The need to conform to the group and the need to defer to the leader of the group are common situations in the persuasion process. Conformity is more likely among those with average rather than high or low acceptance in the group. Also, pressure to conform is greater within a small group than a large group. Other important variables are frequency of contact and degree of mutual liking.

Closely related to the above discussion is the two-step flow of information posited by Elihu Katz and Paul Lazarsfeld.[38] This flow suggests that all information that comes from the media goes first to opinion leaders and then to the masses. Since everyone is a part of some social, work, or family group, everyone is having media messages interpreted for him. Katz and Lazarsfeld suggested the two-step flow as a possible reason for the apparent noninfluence of the media during the political campaigns they studied.[39] Many have attacked the two-step flow as being too simplified or unrealistic. It may be that many people really do not have an opinion leader or that he is simply uninformed on many subjects. Also, research has shown in studies of the process of innovation that the flow of information is never so simple as a two- or even three-step process. Depending on what messages are being sent, there may be quite a few steps in the process, that is, opinion leaders may have opinion leaders. Sometimes individuals may have more than one opinion leader and their leaders may disagree on a given issue. All of this suggests that the two-step flow is a highly simplified version of information flow and possibly a very inaccurate one for the information flow concerning politics.

Social Categories Theory and the Sociocultural Model

The social categories theory suggests that people who have a number of similar characteristics will have parallel communications perceptions and folkways. They will tend to perceive messages from the media in similar ways; their individual perceptual screens will react in the same manner to communications.

DeFleur, in his review of theories of attitude change, notes that the social categories theory and especially the sociocultural model is used in most advertising campaigns. He comments, "Existing theories of persuasion (and of adoption of innovation) see group or interactional phenomena largely in terms of obstacles to persuasion, and not in terms of possible tools to be used in achieving desired affects."[40] Group norms are extremely important in defining and modifying the behavior of individuals, as Muzafer Sherif has shown in many laboratory experiments.

Margaret Mead has described societies having rigid and deeply institutional cultures as providing the individual with ready-made reality against which one interprets new phenomena. The organization man,[41] the other-directed man,[42] and man escaping from freedom[43] are themes present in a few outstanding commentaries on modern man. They all point to man's need for direction and his longing to be a part of the group, to conform and partake of the group's activities. As figure 15 suggests, new definitions can be given the sociocultural processes in groups utilizing the mass media.

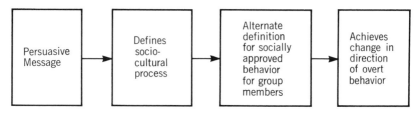

SOURCE: From the book *Theories of Mass Communication* by Melvin L. DeFleur, p. 123. Copyright © 1966 and 1970 by David McKay Co. Inc. Published by the David McKay Co. Inc. Used with permission of the publishers.

Figure 15
Socio-Cultural Model

The way the sociocultural model works is fairly straightforward. Let us take cigarette advertising, for example. The message usually shows how manly, attractive, and intelligent the men or women are who smoke. Indirectly, the advertisement is suggesting that the smoking of cigarettes helped these smart, attractive people get that way. It also suggests that those who do not smoke are somehow deviants, antisocial, or undesirable. The overall reward is social approval by one's peers. Part of the success of these advertisements is suggested by the belief of many children that it is "grown up" to smoke.

This group-related message, of course, negates the effect to the two-step flow of information and the influence of the opinion leader since it is, in effect, using him. How does it relate directly to political slogans? The trend recently has been the use of group-related advertisement — blacks in a black area, Jews in a Jewish area, farmers in a farm area. The group or opinion leader can be an important additional force in changing attitudes and changing subsequent behavior. If communications can penetrate the group, then the all-important environment is undergoing change, resulting in a high probability of both changed attitude and changed behavior.

Theory of
Cognitive Dissonance

Leon Festinger's theory of cognitive dissonance predicts that inconsistencies between cognitive elements of an attitude will not be tolerated by the individual if the consistency is above a certain magnitude.[44] Cognition is any knowledge, opinion, or belief about the environment, about one's self, or about one's behavior.[45] Dissonance is a relationship with two positions being in disagreement when one is the opposite of the other.

For example, one can smoke cigarettes and still think they cause cancer. When this dissonance becomes great (Cancer Society warnings, doctors' or family warnings), there is great pressure to reduce the dissonance by rationalizing the information about cancer or by attempting to quit smoking. The sources of dissonance can be varied: exposure to new information, realization of logical inconsistency, cultural values, or conflicting past experiences.

Another example concerns the application of dissonance theory to voting behavior. During the 1968 presidential election campaign, there were many strong Democrats who did not like Hubert Humphrey. A citizen faced with this dilemma might resolve his problem in a number of ways: he could rationalize a vote for Humphrey by emphasizing Humphrey's partisan qualities, ignoring the personal qualities or positions he found distasteful; he could decide not to vote; or he could vote for an opposing candidate either from the major party or one of the minor third-party's candidates on the ballot. Some evidence does suggest that dissonance produces partisan irregularity and voting instability. After examining the effect of conflicts among partisan attitudes, a form of dissonance, Angus Campbell states that:

Not only does the degree of attitude consistency affect the time of the individual's vote decision; it affects other aspects of behavior as well. The person who experiences some degree of conflict tends to cast his vote for President with substantially less enthusiasm; he is much more prone to split his ticket in voting for other offices, and he is somewhat less likely to vote at all than the person whose partisan attitudes are entirely consistent.[46]

Play Theory of
Mass Communications

The play theory suggests that media exposure does not demand intense or even a moderate ego involvement. One becomes absorbed in the media, losing all sense of self. William Stephenson suggests that communication-pleasure is a direct consequence of personal experience with the nonserious, nonwork communication situation.[47] The nonserious, nonwork environment of the media is the norm. He says:

Playing is pretending, a stepping outside the world of duty and responsibility. Play is an interlude in the day. It is not ordinary or real. It is voluntary and not a task or moral duty. It is in some sense disinterest, providing a temporary satisfaction. It is the thesis of this book that at its best mass communications allows people to become absorbed in subjective play.[48]

The effect television has on politics is to allow the electorate to play vicariously at the game of politics. From the television experience in particular, many voters derive an actual vicarious sense of participation in the political process. Thus, many commentators have observed that the masses of citizenry feel a direct part of civil rights protest, urban riots, and wars in foreign lands, even though they could not possibly be a physical part of the action. One might speculate that the seeming increase in willingness to protest or influence policy directly via street demonstrations, sit-ins, or confrontations with policy makers is a direct result of this communication-induced sense of vicarious participation.

The play theory suggests that individuals view the mass media in terms of nonserious, noninvolving messages. If we extend this to the political campaign situation, we see a relatively serious, sometimes thought-provoking, work-related atmosphere. People are told they should become informed; they should listen to the candidates' positions; they should decide rationally how to vote — all of which is serious and hard work. In such situations, especially when citizens are presented with a great overload of messages (many political advertisements are usually programmed most heavily in a small time period), they are likely to "tune out" and ignore the messages. Perhaps this is one of the reasons for the finding that few attitudes are really changed by the mass media. Certainly it is unrealistic to expect that the citizenry would rationally listen to the bombardment of communications and sift through all the contrasting messages to make a decision.

Two theories relate to the actual voting decision. The first is the cross-pressure hypothesis, which indicates how voters are likely to react given conflicting pressures, sometimes inspired by the mass media. The second is the Downsian theory of voting which applies the rational man model of economics to the voting situation.[49]

Cross-Pressure
Hypothesis

Psychological tensions which result from the holding of conflicting attitudes are only one form of cross-pressure to which the voter might be subjected. In advancing the cross-pressure hypothesis, Lazarsfeld, Berelson, and Gaudet distinguish three types of cross pressures: (1) conflicting evaluations of political objects; (2) conflicts arising from tensions between the various social statuses a person might occupy; and (3) conflicts arising from the primary groups of which the individual voter is a member.[50] Cross-pressures would also arise in the event of cross-pressures between these types of influence, for example, as would be the case if primary and secondary group pressures on the vote ran in the opposite directions. The effect of social and primary group cross-pressures on voting regularity is the same as attitudinal conflict. According to Lazarsfeld and Berelson:

While theory regarding these cross pressures is not yet particularly advanced, an impressive series of empirical results has been accumulated over the last fifteen years of research. An individual who is characterized by any type of cross pressure is likely to change his mind in the course of the campaign, to make up his mind late, and occasionally, to leave the field and not to vote at all.[51]

Downs' Rationalist Theory
of Voting

In Downs' theory, a rational citizen decides whether to vote or not on the basis of four factors: (1) the expected utility incomes which would attend various outcomes; (2) the probability of having an impact on the outcome of the election; (3) the cost of voting in terms of the time and expense it would take to go to the polls, the cost of the information needed to reach a decision, and the cost of the anguish associated with arriving at a choice; and (4) the extent to which he associates voting with the maintenance of democracy.[52] To these factors might be added the social reward which society metes out for voting or the social costs which a citizen might incur if his voting would anger or estrange a member of his family, a friend, a co-worker, or an employer.

Downs' theory suggests that "issues do count" and, moreover, citizens vote on a rational basis just as citizens purchase economic goods based upon cost of the good, desirability of them to the citizens, and the citizens' resources. There are a number of testable propositions that one can derive from the rational man model of voting behavior.[53]

The first proposition is that the rational voter will seek information on those issues which are salient to him. His perceptual screen will eliminate information on many unimportant issues and focus on information about the important ones.

The second proposition is that the rational voter as a voter will attempt to maximize his policy/issue preferences through his choice of candidates or parties contesting an election. Both the candidates and parties must offer some choice. If they do not, the rational voter can vote for either if they agree with his preferences or abstain (become alientated) if they disagree.

Third, rational voters, each attempting to maximize his policy preferences through the casting of his ballot and campaigning, will collectively influence and perhaps determine the policy decisions of the men elected to run the government. That is, those elected will perceive clearly the policy mandate given them by the voters and act on it through legislation and policy implementation.

Finally, the actions and policies of an incumbent government or legislator will be directed at maintaining his support to continue his success in the next election.

In an attempt to test the rational model, David M. Kovenock, Philip L. Beardsley, and James W. Prothro investigated status, party, ideology, issues, and candidate choice in the 1968 presidential election.[54] They use a recursive (one-way causation) model and employ five general variables: candidate choice (the dependent variable); issue proximity; partisan proximity, proximity on liberal-conservatism, and social status. Their findings indicate that issues played a central, even causal, role in determining candidate choice in 1968. Specifically they found that issue voting (the rational-choice voting) and party identification are of equal importance in explaining votes for and against Nixon and Humphrey and that the issue variable is vastly more important than the party variable in explaining the voters' decision for or against Wallace.[55] They also attempt to test the causal role of public opinion in candidate choice.

The increasing importance of issue-rational voting was discussed at length in chapter 3. The important point is that economic behavior models can be applied to voting behavior and governmental policy making if rationality is assumed. One of the problems with this model is that it assumes perfect information, and while voters are becoming more informed, they still are relatively uninformed about many candidates and issues.

The public choice literature discussed in chapter 1 on linkages applies the rational man model directly to public decision making. While one still has the indivisibilities problem, since he can work for only one candidate, one's vote based on his attitude preferences can be measured and predicted. The skill with which Gallup and Harris predict the vote on the basis of attitudes indicates that public opinion can be used to solve the indivisibilities problem and to predict the marginal utility of public goods as the marginal utility of private sector goods are now predicted.

Model of Voting Influence

Figure 16 indicates both the proximate and distant influences on voters' attitudes. Figure 17 indicates that there are three kinds of voters: the early deciders, approximately 65 percent of the elec-

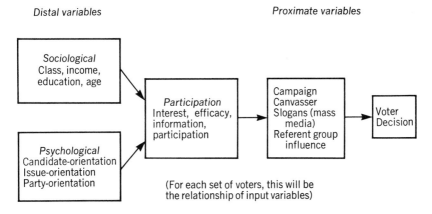

Figure 16
Voter Influence Model

torate; the late deciders, about 20 percent of the electorate; and the last-minute deciders, almost 15 percent of the voters.[56] The three different sets of voters are influenced in different ways by the social and psychological variables listed. This is an important point, one reiterated by many campaign specialists who wage separate campaigns for the three categories of voters and even break the categories down further into racial, ethnic, and religious groups.

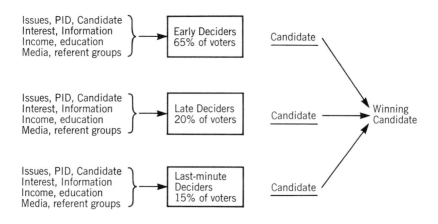

Figure 17
Models of Voter Decisions

Conclusions

The theories of media effect were discussed on three levels of analysis. The first was the societal level in which we examined the effect of the electronic age on society itself. McLuhan suggests that television and other electronic media, especially cable television, are changing the way people think about society and the way they think about politics. Second, we looked at the impact of the media on political theory and its special importance to developing countries.

Finally, we studied the effects the media have on changing attitudes and behavior related to those activities. Voting studies have generally found that few voters have their minds changed by the media. Instead, opinion leaders through a two-step flow of information seem to be responsible for the attitude change that occurs. However, laboratory experiments have shown that significant attitude change can be achieved through persuasive messages. One possible path out of the conflicting findings is the sociocultural model of persuasion that actually uses the opinion leaders and group norms to make the message more persuasive and possibly change the attitudinal environment to the extent that the change becomes permanent and results in different behavior. Also discussed were some models of voting behavior that pinpoint the groups of voters most likely to change.

NOTES

1. Marshall H. McLuhan, *Understanding Media: The Extensions of Man* (New York: McGraw-Hill, 1964).

2. Karl W. Deutsch, *The Nerves of Government* (New York: Free Press of Glencoe, 1966). See also his *Nationalism and Social Communication* (Cambridge, Mass.: The MIT Press, 1966).

3. Lucian W. Pye, ed., *Communications and Political Development* (Princeton, N.J.: Princeton University Press, 1963).

4. Daniel Lerner, *The Passing of Traditional Society: Modernizing the Middle East* (New York: Free Press of Glencoe, 1958).

5. McLuhan, *Understanding Media*, pp. 46-47.

6. Marshall H. McLuhan and Quentin Fiore, *The Medium is the Massage* (New York: Random House, 1967), p. 100. For a number of insights on the effects of the electronic media on war and peace see their *War and Peace in the Global Village* (New York: McGraw-Hill, 1968), especially "Education as War," pp. 148-74. On page 99, McLuhan states, "Every new technology necessitates a war."

7. Ibid., p. 24.

8. Jack Newfield, *The Village Voice*, October 1970.

9. McLuhan and Fiore, *Medium is the Massage*, p. 72.

10. McLuhan, *Understanding Media*, pp. 299-300.

11. Ibid., p. 301.

12. Ibid., p. 114.

13. A. D. Whitehead, cited in McLuhan and Fiore, *Medium is the Massage*, p. 78.

14. Norbert Weiner, *The Human Use of Human Beings: Cybernetics and Society* (Boston, Mass.: Houghton Mifflin, 1950), p. 9. See also his *Cybernetics: Or Control and Communication in Animal and the Machine* (New York: Technology Press, Wiley, 1948). In *The Nerves of Government*, Deutsch offers an extended investigation into cybernetics, pp. 74-140. See especially pp. 110-26.

15. Deutsch, *Nerves of Government*. See also his "Communication and the Political System," in *The Integration of Political Communities* ed. Philip F. Jacobs and James V. Toscano (Philadelphia, Pa.: Lippincott, 1964). On p. 49 he states, "by viewing nations as communications systems, one can generate verifiable evidence to examine both descriptive and qualitative assertions about nationalism, about sovereignty, and about the merger of states."

16. Deutsch, *Nerves of Government*, p. 125.

17. Karl W. Deutsch, "Social Mobilization and Political Development," *American Political Science Review* 55 (September 1961): 493-514.

18. Deutsch, *Nerves of Government*, p. 126. Used by permission of the publisher.

19. Ibid., p. 146.

20. Ibid., p. 147.

21. Ibid., p. 151.

22. Ibid., p. 162.

23. Ibid., p. 161.

24. Lerner, *Passing of Traditional Society*, p. 400. Used by permission of the publisher.

25. Donald R. Matthews and James W. Prothro, *Negroes and the New Southern Politics* (New York: Harcourt Brace Jovanovich, 1966), p. 261.

26. Lerner, *Passing of Traditional Society*, p. 412.

27. Deutsch, *Nerves of Government*.

28. James V. Toscano, "Transaction Flow Analysis in Metropolitan Areas," in Jacobs and Toscano, *Integration of Political Communities*, pp. 109-14.

29. Pye, *Communications and Political Development*, p. 11.

30. David C. McClelland, *The Achieving Society* (Princeton, N.J.: Princeton University Press, 1961).

31. Gabriel Almond and Sidney Verba, *The Civic Culture* (Princeton, N.J.: Princeton University Press, 1963). See also Almond and G. Bingham Powell, *An Analytic Study of Comparative Politics* (Boston, Mass.: Little, Brown, 1966).

32. Wilbur L. Schramm, *Mass Media and National Development* (Stanford, Calif.: Stanford University Press, 1964), p. 37.

33. Deane E. Neubauer, "Some Conditions of Democracy," *American Political Science Review* 41 (December 1967): 1002-9.

34. The attitude change literature is a vast one and has been examined in some depth in previous chapters, especially chapter 3. There are a number of central books to which the reader can refer. See Chester I. Insko, *Theories of Attitude Change* (New York: Appleton-Century-Crofts, 1967); Philip G. Zimbardo and Ebbe B. Ebbesen, *Influencing Attitudes and Changing Behavior* (Reading, Mass.: Addison-Wesley, 1970); John W. Bowers and Donovan J. Ochs, *The Rhetoric of Agitation and Control* (Reading, Mass.: Addison-Wesley, 1971); Milton J. Rosenberg et al., *Attitude Organization and Change* (New Haven, Conn.: Yale University Press, 1960); Carl I. Hovland, Irving L. Janis, and Harold H. Kelley, *Communication and Persuasion* (New Haven, Conn.: Yale University Press, 1953); Carl I. Hovland and Irving L. Janis, eds., *Personality and Persuasibility* (New Haven, Conn.: Yale University Press, 1959); and the classic by Harold D. Lasswell, ed., *The Language of Politics* (New York: George W. Stewart, 1949).

35. Harold Mendelsohn and Irving Crespi, *Polls, Television, and the New Politics* (Scranton, Pa.: Chandler, 1970), p. 297.

36. Leon Festinger, "Behavioral Support for Opinion Change," in *Dimensions of Communications*, ed. Lee Richardson (New York: Appleton-Century-Crofts, 1969), p. 114.

37. Melvin L. DeFleur, *Theories of Mass Communication* (New York: McKay, 1966), p. 120.

38. Elihu Katz and Paul Lazarsfeld, *Personal Influence*, 2d. ed. (New York: Free Press of Glencoe, 1964), p. 127.

39. Ibid., p. 129.

40. DeFleur, *Theories of Mass Communication*, p. 133.

41. William H. Whyte, Jr., *The Organization Man* (Garden City, N.Y.: Doubleday, 1957).

42. David Riesman, *The Lonely Crowd: A Study of the Changing American Character* (New York: Anchor, 1953).

43. Erich Fromm, *Escape from Freedom* (New York: Holt, Rinehart and Winston, 1941).

44. Leon Festinger, *A Theory of Cognitive Dissonance* (Stanford, Calif.: Stanford University Press, 1967).

45. Ibid.

46. Angus Campbell et al., *The American Voter: An Abridgement* (New York: Wiley, 1964), p. 46.

47. William Stephenson, *The Play Theory of Mass Communication* (Chicago, Ill.: University of Chicago Press, 1967), p. 46.

48. Ibid.

49. Anthony Downs, *An Economic Theory of Democracy* (New York: Harper and Row, 1957). See especially chapter 3 and chapter 14.

50. Paul F. Lazarsfeld, Bernard Berelson, and Hazel Gaudet, *The People's Choice*, 3rd ed. (New York: Columbia University Press, 1968).

51. Bernard Berelson, Paul F. Lazarsfeld, and William N. McPhee, *Voting* (Chicago, Ill.: University of Chicago Press, 1954), p. 284.

52. Downs, *Economic Theory of Democracy*.

53. Downs outlines a simple model of rational voting behavior. He adopts the following notation:

U — Utility or benefits received from the government during some period of time
A — The incumbent party
B — The opposition party
t — A time period
E — Expected value

The rational voter, according to Downs, compares the benefits he expects to receive from party A, $E(U^A{}_{t+1})$, with those he expects to get from party B, $E(U^B{}_{t+1})$. This comparison is called the expected party differential *(EPD)*:

$$EPD = E(U^A{}_{t+1}) - E(U^B{}_{t+1})$$

If the *EPD* is positive, i.e., if $E(U^A{}_{t+1})$, is greater than $E(U^B{}_{t+1})$, then he votes for party A's candidates; if it is negative, i.e., $E(U^A{}_{t+1})$ is less than $E(U^B{}_{t+1})$, he votes for party B; and if it is zero he abstains from voting. In short, the voter simply picks the party which offers him the most.

54. David M. Kovenock, Philip L. Beardsley, and James W. Prothro, "Status, Party, Ideology, Issues and Candidate Choice: A Preliminary Theory-Relevant Analysis of the 1968 Presidential Election" (Paper prepared for the International Political Science Association, Munich, Germany, August, 1970).

55. Ibid., p. 23.

56. Campbell et al., *The American Voter*, p. 42.

8　The Mass Media and Political Change: An Empirical Test

The Problem

The effect of the mass media on the mass audience has been a subject of controversy since the widespread distribution of radio, television, and newspapers. In the political sphere, the use of mass media persuasion techniques has become a central part of a candidate's campaign. Many studies have investigated the influence of the media ranging from the sophisticated studies of Carl Hovland and his associates to the impact analysis of advertising firms testing the effectiveness of their commercials. In fact, the popular cliché of the communications industry is Marshall McLuhan's "the medium is the massage."

Propaganda has always been an important consideration in politics. In international relations, the "war of words" is an important part of foreign policy and military strategy. On every important issue, the government uses all its information outlets to encourage support for governmental policies. Public relations people in politics attribute political success to their skillful use of the mass media.[1] Stanley Kelley's in-depth analysis of the impact of propaganda on politics presents some meaningful case studies on the possible impact of public relations in political campaigns.[2] One conclusion to draw from Kelley's work is that skillful use of the mass media can be the key to success in a given campaign. Yet, studies such as *Voting* and *The People's Choice* conclude that the mass media have little effect on the electorate.[3] In direct contrast, Carl Hovland's studies show that forceful messages can have a strong impact on people's opinions.[4] In an interesting analysis of the 1960 Survey

Research Center's work gauging the effect of the Kennedy-Nixon debates, Philip Converse found that those who had seen the debates were much more likely to change their preference than those who did not see the debates.[5] He concludes that political information can have a strong impact on elections. The effect of mass communications on politics is still a mystery eluding social science discovery.

The Theoretical
Framework

There are two significant theoretical frameworks in which the mass media or communications have importance. The first is the impact of communications on attitude change. This theoretical aspect relates to specific problems within the society — problems of influence, policy implementation, and feedback. The election of political candidates, the government management of information, the impact of reporters on policy, and the general impact of mass communications on decision making in the presidential, legislative, and judicial areas are the relevant areas of inquiry. Much has been written concerning the importance of mass media on policy.[6] While many have researched the power of communications, almost no one has attempted to measure statistically the independent impact of the media on political attitudes and political policy. This virgin area of political science needs a great deal of systematic inquiry.

The second important, and perhaps crucial, theoretical problem with which communication has great import is developmental theory. Again, many scholars have stated that mass communication has a mysterious positive impact upon the modernization of traditional societies. Daniel Lerner comes closest to assessing the importance of mass communication and its relation to societal modernization.

He suggests that the media reorient desires and new satisfactions of citizens.[7] They depict situations in which the "good things" of life — of which most Middle Easterners never dreamed before — are taken for granted. They portray roles in which these richer lives are lived and provide clues as to how these roles can be enacted by others. In a similar assessment, Donald Matthews and James W. Prothro comment on the modernization effect of the mass media on southern blacks. They find that exposure to the mass media increases both political motivation and politically unmotivated activity in politics.[8] These two empirical findings suggest that mass communications are contributing to the modernization of the South. Again, new roles and opportunities suggested by the media change the political and social environment of both the black and white people of the developing South. While the comparison of the South with traditional Middle Eastern society is rather farfetched, the basic point is sound and meaningful — mass communications tend to modernize communities and individuals simply by familiarizing them with the world in which they live.

Others scholars see the pattern of communications within the society as a basic means to differentiate society. Lucian Pye explores this line of reasoning and argues that in a traditional society there is little information outflow or feedback; the masses depend on village wisemen for all their information about the outside world.[9] In a traditional society there are usually one or two means of mass communication available to the general public with the distribution tending to be somewhat limited. However, in the modern society, there is a differentiated mass communications structure with wide distribution to the masses. Deutsch sees the process of communication in a society as an indicator of societal cohesion. Thus, one measure of social cohesion is the speed and accuracy with which information is received and transmitted on wide ranges of different topics.[10]

Discovering the impact of mass communications has great importance to modernization theory. Its practical applications are quite exciting, for here is a tool that is available for all and can be used by underdeveloped countries; a tool that can reflect the degree of modernization of the total community, the social cohesion of the community, and many other aspects of life in that community. Indeed developmental theory may some day be based entirely on communication theory.[11]

Hypothesis

The hypothesis to be tested is that the mass media significantly affects political attitudes and participation. The null hypothesis is that the mass media have no significant effect on political attitudes and participation. Alternative hypotheses would say that education, mobility, and/or income account for political attitudes and participation.

Control
Variables

This study will control for education, income, and geographic mobility.

Definitions

1. Mass media—newspapers, television, radio, magazines. This measure is operationalized from 0 to 4, depending on the total number of media used by the respondent.
2. Political attitude—feelings about the political process. All the attitude measures are indexes comprised of answers on several questions. For a complete description, see Matthews and Prothro, *Negroes and the New Southern Politics*, "Scales and Indexes," pp. 523-29.
3. Change—a significant (statistically) increase or decrease in political attitudes.

Data

The data used here are from the southwide sample of southern voters directed by Matthews and Prothro in their survey.

The Variables
Analyzed

While the analytic procedure of going down from elementary to more sophisticated statistical analysis is somewhat pedantic, it is excellent pedagogically. This is especially true in analyzing such a difficult area as the mass media effect on political attitudes. Therefore, we hope to be rewarded with a thorough, understandable explanation of the findings.

A more difficult but still solvable problem is the assumption of interval scale for the correlation and regression analysis. While the ordinal scale is probably more appropriate, a number of the indexes approach interval scale. Since this is so and since statisticians such as Hubert Blalock[12] argue that if one approaches interval scale, one should use it, we feel justified in utilizing both Pearson's r and regression. The argument Blalock and others make essentially is that if one assumes ordinal scale with interval variables, one imposes an ordinal distribution on the variable that may affect the findings significantly. Likewise, if one assumes interval scale on ordinal variables, a similar problem develops. Since we believe the variables approximate interval scale, we feel justified in assuming interval scale and using some more powerful statistics for analysis.

In their analysis, Matthews and Prothro show that exposure to the mass media favorably affects political participation, political interest, political information, sense of civic competence, and attitudes toward change. They conclude that exposure to the mass media increases political motivation and politically unmotivated activity (such as feelings of civic competence).[13]

While their data support most of the conclusions and speculations they make, there are at least three levels of statistical analysis they failed to utilize: (1) chi-square analysis to see the statistical significance of the variable comparisons; (2) correlation analysis to see the direction of the relationship; and (3) regression analysis to measure the explanatory power of the variables. If one is going to talk about the effect of communications on social change or modernization theory, then such statistical analysis is relevant and necessary. It is only through such systematic inquiry that the real impact and importance of mass communications can be discovered.

In this secondary analysis of the southwide black data, we will explore the significant chi-square relations, the *Pearson r* correlations, and the explanatory power of the control variables (R^2) on the significant political variables. We have controlled for geographic mobility, income, and education. Geographic mobility was chosen rather than region-subregion or urban-rural because travel has much more influence on attitudes than place or area residence. One can live in an urban or peripheral South area and still be extremely parochial; it is much more difficult to remain so when one travels extensively.

In order to facilitate discussion and preclude the presentation of too many individual relationships, we will present only the significant relationships, controlling for income, education, and geographic mobility. The answers to the different political questions can be found in the discussion. For example, when we present the significant chi-squares between exposure to the mass media and other variables, we will indicate what is meant by low, medium, or high mobility, but we will not present the actual table from which the relationship is taken. Such a presentation would take too much space and be too disparate for the trend analysis desired.

The first impression one gets from table 8-1 is that the greatest number and the most significant relationships occur within the medium mobility category, which has the largest number of respondents ($N = 445$). One can conclude that, in this table, the impact of the mass media is greatest for the greatest number of southern blacks.

Table 8-1

A comparison between blacks' exposure to the mass media and selected variables, controlling for geographic mobility.

Low Mobility (within state)
($N = 93$)

Exposure to the mass media
with political interest .... p > .05 < .10
with psychological forces .... p > .05 < .10

Medium Mobility   (outside South, within
($N = 445$)   continental United States)

Exposure to the mass media
with political interest .... p < .001
with attitude toward change .... p < .01
with psychological forces .... p < .01
with civic competence .... p < .02
with political information .... p < .02
with political participation .... p < .05
with community rating today .... p < .05
with community rating in 5 years .... p > .05 < .10

High Mobility   (outside continental
($N = 76$)   United States)

Exposure to the mass media
with community rating today .... p < .05
with community rating in 5 years .... p > .05 < .10
with psychological forces .... p > .05 < .10

The most significant chi-square for the medium mobility group is exposure to the mass media with political interest ($p < .001$). The exposure to the mass media variables varies from zero (no regular exposure to any medium) to four (regular exposure to newspapers, magazines, radio, and television); the political interest variable varies from zero (no interest) to two (a great deal of interest). This strong relationship is consistent with the Matthews and Prothro findings concerning the independent effect of the media on political interest.[14] Mass communications are also important to political interest, though not statistically significant, in the low mobility category.

Other significant chi-squares in the medium mobility category are attitude toward change (p < .01), psychological forces (p < .01), political information (p < .02), and sense of civic competence (p < .02). The attitude toward change variable ranges from one (most favorable) to six (most unfavorable); the psychological forces variable is a composite of eight psychological factors, the weighting varying from zero (no psychological influences associated with participation) to thirteen (all eight factors relating to participation); the political information variable relates to a score of correct answers to seven political information questions (a high score indicates the most information); and the civic competence index relates to three hypothetical "take action" questions, the scores ranging from zero (no action in all three situations) to three (direct action every time).

Both political participation (p < .05) and community rating today (p < .05) are significantly associated to mass communications. The political participation variable is a scale ranging from one (no political activity) to five (talking, voting, campaigning, and holding office) while the community rating today variable varies from one (worst possible race relations) to ten (ideal race relations). The other important association is community rating in five years (p > .05 < .10) which ranges from one to ten exactly as community rating today.

In each mobility category, psychological forces are important. We can conclude that as the individual feels more certain about himself (as measured by the eight psychological characteristics), he tends to expose himself more to the mass media regardless of how mobile he is. In this respect, the media have an independent effect on the strength of the blacks' psychological forces.

Other variables which relate to the media are political interest, community rating today, and community rating five years hence. The political interest variable is highly significant for those with medium mobility (p < .001), important for those of low mobility (p > .05 < .10) but has no relationship to blacks with high mobility. Perhaps those blacks with such high mobility are all politically interested. For the great majority of the respondents, however, the mass media have an important relationship to political interest. Since interest in politics increases exposure to the mass media, we can see the importance of mass communications experts in political campaigns. If the voter is more interested, he is more likely to vote as Campbell's findings indicate.[15] How this "new voter" votes becomes a crucial variable in an election, especially a close one.

For those in the medium and high mobility categories, the mass media have an important effect on the community rating today and the community rating in five years. Since the community rating refers to how one feels about his community racial situation in relation to the ideal, we can conclude that the mass media increase blacks' satisfaction with their home situation perhaps because they see just how bad the racial conditions of other areas are.

When one looks at the entire table, only the psychological forces variable is consistently significant, although political interest, community rating today, and community rating in five years is significant for two categories. Nonetheless, the impressive array of statistical significance for many crucial political attitudes is very important. No causality is inferred or intended here; however, these results coupled with the more sophisticated analysis should give us a clear trend of media effect.

The only consistently significant relationship in table 8-2 concerns the political interest variable. In each education category, the significance is $< .01$, which indicates that in only one out of one hundred times would this happen by chance. Again one sees that the media have an independent effect on the politicization of the citizenry. Since the two variables controlled for (education and mobility) are relatively hard to distribute (education requires a long time process and mobility requires money, motivation, and time), perhaps the easiest way to make a society a participatory one is to make the media available to all the people. Lerner discusses the impact of widespread media distribution (primarily radio) in transforming traditional societies such as Turkey and concludes that the radio plays an important part in the spread of new ideas and the breaking of traditional patterns of behavior.[16]

Two other variables which are important in both the medium and high education categories are the psychological forces variable and political participation variable. The significant relationship in the high education category might be due somewhat to its increased range. In order to have a good number of respondents, high school graduates were included in the high education category. Since the average education level of the black in the South is very low, high school graduates can be considered to have high educational achievement.[17] In both categories, blacks psychological forces and their political participation relate significantly to the

Table 8-2

A comparison between blacks' exposure to the mass media and selected variables controlling for education.

Low Education (0–8th grade)
($N = 360$)

Exposure to mass media
with community rating today .... $p < .05$
with political interest .... $p < .01$

Medium Education   (9th – non-high school
($N = 82$)   graduate)

Exposure to mass media
with political interest .... $p < .01$
with psychological forces .... $p < .01$
with group memberships .... $p < .05$
with political participation .... $p < .05$
with community rating in 5 years .... $p > .05 < .10$

High Education   (graduate high school;
($N = 171$)   college training)

Exposure to mass media
with political interest .... $p < .01$
with attitude on segregation/integration .... $p < .01$
with psychological forces .... $p < .05$
with political participation .... $p > .05 < .10$
with community rating today .... $p > .05 < .10$
with attitude toward change .... $p > .05 < .20$

mass media. Perhaps they become concerned with what they see, read, and hear and consequently feel motivated to do something about intolerable situations. The rapid increase in the participation within the civil rights movement by blacks must be due, as many have suggested, to the mass media spotlighting the movement to blacks. Many opposed to the civil rights movement have often spoken with some vehemence about the encouragement by the mass media of such activities.

Matthews and Prothro report an overwhelming black choice for integration. The 1964 Survey Research Center study indicates that only 7 percent of the black respondents choose segregation when given the choice between integration-segregation or something in between.[18] In the high education category, blacks' attitudes on segregation/integration related significantly to exposure to the mass media. This finding relates to the inclusion of high school graduates in the high education category. For high school graduates, the media do have an important relationship to attitude change on the segregation/integration question.

The relationship of the media to attitude change is an intriguing question. In the high education category, the media have an important relationship to both the segregation/integration variable and the attitude toward change variable. While not too important in this category, attitude toward change is significantly related to the mass media in the medium mobility category. If attitude change can be successfully realized merely through exposure to the media, what amount of change can be obtained with directed, intensive messages through the mass media? What is the influence of the media on attitude change — how much, under what conditions, and in which direction? This type of inquiry bears directly on a general political problem — getting elected to office. If we can show that the individual's attitude toward change can be significantly altered through an exposure to the mass media, then we have answered one part of this question — the mass media *can* change attitudes significantly. Of course, qualifications such as the amount of attitude change vary indirectly as the intensity of attitude held would have to be included; however, the mere assertion that the media have a significant relationship to attitude change is an important step forward.[19]

One might argue that since the attitude toward change variable is significant for only one of the categories, we are overstating the media effect. Again, the trend and overall picture is the important point. The number and diversity of attitudes significantly related to mass media exposure indicates important media effect.

We will now look at table 8-3 which controls for income. In the low and medium income categories, political interest and psychological forces were the most significant variables. For the low income group, political interest was significant to the $p < .001$ level while in the medium income category, it was significant to the $p < .01$ level, both very important.

In the low income group, the attitude toward change variable and the segregation/integration variable were both significant ($p < .05$). Attitude toward change was also important in the medium income category. Since the segregation/integration variable reflects attitude change toward a given issue, there were three instances of a significant relationship between the media and attitude change under controls for income category. While there are less significant relationships reported in table 8-3, there are still a number of significant results and, we believe, considerable justification for stating that the trends continue to be the same. The independent effect of the media on political interest and participa-

Table 8-3

A comparison between blacks' exposure to the mass media and selected variables, controlling for income.

Low Income (to $2,999)
($N = 433$)

Exposure to mass media
    with political interest .... $p < .001$
    with psychological forces .... $p < .01$
    with attitude toward change .... $p < .05$
    with segregation/integration .... $p < .05$
    with political information .... $p < .05$
    with political participation .... $p > .05 < .10$

Medium Income (3-$4,999)
($N = 106$)

Exposure to mass media
    with political interest .... $p < .01$
    with psychological forces .... $p < .05$
    with attitude toward change .... $p > .05 < .10$

High Income ($5,000 and above)
($N = 64$)

no significant relationships

tion ($p > .05 < .10$) along with attitude change is confirmed again.

Since we are interested in trends in significant relationships, figure 18 presents a bar diagram indicating the number of times a given variable had a significant relationship with exposure to the mass media. In all, there were nine categories in which a variable could have significance.

Figure 18 gives the best indication of trends in the findings. In seven of the nine control categories, political interest and psychological forces are significantly related to exposure to the mass media. In four categories, the political participation variable, the attitude change variable, and the community rating today variable are significantly related to mass media exposure. Each of these trend variables shows that means of communication are important for politicizing the electorate and changing its attitudes.

The two aspects in which the mass media have the most importance — attitude change and developmental theory — have been shown significant. In order to discover the direction of the relationship and its predictive level, *Pearson r* correlations and regression analysis were used.

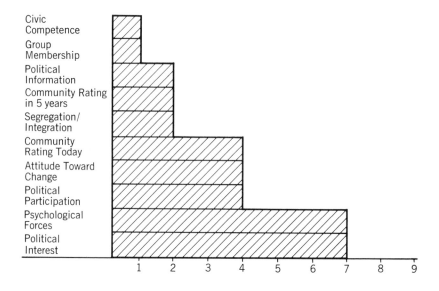

Figure 18

The number of times a variable was significant in each of the nine control categories.

Correlation Analysis

In table 8-4, every variable thought significant after employing chi-square tests has good positive correlations with exposure

Table 8-4

A comparison between exposure to the mass media and selected variables.

Variable	Pearson "r" correlation
Psychological forces	.30
Information score	.26
Political participation	.25
Education	.24
Income	.24
Political interest	.24
Change	.21
Civic competence	.19
Group memberships	.17
Community rating in 5 years	.14
Community rating today	.15
Mobility	.13
Segregation/Integration	.02

to the mass media except the segregation/integration question. Since the blacks' feeling is overwhelmingly in favor of integration, perhaps the variable just does not vary much. In an analogous situation, Matthews and Prothro found that white political participation did not vary a great deal because of the high rates of political participation of most white southerners.[20] We included the control variables — education, income, and mobility — to show that these variables do relate to the media themselves. Their use as control variables is consistent with the Matthews and Prothro analysis and the voting studies directed by the Michigan Survey Research Center.

Table 8-4 shows that the "psychological forces" variable, the "political participation" variable, the "political information" variable, and the "political interest" variable have the strongest positive relation with the mass media. Except for political information, this table is consistent with the strength and frequencies of the chi-square relationships. For example, figure 18 indicated that political interest and psychological forces were significantly related to the mass media in seven of nine categories. Political participation was significantly related in four of the nine categories and all the relationships with the three variables were p < .05.

In table 8-5, the relationships with the key political variables (participation, interest, and information and psychological forces) and the "change" variable are consistent in all categories of mobility, showing a strong independent effect of exposure to the mass media. Three variables vary directly in correlation with the media as mobility increases. Group membership adds almost .20 in moving from low to high mobility. We could hypothesize that high mobility significantly increases the effect of the media on one's motivation to join groups. In both civic competence and community rating today, the blacks who are very mobile tend to be influenced much more by the media than the low mobiles. A snowball effect probably is present here. As one becomes able to travel extensively, he exposes himself to more media, feels more assertive about himself, and understands the position of his community as it relates to other areas of the country and the world. The most important conclusion to be made from table 8-5 is that the mass media have an important and consistent relationship to political variables and the attitude change variable.

With education controlled, exposure to the mass media retains its important relationship to political and change variables, with the stronger relationships residing in the medium and high edu-

Table 8-5

The correlation between selected variables and blacks' exposure to the mass media, controlling for geographic mobility.

Variable	Low Mobility	Medium Mobility	High Mobility
Political interest	.32	.21	.18
Political participation	.26	.21	.28
Attitude toward change	.23	.17	.15
Psychological forces	.21	.29	.29
Political information	.18	.24	.25
Group membership	.14	.13	.32
Segregation/integration	.10	−.06	.10
Community rating in 5 years	.04	.18	−.06
Community rating today	.03	.15	.23
Civic competence	.03	.20	.24

cation categories (table 8-6). The medium education category contains the strongest relationships in eight of the ten variables. We might hypothesize that the mass media have their greatest impact on blacks who have gone to high school but who have not yet graduated. While the increase in correlation is not extremely large with each variable when compared to high education, intuitively such a hypothesis seems correct. Those blacks with enough education to make them aware of the world around them would seem more influenced by exposure to the media than either the low education respondents, who probably border on illiteracy, or the respondent with high education, for whom wide exposure to the mass media would be common to most and therefore would tend to vary less significantly.

In applying this finding to moderization theory, one would conclude that communications have the greatest effect on those with some understanding of, or empathy with, the world around them.

Table 8-6

The correlation between selected variables and blacks' exposure to mass media, controlling for education.

Variable	Low Education	Medium Education	High Education
Political participation	.21	.34	.17
Political interest	.15	.38	.30
Psychological forces	.14	.51	.34
Civic competence	.12	.17	.22
Political information	.12	.24	.33
Attitude toward change	.09	.27	.12
Group membership	.07	.31	.22
Community rating in 5 years	.06	.38	.03
Community rating today	.01	.36	.21
Segregation/ integration	−.004	.04	−.24

The influence would vary directly as the understanding increases, until the respondent is sufficiently sophisticated to judge the content of the communication for himself.

One can conclude again that the mass media have an important and consistent effect on attitudes toward change and the political variables. The most interesting category in table 8-7 is in the high income correlation group. Excepting the two community rating variables, the high income correlations are consistently and even dramatically lower than those of the medium and low income category. The correlations of the political interest and political participation variable are almost nonexistent. High income appears to prevent the effectiveness of exposure to the mass media more than any other category.

The high relationships between community rating and the mass media show a satisfaction of the respondent with his situation in the community. As he becomes more aware of the problems of blacks elsewhere in the United States, the successful black becomes more satisfied with his own community. Since one tends to hear only bad (i.e., newsworthy) news comments about racial tensions and problems in other communities, the blacks with high income would tend to rate their community better as they hear, read, and see more about other community situations.

Table 8-7

The correlation between selected variables and blacks' exposure to the mass media, controlling for income.

Variable	Low Income	Medium Income	High Income
Psychological forces	.23	.37	.17
Political information	.21	.26	.14
Political participation	.20	.31	.002
Political interest	.19	.36	.03
Civic competence	.16	.20	.15
Group membership	.15	.16	.01
Attitude toward change	.15	.23	.14
Community rating today	.09	.22	.39
Community rating in 5 years	.09	.19	.23
Segregation/ integration	−.03	−.06	−.07

Regression Analysis

We have shown consistent and statistically significant relations between exposure to the mass media and selected variables, when controlling for education, income, and mobility. In each of the control categories, exposure to the mass media has an important independent effect on political interest, information, and participation and an important effect on the attitude change variable. All the important correlations (20 percent or better) were positive. As one's exposure to the media increases, his political interest and attitude toward change increase as well.

Education, income, and mobility have been used as control variables in this study and many other attitude studies because they themselves account for a great deal of attitude variation. Table 8-4 indicated that most correlate well with mass media. An interesting line of analysis would be to see how predictive these control variables are, how they rank in predictive power, and how they relate to mass media in prediction. If the media variable does have a significant effect on attitudes, one might expect that media, in some cases, would explain more variance than some of the control variables.

The next set looks at the predictive power (R^2) of the education, income, mobility, and media variables as they affect ten variables which were found to be significant statistically through chi-square analysis (table 8-8). The regression program used for this analysis selects the most predictive variable, then the next most predictive variable and so on. In doing this, the program gives Pearson r correlations, partial correlations, and R^2 values. One can find out not only the effect of education on political interest but also the effect of income on political interest when education is held constant, and how much variance education explains.

Table 8-8

Predicting blacks' psychological forces using the income, education, mobility, and mass media variables.

Variable	R	R^2	Increase in R^2
Education	.451	.204	.204
Income	.518	.268	.065
Mass media	.542	.294	.026
Mobility	.555	.308	.014

NOTE: All relationships are rounded to three places.

As mentioned before, the psychological forces variable is a composite weighting of the results from eight other variables (strength of partisanship, political interest, political information, sense of civic competence, sense of deprivation, sense of racial inferiority/superiority, attitude toward change, and awareness of local intimidation). Summing these weights for each respondent yields a composite score ranging from 0 (no psychological influences associated with participation) to 16 (all eight psychological factors strongly in support of participation).

In table 8-8, the education variable is more predictive than income, mass media, and mobility. Even after education and income are included in the regression equation, the mass media still explain 3 percent of the variance. Mass media are more important than geographic mobility in predicting this variable. While not overwhelming, the independent effect of exposure to the mass media is still important.

The psychological forces variable is somewhat analogous to an overall efficacy index. The ability to make strong judgments and the feeling that one can carry these determinations to consummation along with the effect of one's community is the essential direction of this variable. That the mass media can contribute to such feelings has great import for those interested in creating a participatory government. In an "Almond and Verba" line of analysis, this contribution of the media would be very important to political development.

As expected, we can see from table 8-9 that education is the most predictive variable when one explains political information. The mass media explain only 1 percent, but this is as expected since political information had only two significant chi-square relationships with exposure to the mass media as figure 17 indicated. Mass media does explain almost as much variance as geographic mobility and 62 percent of the variance explained by income. The explanatory power of the mass media is small when compared to education but large when compared to income and mobility.

Table 8-9

Predicting blacks' political information, using the income, education, mobility, and mass media variables.

Variable	R	R^2	Increase in R^2
Education	.484	.234	.234
Income	.508	.258	.023
Mobility	.523	.273	.016
Mass media	.534	.287	.014

Again, in table 8-10 education is the most predictive variable. While mass media explain only 1 percent of the variance after education and income are held constant, they still explain twice as much variance as does the mobility variable. One might conclude that mobility is simply not too important. However, one of Matthews and Prothro's tables indicates the effect of mobility on racial attitudes, controlling for education.[21] Of white respondents who had low education and travelled only within the South, 89 percent chose strict segregation, while only 8 percent desired something in between or integration. Of low educated white respondents who travelled outside the United States, only 57 percent chose strict segregation while 34 percent preferred something in between or integration. This finding indicates an important relationship between geographic mobility and attitudes toward segregation by white southerners.[22] Mobility is an important variable and the ability of the mass media to explain more variance than mobility is an important finding in itself.

Table 8-10

Predicting blacks' attitude toward change, using the income, education, mobility, and mass media variables.

Variable	R	R^2	Increase in R^2
Education	.362	.131	.131
Income	.405	.164	.034
Mass media	.416	.173	.009
Mobility	.421	.177	.004

While income is the most predictive variable in table 8-11, the interesting result is that the mass media explain more political participation variance than both the mobility and education variables. If exposure to the mass media has an important bearing on whether or not the respondent participates in politics, then the skillful use of the media has great importance for political actors (candidates seeking office) and for governments themselves. We could hypothesize that one important and available means that a developing country might use to increase the political participation of the electorate is to make the media available. The mass distribution of radios could be as important as massive school construction efforts. Lerner notes that significant change in Turkey was the result of widespread accessibility of the radio. No longer did the villagers depend exclusively on the village elders for information about local and national matters. The government made such information available to anyone who wanted to listen. Lerner concluded that the availability of this independent informational source contributed greatly to the modernization of traditional Turkey. New ideas, new machinery, and new expectations resulted from the exposure to the radio, according to his analysis.[23]

Table 8-11

Predicting blacks' political participation, using the income, education, mobility, and mass media variables.

Variable	R	R^2	Increase in R^2
Income	.312	.097	.097
Mass media	.362	.131	.034
Mobility	.387	.150	.019
Education	.400	.160	.010

Table 8-12 shows that the mass media variable predicts more political interest than education, income, or mobility. Campbell shows that as the individual's political interest increases, his propensity to vote increases. Effective use of the mass media is very important to the individual candidate and anyone interested in encouraging participatory government.

Table 8-12

Predicting blacks' political interest, using the income, education, mobility, and mass media variables.

Variable	R	R^2	Increase in R^2
Mass media	.239	.057	.057
Education	.294	.086	.029
Income	.310	.096	.010
Mobility	.322	.104	.007

For the candidate seeking office, changing attitudes is his most important concern. While table 8-10 indicated that the mass media explain only 1 percent of the attitude toward change, figure 17 showed that attitude toward change and the mass media related significantly in four of the nine categories.

We could hypothesize that skillful use of the mass media can be an important means of gathering votes. Kelly used a case study treatment of several elections in which the mass media did have an important effect.[24] In an assessment of the Nixon-Kennedy 1960 presidential fight, William Rivers states that "Nixon was clearly defeated in the most decisive of the Great Debates, the first—and before an audience of 70 to 75 million."[25] To corroborate his conclusion, Rivers mentions two polls. One by Gallup showed Nixon leading Kennedy by 47 percent to 46 percent before the debates. A week after the debates, Gallup showed Kennedy ahead 49 percent to 46 percent. One could attribute such a small change to sample error. However, Elmo Roper found that nearly four million voters decided how to cast their ballots on the basis of these debates, and three million voted for Kennedy.[26] Such conclusions about the effect of mass communications on voter choice are supported by our findings.

Since mass media exposure is the second most predictive variable and explains almost as much variance as mobility and education together, we could conclude that an increase in exposure to the media is positively related to one's feelings of civic competence (table 8-13). Exposure to the mass media explains very little of the variance of the group membership variable (table 8-14). This finding is consistent with the chi-square analysis which showed only one significant relationship in the nine control categories.

Table 8-13

Predicting civic competence, using the income, education, mobility, and mass media variables.

Variable	R	R^2	Increase in R^2
Income	.225	.051	.015
Mass media	.265	.070	.092
Mobility	.291	.085	.015
Education	.302	.091	.006

The tables dealing with the remaining three variables—predicting community rating today, in five years, and segregation/integration attitudes—will not be presented. The total variance explained is too small to warrant discussion.

Table 8-14

Predicting Group Membership, using the income, education, mobility, and mass media variables.

Variable	R	R^2	Increase in R^2
Education	.255	.065	.065
Income	.288	.083	.018
Mass media	.301	.090	.008
Mobility	.302	.091	.001

Conclusions

The Matthews and Prothro Findings

We will now compare our findings with those of Matthews and Prothro and assess the importance of mass communications to attitude change and modernization theory. Our findings indicate that the overall conclusions of Matthews and Prothro on the effect of mass communications are correct. That is, exposure to the mass media increases both political motivation and politically unmotivated activity. Figure 18 showed that in seven of the nine control categories, political interest and psychological forces were significantly related to exposure to the mass media. Also, political participation and attitude toward change had important chi-squares in four of the nine categories. The regression analysis showed that the mass media explained more variance than mobility for psychological forces; they explained more variance than mobility and education combined for political participation; and they explained more variance than education, income, and mobility for political interest.

There is one conclusion made by Matthews and Prothro which seems inconsistent and empirically questionable. They state, "twenty-four per cent of the adults with little exposure to the media have some interest in politics, but only about 15 per cent of this group are politically active." On the basis of this approximately 9 percent difference, they conclude, "greater political motivation than activity seems to be associated with little media exposure."[27] This finding disagrees with previous results that indicated a strong association between the media and political interest, information, civic competence, and so on. It is inconsistent with the total meaning of their work and rests totally on a questionable 9 percent difference.

When relating their findings concerning the influence of mass communications on southern blacks to the concept of modernization, Matthews and Prothro make one statement which, while valid, is somewhat misleading. They state that "the more apathetic, under-educated, impoverished, and rural Negroes are the ones whose rate of political participation seems most responsive to media exposure.[28] The statement is based on findings in their tables. More specifically it is based on a percentage that indicates the "participation rate of the highest exposure group as a percentage of the rate of the lowest exposure group." Thus, they find that in the peripheral South, 84 percent of urbanites exposed to all four media are politically active and that only 48 percent of the urbanites exposed to zero-one media are equally active. This gives them a percentage increase of 36 points but a higher/lower exposure ratio of 175 percent.

For those blacks living in rural areas in the peripheral South, 60 percent of those exposed to four media are politically active while only 30 percent of those exposed to zero-one media are equally active. While there is only a 30 percent point difference, there is a higher/lower exposure ratio of 200 percent. They conclude that the media affect the rural more than the urban dweller as far as political participation is concerned. Further analysis of both their tables shows this conclusion to be misleading. For example, if one were to group the middle income brackets together, one would get a higher/ lower exposure ratio of 370 percent instead of 97 and 154. If one would compare percentage point difference between the higher/ lower exposure categories or group the data slightly differently, the tables would support a conclusion that says exposure to the mass media affects those in the middle income, education, and urban categories more than those in the bottom categories.

This finding about the greater impact of the media on those in the middle categories tends to substantiate our findings. The greatest majority of our significant findings are in the middle brackets. This is true not only for low income, but this category also includes all blacks with incomes up to $3,000, which would include some blacks who are really middle income by southern black standards. A more correct statement by Matthews and Prothro would be that exposure to the mass media is most meaningful to those in the medium and low categories.

One interesting finding in Matthews and Prothro's work is that income is more strongly related to black political participation than education. In fact, in table 8-11, we found that of the 16 percent variance explained, income explained 9.7, the mass media 3.4, mobility 1.9, and education only 1.0 percent. This finding confirms the speculation of Gabriel Almond and Sidney Verba concerning the effect of economics on political culture. They remark,

the striking economic improvements in recent times in Italy hold out some prospect of changes in social structure and political culture. Rapid industrial development will certainly weaken traditionalism, and rising standards of living, assuming equitable distribution, may increase social trust and confidence in the political system.[29]

While economics is important, it still expains only 10 percent of the political participation variance. Thus, a strictly economic interpretation of political culture is too narrow.

While Matthews and Prothro feel that income, education, subregion, and the mass media have an independent effect on black political activity, their data analysis does not allow them to rank the variables, while our analysis does. In predicting political interest, table 8-12 showed that the mass media rank first, then education, income, and mobility. As just discused, for political participation prediction, we find that income is most predictive, then mass media, mobility, and education.

This conclusion would have more meaning when related to Lerner's modernization theory. He associates the importance of media exposure to empathy skills. He states that the media give people new ideas and new conceptions of the world around them, but the modernization effect of these new ideas and conceptions varies directly with their differential empathy skills.

For empathy . . . is the basic communication skill required of modern man. Empathy endows a person with the capacity to imagine himself as proprietor of a bigger grocery store in a city, to wear nice clothes and live in a nice house, to be interested in "what is going on in the world" and to "get out of his hole."[30]

It would seem much easier for those in middle income, education, and mobility categories to have such empathy. They already know some of the comforts of life, some of the alien ideas to which the media refer, and something about the political process. Those without such conceptions would have to be taught completely new ideas and values first before the media could have an important effect.

While the media have more important political effects for those in the middle categories, mass communications are also very important for the impoverished's attitude toward change. Table 8-10 indicated that education is the most predictive variable, then income, mass media, and mobility. Table 8-14 showed that in predicting blacks' civic competence, income is first, then mass media, mobility, and education. Thus, exposure to the mass media actually explains *more* variance than income, education, or mobility for certain variables. This finding is the most significant in this study.

Implications

Implicit in the previous discussion is the theoretical importance of these findings. If the mass media increase political participation, interest, and information, then skillful manipulation of the media can win elections. Campbell has shown that an increase in interest in a political campaign means an increase in voter turnout; also, that only 75 percent of the electorate has any party identification and that even these 75 percent do not vote always for the party with which they identify (especially weak identifiers).[31] Therefore, skillful use of mass communications will turn out many unaffiliated or weakly affiliated voters who then will vote for the person (candidate) they know through an intensive media campaign. This is the theory that Hal Evry says has won for him thirty to thirty-four political contests.

While the process is not really that straightforward since both opposing candidates can have skillful public relations men, the implication that the mass media are crucial in any election is overwhelming if we accept the findings in this study. The mass media as a crucial variable are exactly Kelley's point when he relates case studies indicating the importance of mass communications in elections.

The relation of these findings to modernization theory is equally important. The mass media contribute to the dissemination of new ideas and techniques. The media are a developing nation's most useful tool to modernize its society. The mass media are available to all, relatively inexpensive, and very effective in modernizing the political and social attitudes of the citizenry. All the billions in the world would not be enough to modernize a developing country if its people were not willing to make the necessary cultural changes.

While this study is an important step forward in the measurement of the impact of mass communications on society, much more work has to be done. A similar study should be done with Matthews and Prothro's southern white respondents. A factor analysis could be done on both groups of respondents to discover the underlying factors. New surveys could ask similar questions on mass communications so that the findings in this study could be replicated.

NOTES

1. In a letter to this writer (June 28, 1966) Hal Evry, director of Public Relations Center, Inc., related his philosophy about winning political campaigns. He refuses to allow his candidates to make speeches, kiss babies, shake hands, or do any of the traditional campaign activities. His strategy is to figure out what the people want, then hit them early and hit them hard — with advertising, posters, bumper strips, letters, publicity stories, television spots—anything at all but speeches. He claims success in over 90 percent of his campaigns.

Evry's entire letter is printed in chapter 2. The literature regarding the effect of the mass media on the political process is a vast one and has been cited in previous chapters. Dan Nimmo's *The Political Persuaders* (Englewood Cliffs, N.J.: Prentice-Hall, 1970) is one of the better books describing the media effects on political campaigning.

2. Stanley Kelley, Jr., *Professional Public Relations and Political Power* (Baltimore, Md.: Johns Hopkins Press, 1956).

3. Paul F. Lazarsfeld, Bernard Berelson, and Hazel Gaudet, *The People's Choice,* 3rd ed. (New York: Columbia University Press, 1968). See also Peter Rossi, "Four Landmarks in Voting Research," *American Voting Behavior,* ed. Eugene Burdick and Arthur J. Brodbeck (Glencoe, Ill.: Free Press, 1959), pp. 5-54.

4. Carl I. Hovland, *The Order of Presentation in Persuasion* (New Haven, Conn.: Yale University Press, 1957).

5. Philip E. Converse, "Information Flow and the Stability of Partisan Attitudes," *Elections and the Political Order,* ed. Angus Campbell et al. (New York: Free Press, 1965), p. 130. Converse's thesis has been challenged somewhat in Edward Dreyer's article, "Media Use and Electoral Choice: Some Political Consequences of Information Exposure," *Public Opinion Quarterly* 35 (Winter 1971–72): 544-53. Converse told us that those who received the smallest amount of political information were the most stable of voters throughout the campaign. But Edward Dreyer has recently demonstrated that the old relationships have been reversed. The least exposed (the TV dependents) are the least stable, at least since the early sixties. There simply are no more "no media" voters. (Interestingly enough, Michigan's Survey Research Center has dropped the "no media" code.)

6. To name only a few: Kelley, *Professional Public Relations;* Richard E. Neustadt, *Presidential Power* (New York: Wiley, 1960); and Donald R. Matthews, *U.S. Senators and Their World* (New York: Vintage Books, 1960), especially chapter IX.

7. Daniel Lerner, *The Passing of Traditional Society* (New York: Free Press, 1958). Used by permission of the publisher.

8. Donald R. Matthews and James W. Prothro, *Negroes and the New Southern Politics* (New York: Harcourt, Brace, and World, 1966).

9. Lucian C. Pye, *Communications and Political Development* (Princeton, N.J.: Princeton University Press, 1963), pp. 3-29.

10. Karl W. Deutsch, *The Nerves of Government* (New York: Wiley, 1965), pp. 145-62.

11. Many believe that communications theory has a good probability of becoming a true paradigm for political science. For a good review of the literature see M. Margaret Conway and Frank B. Feigert, *Political Analysis: An Introduction* (Boston, Mass.: Allyn and Bacon, 1972), pp. 221-39.

12. See Hubert M. Blalock, Jr., *Social Statisics,* 2d ed. (New York: McGraw-Hill, 1972). See also his *Theory Construction* (Englewood Cliffs, N.J.: Prentice-Hall, 1969).

13. Matthews and Prothro, *Negroes and the New Southern Politics,* pp. 237-61.

14. Ibid., p. 257.

15. Angus Campbell et al., *The American Voter: An Abridgment* (New York: Wiley, 1964), p. 56.

16. Lerner, *Passing of Traditional Societies,* pp. 119-43.

17. Matthews and Prothro, *Negroes and the New Southern Politics,* p. 76.

18. Ibid., p. 351.

19. Carl I. Hovland, "Results from Studies of Attitude Change," *Public Opinion and Communications,* ed. Bernard Berleson and Morris Janowitz, 2d ed. (New York: Free Press, 1966), p. 668.

20. Matthews and Prothro, *Negroes and the New Southern Politics.*

21. Ibid., p. 347.

22. Lerner, *Passing of Traditional Society,* pp. 19-43.

23. Ibid.

24. Kelley, *Professional Public Relations.*

25. William Rivers, *The Opinion Makers* (Boston, Mass.: Beacon, 1965), p. 96.

26. Ibid.

27. Matthews and Prothro, *Negroes and the New Southern Politics,* p. 257.

28. Ibid., p. 261.

29. Gabriel A. Almond and Sidney Verba, *The Civic Culture* (Boston, Mass.: Little, Brown, 1963), p. 309.

30. Lerner, *Passing of Traditional Society,* p. 412. Used by permission of the publisher.

31. Campbell et al., *The American Voter,* p. 56.

9 The Wired Nation: Social and Political Implications

The potential of cable television (CATV) is reverberating throughout communication technology and may change the very nature of our lives in America and even the world. The prospect of a wired nation or even a wired world, where communications are instantaneous with anyone, where essential services such as mail, shopping, banking, telephones, and voting can be handled easily by cable TV, poses as the dawn of massive social, economic, and political change on the American horizon.

Cable Television in Historical Perspective

Cable television enhances the ability to transmit signals by many times the present "over the air" capabilities of electronic media. A single coaxial cable can carry from twenty-eight to thirty-five television channels. If more channels are needed, more cables can be wired to the home. The possibilities of receiving and transmitting programs becomes enormous. With cable, the possibility of a two-way system becomes an immediate reality. Programs can emanate from the home or clubhouse to any preselected audience.

However, the history of cable television in America is one of simple utility. Cable systems were set up almost simultaneously with the birth of the national television networks. Because some communities were too small to warrant a television station or located in mountainous areas where signals from nearby areas were impossible to obtain, cable systems were organized, primarily by television-radio store owners who wanted to sell their products. The first cable system was set up in Lansford, Pennsylvania, in 1949 by Robert J. Tarlton, the owner of a local radio sales and service shop.[1] He organized the Panther Valley Television Company to erect a large tower to receive television signals from Philadelphia. Subscribers paid a $125 installation feed and for $3 per month received television pictures that were often clearer than those received by people living in central Philadelphia. From this insignificant beginning, a whole new technology developed, and today there are over 2,780 systems serving six million subscribers. Most of the systems are in small communities; however, the large cable operations have established some limited systems in New York and other metropolitan areas. The primary function of the large city cable systems is to televise sport events to subscribers.

As figure 19 indicates, the projected growth of cable television is enormous. Some suggest that within ten years the entire country will be wired. They argue that, like television, once the cable system gets into the major media markets, everyone will want it and it will be simply a matter of how much time it takes to physically build the system.

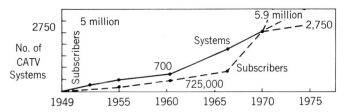

SOURCE: From *On the Cable: The Television of Abundance,* report of the Sloan Commission on Cable Communications, p. 31. Copyright 1971 McGraw-Hill Book Company. Used with permission of McGraw-Hill Book Company.

Figure 19
Historical Growth of the Cable System

Many of the present beneficiaries of cable are resort tourists who visit beach areas that cable in outside channels. Although Atlantic City, New Jersey, is large enough to support its own television station, it cables in all the New York and Philadelphia channels. One channel is exclusively for weather reports from all over the country. An unattended camera is simply focused on weather reports being teletyped in. However, the real significance of this revolutionary device remains unknown to the mass public.

What Is
Cable Television?

The pure cable system dispenses entirely with the regular television's electromagnetic radiation.[2] At its center lies the coaxial cable, which consists of a small diameter inner conductor, a large diameter outer conductor, a plastic foam to keep them apart and to maintain an electric field between them, and an outer sheath to protect the entire cable from the weather or whatever else might affect the operation of the system.

The coaxial cable used to transmit television signals carries all frequencies between 40 million and 300 million cycles per second.[3] Since a television signal requires a band width of 6 million cycles per second, a single coaxial cable can carry approximately forty channels of television. If more channels are needed, extra cables can be attached so that an almost unlimited number of channels can be accessible to the wired home. Because the cable must perform the entire task of carrying the signal from the point of origin to the set, the home must be physically attached like a telephone hookup. While the number of channels available becomes almost unlimited, the actual physical plant hookups are expensive. To wire the nation would cost several billion dollars, and some experts consider this figure quite low. However, since the possibilities are enormous and the profitability equally inviting, major private firms are quite willing to make the massive investment.

Regulation by the
Federal Communications Commission

The Federal Communications Commission, the agency that allocates channels and directs American communication policy, is caught in a bind. Although an independent agency (because its commissioners serve six-year terms and are appointed by more than one president), it has always been quite political. Dean Burch, Nixon's former appointee as chairman, was no exception, although he received very limited direction from the White House. The most outspoken individual on the Commission was Nicholas Johnson, an appointee of Lyndon Johnson. It should be noted that Johnson was a particularly beneficent recipient of FCC rulings since the Commission allowed Johnson's Austin television station to be the only station in that city until the mid-sixties. The former president's personal fortune was in large part attributed directly to this favorable situation for his company.

Nicholas Johnson, whose term expired in 1973, appeared to be keenly aware of the potentialities of cable TV, both as a community service vehicle and as a fantastically profitable enterprise. To get an idea of the profitability one only has to refer to an October, 1968, report of the investment firm of Drexel, Harriman, Ripley entitled "Industry Report on Community Antenna Television (CATV)."[4] The report offers a hypothetical case of a cable system constructed in a small community of 30,000 to 40,000 people, of whom approximately 20,000 might subscribe. The density would be assumed at 100 homes per square mile. The town would require 100 miles of cable, at a cost of $4,000 per mile, or $400,000. A good antenna would be $75,000 while legal fees and marketing would be about $85,000, for a total initial investment of $560,000. The system would be depreciated over ten years, and the cable operator would have borrowed $400,000 at 7.5 percent interest.

When the system has signed up 5,500 subscribers or 55 percent of potential, after all costs are met, depreciation is accounted for, and interest and taxes are paid, it will be producing an annual profit of $167,000. At that rate, the entire investment could be settled in less than four years. The possible profits from a larger system in major metropolitan areas simply boggles the mind. If some or most of the profit could be directed toward public treasuries, then a great community service could be realized.

Almost everyone with the ability to read and count is aware of the fantastic profits to be made. AT&T, Comsat, Western Union, Time-Life, and other large companies have developed cable systems for market. Politicians have covertly organized to get cable franchises. A recent ruling in Baltimore County, Maryland, that gave a cable company with several politicians as directors a franchise almost to perpetuity is an excellent example.[5] There were several applicants for the franchise, all of which espoused community service goals. However, after brief considerations and no public hearings, the franchise was awarded to the political group, an award certain to make those politicians quite wealthy. Although the ruling is being challenged by the losing companies and some citizen groups, the "gold rush" fever is certainly evident.

The problems and pressures on the FCC are enormous. The television broadcast structure, already greatly profitable to both the networks and the television station owners, is fighting desperately to keep cable television out of the major media markets or, at least, have it establish its own cable systems. The social and political potential of a wired nation is vast and perhaps overwhelming to a commission appointed primarily because of loyalty or friendship to a president.

The 1970 regulations proposed by the FCC relate to this epic business and community struggle.[6] While satisfying no group completely, the commission did establish some reasonable guidelines for cable development. It proposed: (1) a complex formula that would permit cable systems in the top 100 markets to import two distant signals, and sometimes three; (2) urban cable systems would be required to provide a minimum of twenty channels and for every commercial TV signal carried, the system would have to provide a channel for transmission of essentially community-related programs. Excess channels would be available for lease to all potential users. Special channels would be given to state and local government in addition to an exclusive channel for educational programs of the school systems; and (3) local franchising authorities would be required to set "reasonable deadlines" for construction and operation of cable systems after the franchise has been granted.

The broadcast industry was upset with the possible intrusion of cable in its prime television markets, so it appealed to the White House for aid. President Nixon responded by appointing a cabinet-level committee on cable, headed by Clay T. Whitehead, director of the Office of Telecommunications Policy, to review the entire matter. After some deliberation the cable interests and the broadcasters settled on a compromise. They agreed to accept a Whitehead-sponsored plan that follows FCC's distant signal proposals in most respects but gives the broadcasters more power to control the showing on cable of special programming specially purchased by the broadcasters.

On February 3, 1972, the FCC finally issued the new cable rules.[7] Essentially the rules enunciate the above agreement in addition to keeping cable systems severely restricted from the top fifty markets. Throughout America the cable rush has started with franchise groups springing up by the hundreds. The state and federal governments will eventually have to make general policy, especially if some or most of the cable profits are to go to public treasuries. However, the American pattern is to let chaos prevail and then intervene. The enormous profits to be made should energize politicians to do more than form their own cable franchise systems, however. If cable were kept as a limited or complete public trust, the mountainous profits from this system could fund many worthwhile social programs. Of course, greedy businessmen and established monied interests would oppose this vigorously. However, it would seem most rational and reasonable to insure at least a partial public ownership of all cable systems in America. In Arlington County, Virginia, the cable system was awarded to a group which promised 4 percent of gross receipts to the municipal government.[8] Given the profit possibilities, such a return to the public seems quite small; however, the demand by local government to share in this bonanza is quite natural and justified. The danger is that the limited vision and parochial attitude of local legislators, in addition to outright greed, will prevent many other localities from getting even 4 percent of gross receipts.

In January, 1974, the Cabinet Committee on Cable Communications submitted a report of recommendations to President Nixon. It developed a comprehensive new national policy for cable communications that would be free of private or governmental barriers to its use.[9] As Chief Justice Warren E. Burger stated:

> The almost explosive development of CATV suggests the need of a comprehensive reexamination of the statutory scheme as it relates to this new development, so that the basic policies are considered by Congress and not left entirely to the courts.[10]

There are twelve major recommendations set forth by the committee. We will elaborate on the major policy suggestions. There are four major recommendations concerning the distribution of cable systems. Major communications companies such as American Telephone and Telegraph, CBS, NBC, and ABC have long desired entry into the lucrative cable field. In recommendation 3, the committee says "there should be no restrictions on either cross-media ownership of cable systems."[11] However, in other recommendations, it disallows telephone companies' applications and suggests that control of cable distribution facilities should be separated from control of programming. The chief recommendation in this section allows CBS and other broadcast networks to develop their own cable systems. The committee also suggests that it would be unwise, although not prohibited, for municipalities to function as cable operators.[12] This "pro-business" attitude shows that the capital risk might be too great; however, any brief review of profit potential indicates that such a suggestion is inappropriate since the public should benefit directly from cable systems and governments at all levels have the capital potential to develop their own, highly profitable systems.

The second group of recommendations involves programming. The suggestions indicate that government should have no control or censorship over programming[13] and that incentives to create programming for cable should be fostered by full applicability of the copyright laws to cable channel users.[14] The copyright policy has been a great source of dispute between the major broadcasting networks and present cable operations. Present cable operations simply rebeam the signals from ABC, NBC, and CBS to remote areas for a fee. The broadcasters argue that the programs are theirs and cannot be rebroadcast except under express permission and fee. The cable operators say that their customers cannot receive the signal because of their remote location so that all the cable companies are doing is to allow the free signal to reach homes that would be unable to get any television at all. They argue, in effect, that their companies are increasing the exposure of the programs of the major networks and, in so doing, are giving additional financial benefit to the networks at no cost to them.

Monroe Price and John Wicklein indicate the major victory this represents for the profit-hungry major broadcast networks.

As cable became a threat to their interests, over-the-air broadcasters sought and received support against the cable companies from the Federal Communications Commission. The FCC was set up originally to regulate the broadcasters on behalf of the public interest. But as broadcasting grew and waxed powerful, the FCC became more attuned to the industry it was supposed to regulate than it was to the interests of the public. It has bent a sympathetic ear to industry complaints, especially in matters affecting profits.[15]

Overall the Cabinet Committee's report suggests very limited involvement of the federal government, to include only setting technical standards for cable[16] and applying anti-syphoning restrictions on professional sports programming. Further, it recommended:

1. Prohibition of public utility-type rate-of-return regulation.

2. Prohibition on grants of exclusive franchises.

3. Prohibition on the use of franchise fees as general revenue-raising devices.

4. Prohibition on dedicated "free" channels.[17] At present, FCC rules require that cable operators reserve one channel for educational use and one channel for local government use.

With regard to the consumer, the committee recommends that there be strong legal and technical safeguards to protect individual privacy in cable communications and that special effort be made to insure that cable is available to residents of rural areas and the poor. Finally it suggests that minority groups should be encouraged to own, operate, and develop programs for cable systems. Nicholas Johnson feels that CATV might be a major asset to blacks and other racial or ethnic minorities. He suggests that CATV might be an answer to their discontent in that it offers an end to the "tyranny of banal man-audience programming."[18] Special channels could be devoted to special minority programs with major, prolonged efforts at reaching blacks, Indians, Chicanos, and other emerging minorities.

Cable Television and Services

Besides the obvious benefits of community programming, and two-way reception and better reception, cable can bring: (1) facsimile reproduction service to bring printed material such as publications, library reference material and mail into the home; (2) computer links to provide virtually unlimited access to specialized information; (3) burglary, fire and other warning devices; (4) home-to-office/home-to-school links (lessening the need for travel which possibly could be a tool to help solve our urban transportation problems; and (5) a device to help citizens develop a sense of community pride and participation.

The possibilities are seemingly limitless but the opposition to a nonbroadcaster-controlled cable is very substantial and quite powerful. Besides the broadcast interests, newspapers and especially the telephone companies have expressed great fear. With cable, separate telephone systems are unnecessary. Newspaper teletypes can easily be hooked up to one of the cable channels, so there is a possibility of the substantial reduction of newspapers.

Telephone companies are extremely powerful because they have the power of "eminent domain" and can force landowners to let them put up their apparatus. If the telephone companies want to discourage the cable systems they can be extremely uncooperative and force long delays in the physical process of laying cable lines. The FCC rules issued on February 4, 1970, limit the obstructionist desire of the phone companies.[19] The rules prohibit phone companies from operating, directly or indirectly, a cable system where they provide service. The major companies have already sent letters to the FCC promising that they will cooperate with cable systems operating in the company's jurisdiction for reasonable fees. It has been estimated that it will cost $5 billion to wire the nation.

Political Implications of Cable Television

The Sloan Commission Report[20] spends an entire chapter on politics on the cable. With specific regard to political campaigning, cable appears particularly useful.

In 1968, political costs at all levels of government were estimated to be $300 million.[21] In 1972, the costs were estimated to be $400 million. At least one-quarter of all political spending is directly related to broadcast television and radio. The problem with broadcast political advertisements is that the candidate reaches a population (and pays for it) far greater than his constituency. For example, a candidate for political office in a Connecticut suburb would have to reach twenty million viewers in order to reach the few thousand potential voters he wants to convince.

Cable television eliminates this situation. The cable system is so organized that a political message may be directed to an audience that is almost coterminous with the exact constituency. The cost is significantly reduced and the message reaches the exact audience for which it was intended. The spillover effect and cost is eliminated.

Among other political possibilities are partisan channels devoted exclusively to messages from political parties. While this would be expensive to the parties, it would provide an easy forum for policy pronouncements and simple announcements of party activities. If all the parties choose to use just one channel in a rotating fashion, the cost would be considerably lessened.

With the possibility of one channel devoted exclusively to news programs, teletypes, and commentaries, the public would have the opportunity to become much better informed. Possibly this would result in much higher rates of mass public political participation.

The cable would also expose the entire political process. Public hearings can be televised along with a majority of city council meetings. The city offices might be televised so that the public might become aware of the problems of making up the budget, or school administration problems, or what happens in a typical day of the chief elected office-holder. While the cable is incapable of creating an informed public, it significantly increases the possibility of an informed, interested, and participatory public, especially if the two-way capability is employed so that citizens might register their immediate approval or disapproval of proposed policies.

Finally, cable television would free the political process from the money dilemma. Political campaigning would become much cheaper because of almost free television exposure. The bureaucrats and political leaders could instantly and almost costlessly poll the constituency on various policy matters. The citizen could have a direct role in the policy-making process. All detailed information on various proposals could be made generally available to the mass public and all elected officials. The possibility of rational government could become a reality.

The possible effects of cable television on the opinion-policy process are simply fantastic. The two-way capability suggests that Americans could vote in an election (using some kind of computerized voter registration card) from their living rooms. The electorate could be called upon for instant referenda and opinion polls to see exactly what its opinion is on a given issue. These innovations could be employed, with varying degrees of difficulty, at all levels of government. Finally, the voice of the community could be heard on all issues and used as a means of engendering a sense of community among the citizenry. A neighborhood atmosphere for towns and cities of all sizes is a possibility.

First let us focus on the voting possibilities. A large obstacle to voting is the archaic registration system controlled at the local level. Instead of differing systems for each locality, a central registration could be developed with the ability of the potential voter to register from his home. In addition, a computerized voters' card could be developed similar to the bank card now available to bank customers. With the bank card, a customer can deposit or withdraw money twenty-four hours a day. The voters' card could be sensitized by zip code and Social Security number so that he could be identified and then could vote via cable during the election day, again from his home. Such a process would eliminate the tremendous costs of voting machines and registrars. The greatest advantage would be the convenience to the voter. Long waits at the polls would be eliminated as well as the necessity to rise very early or give up dinner to vote. The present voting-day system coming in the middle of the week is almost designed to inhibit voting by the mass electorate. Many political scientists suggest that poll taxes (now illegal), registration systems, and inconvenient voting days are designed by elites to keep the mass public out of the political process. To date, this has been the effect of the present system. Only the most motivated citizen has the time and the patience to overcome all the legal and physical obstacles to voting.

The potential of CATV for direct democracy and the re-creation of the town meeting is also present. With the cable, citizens could express their opinions directly on all sorts of policy proposals and policy implementations. Legislators would be able to find out instantly the opinions of their constituency, especially if the hearings and the arguments were broadcast in full. In addition, the actual desires of the voters could be ascertained through a referendum. Voters could vote on each issue as easily as the elected council members. Perhaps, with cable, the "withering away of the state" could be a real possibility. Voters could also inform bureaucrats on their wishes with regard to policy implementation. The possibility of eliminating or severely restricting the duties of elected representatives at all levels may be forthcoming. The tasks of government could operate right before the eyes of the electorate.

Several states, most notably California, provide for a referendum on a law after the collection of a large number of signatures on a petition. In this manner, the mass electorate can have a direct influence on certain legislation. To date, the law has worked against its original intention with radical groups of all persuasion petitioning certain legislation for referendum. Companies have been organized with the sole purpose of collecting signatures (at one-half cent per signature) for various petitions. Thus a group or industry with lots of money could bring any law to petition if it desired. With cable, of course, direct democracy could ensue (voters actually voting on each piece of legislation) or some form of referenda system could be implemented easily. It would be easy and almost costless to find out how the community felt about any given issue. The major problem with such a system is that on certain controversial issues, where representatives sometimes give leadership, the community might vote vigorously against an enlightened proposal. For example, on open housing legislation, President Johnson and Congress and some local governments waged a vigorous campaign to allow minorities to live anywhere they pleased. Prejudice and ignorance on the part of the mass public might have prevented that kind of legislation under a direct democracy system.

Opinion polls, which vary in accuracy with the skills of the pollster and which are extremely expensive if done person to person (the only really accurate method), could be taken almost at will with a very high degree of accuracy. In fact, the entire population could be polled if necessary. Very limited populations such as ethnic, religious, or racial groups could be sampled with very little cost and trouble. With the entire population wired for cable, the opinions of the mass electorate or any segment of it could be instantly known. The large costs spent on polls especially during political campaigns would become unnecessary. Constant polls and informational programs could be joined on one station so that citizens could both inform themselves on the issues and almost simultaneously inform decision makers how they felt. With direct links to representatives and top bureaucrats, the enticement to become informed and participatory would be great.

The sense of community that many scholars think essential to participatory democracy would be enhanced by cable television. Small communities, large communities, or segments of large communities could have their own programs and two-way communication system. Persons involved would feel a part of the events even if isolated in terms of geography. Almost every segment of the larger public would be part of some ethnic, racial, religious, or simply social group that would benefit from such an arrangement. The "Little Italys" and "Chinatowns" could be in constant contact with the sons and daughters who had moved to the suburbs or other sections of the cities. Ethnic fairs could be revived as well as other social activities designed to give all a sense of belonging. The social and political issues that affect the group would also be a segment of the activities. The important identification with smaller groups that give one a feeling of community could be realized through the wired nation. Just as important, community groups of all kinds could put on local news shows or any kind of programs as frequently as desired.

The national and international communications system would be similarly expanded. Ethnic, racial, or other groups could easily go on a national network that would tune in persons of similar background throughout the nation and even the world. In fact, international communications could be almost instantaneous. Persons on one continent could talk with or exchange ideas with individuals around the world whenever they desired. In terms of politics, the world community would be much more personal and interrelated than it is now. With an instant communications network, problems of peoples around the globe would become more immediate. In the McLuhan sense, how we go about politics, especially international politics, would be dramatically changed. While the international interchanges will be considerably more difficult to arrange, the possibilities are really immense. Many scholars have suggested that increased exchanges between two countries, in whatever form, generally result in more friendly relations between those countries. With cable television, once the world is wired, those exchange possibilities become infinitely more possible and more varied. The entire world would be reduced to the size of a living room through cable. Of course, the precise effects of this technological revolution remain to be realized and one must keep in mind that it may take ten to thirty years before any such worldwide cable system is functioning. Even then, one would expect that the Communist nations would place severe restrictions on its use and would choose the persons who would have cable capability.

Local Government and CATV

In a survey to determine the growth, impact, and pattern of use of cable television in municipal governments, the International City Management Association (ICMA) questioned 6,223 cities and received 3,211 (52 percent) responses.[22] Only 27 percent of the cities reporting indicated that the question of cable television had not been raised. Another 24 percent reported that the CATV question had been raised but was still under intensive consideration. Forty-one percent had either granted franchises but construction had yet to commence or had granted franchises (34 percent) and construction or operation had commenced.

Table 9-1 shows that 43 percent of the cities between 100,000 and 249,999 had CATV under construction, and 40 percent of the cities between 50,000 and 99,999 also had CATV under construction. While the smaller cities seemed to be much more active, the larger cities were also active with 50 percent of the cities

Table 9-1

Status of Cable Television

Classification	No. of cities reporting (A)	CATV question not raised		CATV question raised, no action		Responsibility for CATV assigned		Planning for CATV underway, no legislation passed		Planning for CATV underway, legislation passed		Franchise awarded, no construction		Construction of CATV underway and/or operational	
		No.	% of (A)	No.	% of (A)	No.	% of (A)	No.	% of (A)	No.	% of (A)	No.	% of (A)	No.	% of (A)
Total, all cities	3,183	851	27	750	24	184	6	61	2	58	2	209	7	1,070	34
Population group															
Over 500,000	16	0	0	2	13	5	31	3	19	1	6	2	13	3	19
250,000–500,000	14	1	7	2	14	3	21	1	7	0	0	3	21	4	29
100,000–249,999	56	3	5	6	11	5	9	4	7	6	11	8	14	24	43
50,000– 99,999	158	18	11	30	19	24	15	3	2	9	6	11	7	63	40
25,000– 49,999	329	53	16	82	25	21	6	14	4	7	2	23	7	129	39
10,000– 24,999	719	138	19	192	27	50	7	12	2	10	1	40	6	277	39
5,000– 9,999	783	192	25	196	25	45	6	15	2	13	2	42	5	280	36
2,500– 4,999	949	353	37	218	23	27	3	8	1	12	1	73	8	258	27
Under 2,500	159	93	58	22	14	4	3	1	1	0	0	7	4	32	20
Geographic region															
Northeast	801	287	36	209	26	39	5	6	1	8	1	41	5	211	26
North Central	1,026	314	31	287	28	49	5	26	3	13	1	63	6	274	27
South	854	190	22	170	20	55	6	12	1	18	2	61	7	348	41

	502	60	12	84	17	41	8	17	3	19	4	44	9	237	47
West															
Metro/city type															
Central	188	8	4	18	10	23	12	9	5	11	6	21	11	98	52
Suburban	1,571	507	32	495	32	86	5	36	2	31	2	90	6	326	21
Independent	1,424	336	24	237	17	75	5	16	1	16	1	98	7	646	45
Form of government															
Mayor-council	1,384	415	30	381	28	59	4	14	1	15	1	92	7	408	29
Council-manager	1,558	329	21	313	20	118	8	46	3	40	3	105	7	607	39
Commission	93	20	22	19	20	4	4	1	1	1	1	6	6	42	45
Town meeting	117	71	61	30	26	1	1	0	0	2	2	5	4	8	7
Rep. town meeting	31	16	52	7	23	2	6	0	0	0	0	1	3	5	16

SOURCE: *The Municipal Yearbook 1974* (Washington, D.C.: International City Management Association, 1974), p. 57. Used by permission of the Association.

between 250,000 and 500,000 having awarded a franchise or having a CATV system under construction.[23] This indicates a massive interest in CATV and portends the coming of the wired city very quickly, perhaps within a decade.

While the question of minority ownership of CATV needs much more study, the ICMA survey addressed itself to this policy (see table 9-2).[24] A large number of responses were "don't know"; however, the larger cities (over 250,000) seemed to be considering this option seriously. Of the eight cities over 500,000 reporting, six said that minority ownership will be or has been considered. Of the eight cities over 250,000 but below 500,000, two reported consideration and one reported a completed consideration.

Table 9-2

Policy Issues: Minority Ownership

Classification	No. of cities reporting (A)	Completed No.	Completed % of (A)	Will be considered No.	Will be considered % of (A)	Will not be considered No.	Will not be considered % of (A)	Don't know No.	Don't know % of (A)
Total, all cities	957	80	8	49	5	297	31	531	55
Population group									
Over 500,000	8	1	13	5	63	0	0	2	25
250,000–500,000	8	1	13	2	25	2	25	3	38
100,000–249,999	33	4	12	3	9	8	24	18	55
50,000– 99,999	70	7	10	2	3	26	37	35	50
25,000– 49,999	138	14	10	10	7	51	37	63	46
10,000– 24,999	255	15	6	12	5	83	33	145	57
5,000– 9,999	233	22	9	11	5	61	26	139	60
2,500– 4,999	189	13	7	4	2	59	31	113	60
Under 2,500	23	3	13	0	0	7	30	13	57
Geographic region									
Northeast	148	10	7	4	3	55	37	79	53
North Central	272	25	9	16	6	70	26	151	59
South	287	21	7	17	6	80	28	169	59
West	250	24	10	12	5	92	37	122	49
Metro/city type									
Central	112	13	12	11	10	30	27	58	52
Suburban	353	28	8	19	5	119	34	187	53
Independent	492	39	8	19	4	148	30	286	58
Form of government									
Mayor-council	297	32	11	13	4	84	28	168	57
Council-manager	621	46	7	33	5	203	33	339	55
Commission	28	1	4	2	7	7	25	18	64
Town meeting	8	1	13	0	0	1	13	6	75
Rep. town meeting	3	0	0	1	33	2	67	0	0

SOURCE: *The Municipal Yearbook 1974* (Washington, D.C.: International City Management Association, 1974), p. 63. Used by permission of the Association.

Cable Television and Education

In a report by the National Cable Television Association, the entire area of CATV impact on education was explored.[25] The immediate benefits to schools and campuses in terms of educational dividends will be in the area of programming. It is possible for schools with cable connections to originate their own programming for their own educational purposes. CATV can help transform passive education into a dynamic feedback, one that continually creates new learning experiences. Of course, one must wait until schools and colleges have developed a "track record" of CATV use before getting too enthusiastic. The modest aid that television afforded educational opportunity suggests that caution is necessary. However, even cautious optimism does little justice to the myriad of possibilities of educational CATV.

Although CATV is still in its infancy both as a system and as an educational tool, a number of CATV-schools hookups are in progress.[26] A few examples of the kinds of working relationships already developed are:

Dougherty County, Georgia: The school system leases a channel from the cable system. Vocational school students help operate the channel, called SET-TV for "Serving Education through Television." They produce regular lesson programs and also programs on local issues.

Casper, Wyoming: The cable system shares its studio facilities with the local school district. Filmed programs are scheduled during school hours on the cable system's local origination channel. Live football and basketball games and taped review courses are also shown on the cable system's channel.

Bainbridge, New York: The Bainbridge-Guilford Central School District owns and operates its own studio facilities. They program elementary school student-produced programs and school sports on a channel provided by the local cable company.

Abilene, Texas: The school district uses the cable company's studio and equipment. Two control room technicians, hired and paid by the school board, are in charge of school programming at the cable studio.

Hagerstown, Maryland: The local cable system constructed a special cable to the studio facilities of the Washington County Board of Education so that their existing in-school closed circuit TV system could be tied into the cable system. Now some of the school district's closed-circuit programming goes to all cable system subscribers.

Moab, Utah: The local school district has been programming from its own studios over a cable channel since 1965. In 1968, the cable system and the school system cooperated to construct a special cable to connect the school studio with the cable system's headend. This connection makes it possible for the school system to program live, tape and film material directly onto the cable system. The school system allocated $12,000 and the cable system provided the labor for construction of this special connection.

Ellensberg, Washington: The cable system provides a link tying Central Washington State College with the cable system's headend. This link allows the college's CCTV system to receive all the CATV system's channels and the CATV system to receive much of the college's programming.[27]

Some other obvious aids will be more flexible scheduling and programming, special programming to meet local interest and needs, improved and more intensive parent-teacher relationships, special programs for the gifted, for the handicapped, and for the slow learners.[28] Cable has some special advantages to the college by making them more accessible to the community. Besides courses and refresher courses for professionals such as physicians, lawyers, and engineers, the research efforts and findings could be applied to community needs.[29] One of the most intriguing possibilities of CATV concerns the wired library. Those who are unable to get to the library or who are too culturally deprived to come in person can have the resources of the library available to them in their own wired homes. Small towns with small libraries may someday be connected to large national library centers (such as the Library of Congress) so that the vast resources of these libraries will be available even to the most remote town.[30]

McLuhan and
Cable

Although Marshall McLuhan deals only generally with electronic media, he makes a number of specific observations that seem a logical extension of the wired nation. First, McLuhan believes that the cities of America have passed their utility and will continue to decline in population and importance. He suggests that the old cities should be preserved for posterity much like Williamsburg, Virginia, is preserved so that future generations can see what city life was like during the age of the cities. The reason for the decline of the cities, according to McLuhan, is simply communications technology. No longer does a company need to be located in the central city; in fact, the roads and access to a company are much better in the suburbs. However, the businessman can locate his company far from the central city (100 to 200 miles away) and still be able to contact everyone he desires and receive all necessary supplies with great ease. The commercial and transportation reasons for the growth of the big cities are no longer apparent. Moreover, communications technology makes instant interchange with anyone around the world a possibility. So the cries of mayors for more money to improve and regenerate their cities may be simply straws in the winds of change with most of the change being caused by the technological revolution in communications.

McLuhan also suggests that education and the entire process of learning is undergoing great change. Cable television will certainly enhance this change. No longer will it be necessary to have children relate mostly to books since visual presentation and learning processes will be developed. Of course, with the cable, educational systems will have several different channels on which to present programs. Special programs for reading, music, and science could be developed. Entire grades could be taught via the television with teachers available for special consultation. Educational programs developed by the most skillful learning specialists with help from television writers and directors could revolutionize the educational system. Since cable has a two-way capacity, the central headquarters would be able to assess the impact of the program on the children. With such feedback, the programs could be modified to achieve the most impact possible. The children-sponsored program is also a strong possibility. Instead of teaching to children, programs could be developed to teach *with* children and have them as active, even controlling, participants in the planning and staging of the educational process.

For governmental systems, McLuhan suggests that the centralization of both government (in terms of power) and bureaucracy (in terms of implementation) will continue and increase. The need for a central communications system is demanded by the technology, and governments and social systems will conform to the system. Programs that emphasize decentralization, such as revenue-sharing, are doomed to failure. Some observers suggest that revenue-sharing, which is the giving of money to local governments without any directions on how to spend it, will eventually lead to complete federal control. As the program grows, state and local governments will become more dependent on it. Eventually some restrictions will be placed on the money to insure against local irresponsibility. These conditions will be increased until the federal government almost mandates how the money should be spent and how much for each category. The process will be considerably enhanced as the fiscal revolution continues with the federal government doing most or all of the tax collecting and state and local governments doing very little. Eventually the only tax Americans will pay is the federal progressive income tax and all state and local property and sales taxes will be eliminated as regressive and discriminatory.

Dangers of the Cable

As Mike Wallace, the CBS commentator, said on his show "60 Minutes," "At its worst, cable television could invade our privacy, tranquilize our children, and remove us electronically from the flesh and blood world."[31] The Orwellian world of 1984 becomes a possibility. With the nation wired, a central station could turn sets on and off at will. Pictures and sound could be transmitted whenever desired. Of course, the two-way capability of cable offers much more positive aspects than negative; nonetheless, the negative aspects must be considered.

A government with a "Watergate mentality" could easily bug and televise any home in the nation. Safeguards would have to be devised so that people would know when their sets are operating. The information exposed during the congressional impeachment proceedings shows clear and convincing evidence that such dangers must be carefully watched by both Congress and the public. The possible tyranny of an unchecked executive using CATV appears quite possible and even probable if not guarded carefully.

Another possible danger is the rule by mob of government. Instant opinion polls, referenda, and other direct democracy devices may put too much power in the hands of a relatively uninformed electorate. Information will be made available at a very low cost in terms of time or energy, yet citizens still may have to express themselves on emotional issues that more informed persons could judge better. "Power to the people" would become a reality, and some have speculated that such complete power may be unwise. Of course, the political system at present has made it difficult for the masses to effectively participate on even such limited bases as voting, so we are unclear as to what real effects direct democracy may have on government. It would seem that whatever the dangers, such a system should work and citizens could have their opinions immediately considered and could even vote on issues as they arose.

Whatever the eventual social and political effects of cable, it is clear that all human interaction will change dramatically. The medium of cable television itself will transform the social and political processes. It is a technological revolution almost unsurpassed in possible effects and impact. Because it will probably be implemented within a generation, it will change America and the world in a very short time, possibly within fifteen years.

Cable Television and the
Media Influence Model

The media-policy influence model presented in the linkage chapter (1) suggests that the media can initiate change or policy concern themselves. In this case, the media become an environmental change agent, that is, they change the very nature of the total interaction. Cable television threatens to remake the entire opinion-policy process and, in doing so, will make the media themselves the primary causal factor influencing both public opinion and public policy programs. There is little question that CATV will play an important role in the political process. Even now in its infancy, it is being used widely in California electoral campaigns.[32]

Again, in reviewing the influence of CATV on politics and the policy-making process, the media influence model appears useful as a conceptual, analytic tool.

Conclusions

For the present, one can only speculate with cable. It is true that many systems do exist today; however, their impact is minimal and their purpose is mostly to rebroadcast regular signals. At present, very few cable systems take advantage of the social and political possibilities inherent in this technological revolution.

The regulating agency, the Federal Communications Commission, finds itself in a historic struggle with present system owners fighting the television networks and the telephone companies for control and spread of cable. Present rules forbid the cable systems entry into the top fifty media markets. It is only a matter of time, however, before the entire country becomes engulfed by cable. Some estimates are that $5 billion and ten years would be necessary simply to physically wire America. The profits from cable are potentially enormous and some communities are trying profit-sharing or community-controlled systems to put a large part of these profits into community programs.

The possible services offered by this system seem endless and overwhelming. Newspapers can be printed; mail can be sent and received; programs or simply visual telephone calls can be sent and received; library services can be made available; orders and shopping can be done by cable; urban transportation problems can be alleviated; special cultural programs can be televised live; schools can teach via separate cable channels; a sense of community can be enhanced — the list seems endless and it probably is. Essentially this system has the potential to dramatically change our lives.

The possible implications for the political process, from nominations to votes on bills before the legislature, are enormous also. The entire campaign process will be significantly less expensive. Cable channels can be allocated to various parties who can pay a nominal sum to reach the exact audience they desire. The possibilities for the direct influence of public opinion on public policy making are very significant. Opinion polls can be taken instantly; the two-way system means that voters could vote directly on bills; bureaucrats could find out immediately and exactly how the public wants them to implement policy. The "town meeting" and true direct democracy (with the possible elimination of elected representatives) are a distinct possibility. Meetings of elected representatives can be televised directly, cheaply, and while they are happening. No one need leave his living room to be completely informed about what is going on in government.

The dangers of the cable are equally dramatic. The possibility of government spying is very real. Central government could use the cable to turn on sets to see and hear people whenever they desired. This danger is too real to be ignored, and some system that tells people when the set is on must be devised.

Cable television presents so many change possibilities that it is almost frightening. It promises to do what McLuhan and Alvin Toffler[33] suggested the electronic media will do — change the very essence of our lives and the lives of everyone wired.

NOTES

1. Ralph Lee Smith, *The Wired Nation* (New York: Harper and Row, 1972), pp. 3-4.

2. *On the Cable: The Television of Abundance*, report of the Sloan Commission on Cable Communications (New York: McGraw-Hill, 1971), p. 12.

3. Ibid.

4. Smith, *The Wired Nation*, p. 23.

5. Such rulings and circumstances are common throughout the United States. As more and more businessmen and politicians become aware of the profit potentialities of CATV, they have organized themselves into corporations to bid on the franchises. The obvious conflict of interest in many of these awards has been overlooked by the legislative bodies although a number of decisions have been challenged in the courts. One would hope that the FCC would police the franchise awards more closely and even control for public benefit the profits of cable franchises.

6. Smith, *The Wired Nation*. See especially "The Cable and the Regulators," pp. 44-64. See also Federal Communications Commission release 5 August 1971.

7. Ibid., p. 61. The most recent report issued is *Cable Report to the President,* The Cabinet Committee on Cable Communications (Washington, D.C.: Government Printing Office, 1974).

8. Interview with Joseph S. Wholey, Arlington County Supervisor, June 1973.

9. *Cable Report to the President,* The Cabinet Committee on Cable Communications (Washington, D.C.: Government Printing Office, 1974), p. iv.

10. Ibid., p. 50.

11. Ibid., p. 31.

12. Ibid., p. 33.

13. Ibid., p. 37.

14. Ibid., p. 39.

15. Monroe Price and John Wicklein, *Cable Television: A Guide for Citizen Action* (Philadelphia, Pa.: Pilgrim Press, 1972), p. 9.

16. *Report to the President*, p. 40.

17. Ibid., p. 43.

18. Nicholas Johnson, *How to Talk Back to Your Television Set* (New York: Bantam, 1970), p. 140. See also Edward Jay Epstein, *News From Nowhere: Television and the News* (New York: Random House, 1973) and Robert Agranoff, *The New Style in Election Campaigns* (Boston, Mass.: Holbrook Press, 1972).

19. Smith, *The Wired Nation*. For a complete discussion of the CATV problems with telephone companies, see Smith's chapter on "Mysterious Ma Bell," pp. 64-71.

20. *On the Cable*, pp. 115-22.

21. Ibid., p. 116.

22. *The Municipal Yearbook 1974* (Washington, D.C.: International City Management Association, 1974), p. 56.

23. Ibid., p. 57.

24. Ibid., p. 63.

25. *Cable Television and Education: A Report from the Field* (Washington, D.C.: National Cable Television Association, 1973).

26. Ibid., p. 5.

27. Ibid., pp. 5-6. Used by permission of the Association.

28. Ibid., p. 14.

29. Ibid., p. 28.

30. Ibid., p. 33.

31. "60 Minutes," Transcript Volume III, number 1, as broadcast over the CBS Television Network, 18 September 1970, with CBS News Correspondents Harry Reasoner and Mike Wallace, p. 13.

32. Hank Parkinson, "Cable TV — 'Poor Man's' Medium," *Roll Call*, The Newspaper of Capitol Hill, 22 March 1973.

33. Alvin Toffler, *Future Shock* (New York: Random House, 1970). See also his *The Futurists* (New York: Random House, 1972).

10 Some Concluding Thoughts and New Research Avenues

A Review of Findings and the Media Influence Model

For the purpose of relating and focusing the findings, let us review the media influence model first presented in the linkage chapter.

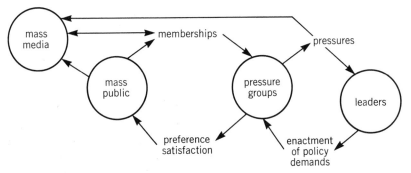

Figure 20
The Media Influence Model

The model subsumes the parties model (parties being considered just another pressure group) and argues that very little individual opinion exists within a developed society apart from group opinions. On any important issue, then, group opinions are the crucial opinion to be considered by elected officials. The model as presented fails to discriminate between the important issues and the day-to-day issues; however, the model seems appropriate for *most* of both kinds of issues. The mass media are presented before the mass public because sometimes the media are the major input to the policy process. The public often needs considerable stimulation before it becomes sufficiently aware of issues to provoke some action. The media often interact simultaneously with each segment in the policy process, setting the agenda for the interaction of leaders with groups and the mass electorate. The arrows point both ways because all three segments often pressure the media to take part. The media then are a catalyst for action, stimulating and encouraging and even rationalizing the opinion-policy process.

While it is difficult to pinpoint the effects of the media, most would suggest that the media played a central role in many vital issues of the 1960s — especially the civil rights movement and the Vietnam War. The mass media are a catalyst for *latent opinion*, energizing it to action; they are also a public lie detector test, indicating by film and commentary whether the statements of governmental leaders are true; and finally they are a quasi-conscience of the American people, setting proper priorities on American policy and attempting to ensure that measures are taken to correct wrongs in America. This latent opinion has been discussed by many, most thoroughly by David Truman. He suggests that a great deal of unexpressed opinion exists in both the elite and mass public that gets expressed only after some event or crisis situation but is not considered by policy makers until it gets energized and then expressed.[1]

With regard to voting behavior, we found that the media never determine the outcome of an election, but they can influence it greatly. This is especially true in primary elections. At the general election level, there will normally be competition from equally qualified and experienced media experts. To a great extent their efforts will cancel each other out, and simply bombarding the voter with larger and larger doses of political advertisements will lead to a quick mental tuning out by the electorate. Ultimately, then, the election will be decided on the issues of the campaign unless one candidate is clearly incompetent or senile.

The case study of Watergate offered a direct look into the relationship between the president and the press and provided direct evidence on the effects of mass media and public opinion on policy makers. The Watergate affair showed that the media influence model has direct applicability. The media's role and mass public opinion's role were crucial to the uncovering of the scandal.

The finding with regard to the influence of the mass media on blacks suggested that they get most of their news from the tele-

vision and that they deeply distrust the white metropolitan newspapers, or at least think the papers worthless. The central
question raised was whether the media caused the riots. The
answer is clearly negative since a whole set of socioeconomic factors could have caused the disturbances. However, the media gave
the riots new significance because they gave the protesters a world
audience and a worldwide airing of their grievances. The media
will continue to be an important weapon in protest politics as
they are an effective, available, and powerful tool when skillfully
employed by protesters.

The implications for the political process of cable television
(CATV), from nominations to votes on bills before the legislature,
are extremely important. The entire campaign process will be significantly less expensive. Cable channels can be allocated to various
parties, who can pay a nominal sum, to reach the exact audience
they desire.

The possibilities for the direct influence of public opinion on
public policy making are very significant, but the dangers of the
cable are equally dramatic.

Future Shock and
Media Technology

Marshall McLuhan has said that, "Future Shock . . . is 'where
it's at'." The whole futurist literature suggests the shattering stress
and disorientation that we induce in individuals by subjecting them
to too much change in too short a time.[2] Alvin Toffler suggests that
instant communications have encouraged this stress and disorientation. Of course, CATV should do similar things to individuals and society. Toffler views voters as so far removed from
contact with their elected representative, with the issues extremely
complicated, that citizens feel excluded from the policy process.[3]
With regard to democracy, Toffler sees more problems in that
democracy is a victim of time-bias as politicians regard policy choice
only until the next election.

Jay Forrester presents some alternative time models that help
predict the consequences of policy decisions for up to fifty years
in the future.[4] The great obstacle for such research is that, even if
the political leader is interested, he is usually concerned only with
his administration or the future election. Long-range decisions that
may be unpopular in the short run are avoided and thus great

opportunities are lost for positive change. The media present change immediate to people and thus tend to affect them more in terms of total environment change rather than a specific immediate effect. However, McLuhan is probably correct in saying that communications technology represents total change for man. For industrialized man the change is swift but not overwhelming; for citizens of developing countries, the effect of this new environment must be enormous. It is usually true that such developing countries are eventually ruled by dictators. A totalitarian government that tells everyone what is right and wrong is more palatable in a world of constant change.

New Research Avenues

There are four main areas for future public opinion-public policy research: (1) the causal role of public opinion; (2) research in public opinion over time; (3) case studies; and (4) more elaborate survey research with some intensive in-depth interviewing.

The causal role of public opinion has been explored in some depth in chapter 1. However, basic research needs to be done on mass and elite attitudes toward public policy. Preferences, intensity of preferences, and priority of policy preference must be established for elites and masses. Such data must be included in complex models that predict both levels and impact of policy decisions.

One of the problems in assessing the effects of mass media and public opinion on given issues or elections is that such research is usually limited to one or, at most, two surveys or one or two years of a case study. Such limited analysis gives only a "snapshot" effect and inhibits conclusive finds. Donald Devine did look at the opinion-policy linkage for a decade but failed to include the mass of case study material that would have substantiated his analysis.[5]

The case study is an important area for opinion-policy research. How an issue develops, what interest groups support it, and when are the critical developments are central questions only available to the intensive researcher. A series of case studies employing an overall model would be most fruitful because they would be structured and comparisons could be made.

Finally, we need survey instruments that really probe the depths of citizen knowledge about issues. While the Comparative State Elections Project did use a questionnaire that produced better data,[6] more effort in designing the best instrument possible is needed. It is clear that citizens are becoming better informed and are willing to spend some of their increasing leisure time to help resolve issues. The in-depth interview and experimental research are natural supplements to survey research. Yet, except for some limited simulation research and even more limited experimental research, there has been little attempt to do work in these areas. Robert Lane's work on the ideology of the working class is one of the more successful attempts at using the intensive interview technique.[7] Yet rarely have these methods been used in conjunction with survey research. Survey research should be used for macro-model building with experimental research used for micro-model building. In-depth interviewing should be used for special areas of interest or an investigation into a deviant case. All in all, the possibilities for future research are manifold.

NOTES

1. David B. Truman, *The Governmental Process.* (New York: Knopf, 1955).

2. Alvin Toffler, *Future Shock* (New York: Bantam, 1970), p. 2.

3. Ibid., p. 483. See also his collection of futurists essays, *The Futurists* (New York: Random House, 1972).

4. Jay Forrester, *Urban Dynamics* (Cambridge, Mass.: MIT Press, 1969).

5. Donald Devine, *The Attentive Public: Polyarchical Democracy* (Chicago, Ill.: Rand McNally, 1970).

6. The project under James W. Prothro surveyed thirteen states intensively in the 1968 presidential election. While the findings are still unpublished, the questionnaire design made significant improvements on the Michigan Survey Research Center study and elicited from respondents much more complete information. David M. Kovenock, Philip L. Beardsley and James W. Prothro, "Status, Party, Ideology, Issues, and Candidate Choice: A Preliminary, Theory-Relevant Analysis of the 1968 American Presidential Election" (Paper presented at the 1970 International Political Science Association in Munich, Germany) elaborate on his design and findings.

7. Robert Lane, *Political Ideology* (New York: Free Press, 1962).

Index